The Society of Equals

The Society

of

Equals

Pierre Rosanvallon

translated by Arthur Goldhammer

Harvard University Press

Cambridge, Massachusetts, and London, England

2013

This book was originally published in French by Éditions du Seuil,
Copyright © 2011, Éditions du Seuil.

Library of Congress Cataloging-in-Publication Data
Rosanvallon, Pierre, 1948–
[Société des égaux. English]
The society of equals / Pierre Rosanvallon ; translated by
Arthur Goldhammer.
pages   cm
Translation of: La société des égaux.
Includes bibliographical references and index.
ISBN 978-0-674-72459-4 (alk. paper)
1. Equality—Sociological aspects.   2. Social structure.
3. Solidarity.   4. Democracy.   I. Title.
JC575.R56613   2013
320.01'1—dc23   2013009718

In memory of
Claude Lefort
(1924–2010)

Contents

INTRODUCTION

The Crisis of Equality

Democracy is manifesting its vitality as a regime even as it withers as a social form. The sovereign citizenry has steadily increased its ability to intervene in government and magnified its presence. Citizens are no longer content to make their voices heard sporadically at the ballot box. They exert an increasingly active power of oversight and control. They assert themselves not just as diffuse opinion but as active minorities and communities of shared ordeals in order to pressure those who govern them and express their expectations and exasperations. The very vigor of their criticism of the representative system demonstrates their determination to keep the democratic ideal alive. This is a characteristic of our times. The aspiration to expand freedom and establish powers responsive to the general will has toppled despots everywhere and changed the face of the globe. But the "people," understood in a political sense as a collective entity that ever more powerfully imposes its will, is less and less a "social body." Political citizenship has progressed, while social citizenship has regressed. This rending of democracy is the major phenomenon of our time, and an ominous threat to our well-being. If it continues, the democratic regime itself might ultimately be in danger.

The growth of inequality is at once an index of this distress and its driving force. It is the stealthy blade that is silently severing the social bond and simultaneously undermining social solidarity. The phenomenon has been explored in numerous statistical studies,[1] including research into the income of well-paid financiers, corporate managers, professional athletes, and celebrities. In the United States, the top 10 percent of earners accounted for 50 percent of total income in 2010 compared with just 35 percent in 1982. In France, the average income of the top 1 percent increased by 14 percent between 1998 and 2006, while that of the top 0.01 percent, the very top of the income scale, increased by nearly 100 percent, whereas the lower 90 percent saw their incomes increase by just 4 percent over the same period. The gap has continued to widen since then, as work published by the French National Institute for Statistics and Economic Studies has shown.[2] What is more, the widening of the gap is a global phenomenon. At the same time, the number of people earning the minimum wage has increased (in France, nearly one in five wage earners is currently paid at close to the minimum wage), while the number of families living below the poverty line has also increased, owing mainly to unemployment and reduced job security.

Along with widening income differentials, we also see an increased concentration of wealth. In the United States, 20 percent of the people own 93 percent of all financial assets (excluding real estate, the value of which has shrunk). In France, the wealthiest 1 percent own 24 percent of the country's wealth, and the wealthiest 10 percent own 62 percent, while the least wealthy 50 percent own only 6 percent of the national riches.[3] To be sure, measuring these inequalities is a complex business that raises important method-ological issues,[4] and the whole question of inequality is clearly broader than a question of income and wealth alone. It would be easy to extend these indications ad nauseam, however, because the literature on the subject is endless. I mention these figures here merely to set the stage and suggest the magnitude of the phenom-enon. The important issue for the purposes of this book lies else-where. It is simply the fact that inequalities have never before been so widely discussed while so little was being done to reduce them. This crucial contradiction calls for explanation, especially since it coincides with the gap between the progress of democracy as regime and the regression of democracy as social form.

The Forms of a Rupture

Rising inequality stands in stark contrast to the earlier reduction of inequality in Europe and America. It is indeed remarkable that the recent increase in inequality follows a lengthy period of reduced income and wealth inequality on both continents. In France, the wealthiest 1 percent owned 53 percent of the national wealth in 1913 but only 20 percent in 1984. In the United States, the top 10 percent of earners shared nearly 50 percent of total income on the eve of the Great Depression but less than 35 percent from 1950 until the mid-1980s.[5] In Sweden, a shining example of inequality reduction, the top 1 percent of earners claimed only 23 percent of all income in 1980, compared with 46 percent at the turn of the twentieth century.[6] These spectacular reductions were achieved by a rapid increase in low incomes, slower growth of high incomes, social transfer pay-ments, and a highly progressive tax system, the upper brackets of which paid steeply increasing rates. Today, this legacy has dissipated, and the current system marks a spectacular break with the past, reversing the trend of the past century.

Why this change of course? Because there has been a veritable revolution in our essential understanding of the democratic ideal. The American and French revolutions did not distinguish between democracy as a regime of popular sovereignty and democracy as a society of equals. In *L'Esprit de la Révolution de 1789*, Pierre-Louis Rœderer, a leading figure of the Constituent Assembly, wrote, characteristically, that "the emotion that stirred the first outbursts of the revolution, aroused its most violent efforts, and obtained its greatest successes was the love of equality. . . . The first motive of the revolution was impatience with inequalities."[7] And Rœderer was by no means a hothead. He was one of the more moderate members of the Assembly, whose ideal was one of democratic liberalism. Hence we should not project onto his words the distinctions and categories that we use today to segment the idea of equality into a series of ever more radical claims ranging from the republican equality of rights to the socialist ideal of actual equality. In Rœderer's day, equality was a single, universal thing. It had no need of an adjective to seem palpable and concrete. Recall, moreover, that equality and liberty, today regarded as antithetical or at any rate in tension with each other, were seen as inseparable at the time of the French Revolution. Indeed, equality was generally considered to be more fundamental. No one in 1789 doubted that equality was the "mother idea" or "rallying cry" of the process that had just begun.[8] The same can be said about the American Revolution. There, too, it was the idea of equality, along with that of independence, that was the key to the political culture of the time. The two revolutions were truly "sisters" in this regard.

4

Consenting to Inequality

The demand for a more active democracy seems to have cut itself loose from the impatience of the beginning. The magnitude of the problem did not go unrecognized, however. For example, many surveys have shown that in Europe, China, and Brazil, a majority—sometimes a vast majority—of people feel that they live in an unjust society,[9] yet they do not act on that belief to issue demands or take political decisions likely to turn things around. Today, it seems as though inequality is implicitly tolerated, although extravagant bonuses and outsized compensation packages have of course been widely deplored in particular cases. Yet a generalized sense that inequalities have grown "too large" or even become "scandalous" coexists with tacit acceptance of many specific forms of inequality and with silent resistance to any practical steps to correct them. Widespread social discontent is thus associated with practical passivity in the face of generalized inequality.

This interpretation is consistent with the findings of a survey conducted in France in 2009 on the "perception of inequality and feelings of injustice."[10] Nearly 90 percent of respondents said that income disparities ought to be reduced, and an even larger percentage felt that a just society ought to guarantee that everyone's basic needs (for shelter, food, health, and education) are met. Yet 57 percent responded that income inequalities are inevitable in a dynamic economy, and 85 percent said that income differences are acceptable when they reward individual merits. Thus there is a global rejection of society as it presently exists together with acceptance of the mechanisms that produce that society. De facto inequalities are rejected, but the mechanisms that generate inequality in general are implicitly recognized. I propose to call this situation, in which people deplore in general what they consent to in particular, the *Bossuet paradox.*[11] This paradox is the source of our contemporary schizophrenia. It is not simply the result of a guilty error but has an epistemological dimension. When we condemn global situations, we look at objective social facts, but we tend to relate particular situations to individual behaviors and choices. The paradox is also related to the fact that moral and social judgments are based on the most visible and extreme situations (such as the gap between rich and poor), into which individuals project themselves *abstractly,* whereas their personal behavior is *concretely* determined by narrower forms of justification. For instance, harsh judgments of the educational system are commonplace, yet individual parents will often circumvent school zoning regulations in order to get their children into better schools.

The evolution of attitudes toward inequality has been furthered by changes in the nature of inequality. Traditional inequalities between social groups have been compounded by inequalities within groups. For example, there is greater variation in the income of different types of managers than there is between the average manager and the average worker. Since this intragroup variation seems to be the result of individual characteristics rather than social causes, it is more readily accepted, especially if it can be related to socially recognized differences of merit. There is a sort of distortion of social judgment. Thus inequality in general can be rejected, while the specific types of inequality that are deemed unacceptable are more limited. Contrast this with class inequalities, which are deemed unacceptable both generally and specifically.

The Crisis of Equality: Understanding It
in Order to Overcome It

Now that a long period of decreasing inequality has come to an end and what I have called the Bossuet paradox has led to widespread acceptance of greater inequality, it is fair to say that we face a crisis of equality. There is an intellectual dimension to this crisis: it reflects the collapse of a whole set of old ideas of justice and injustice. It is also a moral and anthropological crisis, notwithstanding its more apparent economic and social aspects. Hence it must be grasped as a total social fact. It cannot be reduced to a question of unequal income or wealth. It threatens to undermine the very basis of society. We see this in various mechanisms of secession, separatism, and ghettoization that are at work everywhere and have led to what I propose to call a *denationalization* of democracies, a fundamental cause of social distress. We also see it in changing attitudes toward taxation and redistribution, which have weakened welfare states everywhere. The instability is also political, because the Bossuet paradox induces a sense of helplessness. We know more and more about the nature of inequality, yet we do nothing to correct it. "Everything is known and said, yet nothing changes": this seems to be the motto of the modern Leopard. Hence, while we find ourselves facing a deplorable situation, we remain passive, unable to comprehend our paralysis. Our anxiety feeds the search for scapegoats and sends us scurrying toward magical solutions. The instability is political for another reason as well: because the situation in which we find ourselves tends to destroy the very idea of democracy, which was forged to make sense of modern revolution, and this in turn opens the door to political

7

backsliding of one kind or another. And—yet another major political consequence—parties of the left (in the broadest sense of the term), parties that were historically identified with the promotion of equality, have been losing ground.

"Equality" continues to be tossed about as a slogan in speeches and party platforms. Yet even when propped up by resonant adjectives such as "radical" or "real," it has a somewhat empty ring nowadays. The word has somehow become detached from experience, so that it no longer clearly indicates battles that must be fought or goals that need to be achieved. Equality has become a sort of remote deity, which is routinely worshipped but has ceased to inspire any living faith. When used at all, it is generally as a sort of negative incantation—"reduce inequalities"—without a corresponding positive image of a better world. It is no longer a universal value to which everyone can lay claim, as is the case with liberty. Often, it is linked to the reductive idea of fighting overt poverty. The left has lost the historic source of its strength and legitimacy. Hence the reversals that it has suffered everywhere are by no means temporary; they are structural, determined by the breakdown of equality. To be sure, left-wing parties can still win elections, because every election turns as much on the weaknesses of one's enemies as on one's own strengths, but equality is no longer the key to interpreting the actions of the left or mobilizing its troops. It no longer sets the tone for the era. It has lost its revolutionary capacity, in the etymological sense. Democracy itself has been diminished as a result, dragged down by the demons of identity and homogeneity. Hence there is no task more urgent than that of restoring the idea of equality to its former glory. It is the ambition of this book to contribute to that task. To that end, I propose to work in two directions at once, historical and theoretical.

I will explore the historical direction first, because the crisis of equality is the culmination of a lengthy history. It is impossible to understand this crisis as a temporary regression linked to, say, the follies of finance capitalism or the destabilizing effects of unregulated globalization. Nor can it be understood as a straightforward consequence of "neoliberalism," a set of ideas that somehow gained power over people's minds after dictating marching orders to a series of combative governments. These things are not unimportant, yet what is at stake is something much larger. It is a whole era that is coming to an end: an era based on a certain conception of social justice involving redistribution of wealth, forged in the late nineteenth century. We are currently witnessing the consequences and aftershocks of this transition. But in order to understand properly the previous century of redistribution, it, too, must be situated in its proper perspective, as the resolution of a lengthy earlier crisis of equality. This earlier crisis can be traced back to the 1830s, when capitalism began to undo the achievements of the revolution. It attained its acme in the period from 1880 to 1900, the years of the first globalization. This first crisis of equality manifested itself in the rise of nationalism and protectionism along with xenophobic attitudes, which led some to propose principles of identity and homogeneity as answers to "the social question." Redistributive social welfare states came into being as responses to these perverse proposals, offering effective solutions to the social problems of the day. In order to understand the present, we must have these historical precedents in mind, and in the pages that follow I will try to flesh them out. In reviewing this lengthy history, I have found it troubling that the same pathologies that marked the first crisis of equality seem to be making a comeback today. Nationalism, protectionism, xenophobia: all of these things are with us yet again. If we are to overcome this second crisis, we must therefore find a response to today's "social question." But this cannot be done simply by returning to the good old days of redistributive welfare states. Many basic redistributive practices need to be modernized and revived, but we must also go further and rethink the whole idea of equality itself. This is what the social democrats and republicans of the early 1900s did. But they did their thinking in the framework of a corporatist understanding of society, treating institutions of solidarity as mere extensions of an organic vision of the social. We live today in an individualist age and must reformulate things accordingly.

I therefore propose to begin by reexamining the spirit of equality as it was forged in the American and French Revolutions. Equality was then understood primarily as a relation, as a way of making a society, of producing and living in common. It was seen as a democratic quality and not merely as a measure of the distribution of wealth. This relational idea of equality was articulated in connection with three other notions: similarity, independence, and citizenship. Similarity comes under the head of *equality as equivalence:* to be "alike" is to have the same essential properties, such that remaining differences do not affect the character of the relationship. Independence is *equality as autonomy;* it is defined negatively as the absence of subordination and positively as equilibrium in exchange. Citizenship involves *equality as participation,* which is constituted by community membership and civic activity. Consequently, the project of equality as relationship was interpreted in terms of a *world* of like human beings (or *semblables,* as Alexis de Tocqueville would say), a *society* of autonomous individuals, and a *community* of citizens. Equality was thus conceived in terms of the relative position of individuals, the rules governing their interactions, and the principles on which their lives in common were based, and these concepts in turn corresponded to three possible representations of the social bond. The rights of man, the market, and universal suffrage were the underlying institutions. Economic inequalities were seen as acceptable in this framework only if they did not threaten the other modes of relational equality that defined the society of equals. These representations, which were formulated in a precapitalist world, were undermined by the Industrial Revolution, which initiated the first great crisis of equality. In order to overcome the second great crisis, we must recapture the original spirit of equality in a form suitable to the present age. In what follows we will see how the principles of singularity, reciprocity, and communality can restore meaning to the idea of a society of equals and revive the project of creating one. It is these principles that must serve as the basis of legitimacy for new policies of redistribution.

In this book I have been guided more than ever by a desire to maintain a connection between scholarly research and the concerns of citizens. I have sought to explore new horizons by bringing clarity and order to the realm of the thinkable. This book is the work of a historian and political philosopher, but the intellectual stakes are broader. The political point is to demonstrate that the idea of socialism in the twenty-first century will be shaped by the reinvigoration of the democratic ideal through in-depth study of its societal manifestations. The time has come to fight for *integral democracy*, which will come about through the mutual interaction of two ideas that have been kept apart for too long: namely, socialism and democracy. The great intellectual and political debates of the future will involve clarifying the shape and meaning of these two ideas. My only ambition in this book is to lay the cornerstone of this project of refoundation.

I

THE INVENTION OF EQUALITY

The World of Similar Individuals

To understand how the idea of equality came, in 1789, to be identified with the visceral rejection of privilege, there is no better guide than Abbé Sieyès, the author of *Qu'est-ce que le tiers état?* (What Is the Third Estate?). "The privileged individual," Sieyès wrote, "considers himself, along with his colleagues, as constituting a distinct order, a nation of the select within the nation. . . . The privileged actually come to see themselves as another species of man."[1] Half a century later, Tocqueville significantly hit upon the same words to describe the aristocracy: "They scarcely even think of themselves as belonging to the same humanity," he observed in a celebrated remark.[2] He therefore defined democratic society as the opposite of aristocratic society: *une société de semblables,* a society of similar individuals.

The Rejection of "Aristocratic Racism"

Today, it is difficult to understand the aspiration to equality as similarity that existed in 1789 without recognizing the degree to which the nobility of that time was animated by the *spirit of distinc-*

tion. To make sense of this, we can once again start with Sieyès. To justify his argument in the *Essai sur les privilèges,* the father of the first French Constitution appended to his text a damning historical document: a "Petition to the King" by the president of the noble section of the 1614 Estates General. The petition was a response to an appeal by the deputies of the Third Estate to be treated with greater respect. "Treat us as your younger brothers, and we will honor and cherish you," the commoners said to the representatives of the nobility. The nobility, which took this appeal as an insult, replied with a stinging rebuke:

> I am ashamed, Sire, to tell you of the offensive terms in which
> we have once again been addressed. They compare your state to
> a family consisting of three brothers. To what wretched
> condition have we fallen if these words can be taken as true!
> How can so many services rendered since time immemorial, so
> many honors and dignities transmitted hereditarily to the
> nobility and merited by their efforts and loyalty, have been
> reduced to so little? How can the nobility have been linked
> with the vulgar in the closest society that exists among men,
> which is brotherhood. . . . Render judgment, Sire, and in a
> declaration steeped in your justice remind them of their duty
> and order them to recognize what we are, what difference exists
> between us, and tell them that they can in no way compare
> themselves to us.[3]

This petition, intended "to preserve the preeminence of the nobility," was couched in terms that the Third Estate found intolerable. It made explicit the nobility's claim to constitute a superior humanity and stigmatized those who "dared to compare themselves" to these superior beings and "thus misunderstood their own condition."

Since at least the sixteenth century, the nobility in fact openly considered itself to be a separate *race*. To be sure, the meaning attached to this term was different from the one it has today. It was synonymous with lineage or extraction and was typically a part of the language of aristocrats.[4] Although connotations of physiological or ethnic distinctions were absent, the word did denote the idea that certain social qualities are hereditary. Nobles believed that their children were innately equipped to lead. In their eyes, lineages were natural categories. The idea of "race" lay at the root of a hierarchical worldview in which distinctions and conditions stemmed from intrinsic differences. To nobles, this was completely obvious. As they saw it, every social condition corresponded to a certain type of human being. Men shared the same nature but were hereditarily differentiated by their behavior and unequal human value.[5]

From its inception, the Constituent Assembly set itself the goal of destroying these representations and their concrete consequences in terms of tax privileges, exclusive rights, and professional barriers. All but one aspect of this program, the decree adopted on the night of August 4, 1789, is symbolic of the whole enterprise. One cannot leave it at that, however, if the goal is to characterize the spirit of equality that marked the whole period. The aspiration to constitute a society of similar individuals went far beyond denunciation of the aristocracy's most outrageous privileges. Sieyès's attack on privilege aimed at more than just legal exemptions, fantasies of racial superiority, and historical fairy tales. His critique included a much broader range of claims to social superiority and distinction. In his eyes, the "privileged" included all who believed that "they were not made to be confounded, to rub shoulders, to be together."[6] His target was a multifarious propensity to isolation, to separation. The invention of the term "aristocrat," which dates from this period,[7] linked together the many different ways in which commoners experienced social distance, contempt, exclusion, and insuperable social barriers.

America Equally

In fact, this history explains why the stigmatization of aristocracy played as important a structural role in America as in France, even though colonial America had no nobility and none of the legal distinctions that existed in the Old World. Colonial society was nevertheless quite hierarchical, with a very British sense of order and deference, particularly in New England.[8] Although Federalist notables long believed in the need for a "natural aristocracy" (an idea on which they harped incessantly), "equality" soon became the great rallying cry of popular protest. In the colonies of the North as well the South, people voiced disgust with "certain airs of wisdom and superiority" and "affectations of politeness."[9] In Pennsylvania especially, the Revolution was perceived as a conflict between the people and the aristocracy. "Blessed State which brings all so nearly on a level," said ordinary people exasperated by those whom they characterized as "gentlemen."[10] In 1786, representatives of Pennsylvania formally declared that "a democratic government like ours admits of no form of superiority."[11] Years later, one of the most eminent members of the young Constituent Assembly in France was therefore able to link the two revolutions by saying that "like the Americans, we want to regenerate ourselves."[12] The idea of "regeneration" implied a humanity reconciled with itself, rendered equal and one.

A Legacy of Christianity?

How can we explain the advent of this spirit of equality, which animated the revolution of modernity in its three fundamental manifestations (the United States, France, and Santo Domingo)? Did the emergence of a new world suddenly make equality a novel imperative, or did the advent of modernity simply revive the dormant embers of an ancient hearth? And how exactly should we describe the aspiration to constitute a world of similar individuals that stands out as the chief characteristic of this new spirit of equality? The author of *Democracy in America* emphasized the importance of religion in his introduction: "Christianity, which made all men equal in the sight of God, will not shrink from seeing all citizens as equals in the eyes of the law."[13] Was democratic equality thus merely the fulfillment of an old promise? Was the modern revolution merely the heir of the Christian revolution? "The most profound geniuses of Greece and Rome, the most comprehensive of ancient minds, never hit upon the very general yet at the same time very simple idea that all men are alike and that each is born with an equal right to liberty. . . . [I]t took the coming of Jesus Christ to make people understand that all members of the human race are by nature similar and equal."[14] There are many passages of the Bible that might be enlisted in support of this contention. Paul's Epistle to the Galatians (3:28), "There is neither Jew nor Gentile, neither slave nor free, nor is there male and female, for you are all one in Christ Jesus," is among those most frequently cited. In support of this interpretation one might also point to the centrality of the theological argument in the work of John Locke, who sought to prove that the principles of the English Revolution originated in the Bible. In his polemic with Robert Filmer, he devoted long

chapters of his *Treatise of Government* to the defense of radical egalitarianism, citing the categorization of species in Genesis.[15]

The egalitarian aspect of the Gospel message cannot be denied,
but the equality in question is not democratic equality. It is essentially spiritual and not directly related to any social or political
understanding. Although Christianity never stopped preaching
the principle of natural equality, it did not derive any "revolutionary" consequence from its teaching. As evidence of this—but one
example among many—we can look to the first major Christian
treatise of domestic morality, *De Institutione laicali* by Jonas, bishop
of Orleans. Published after the end of Charlemagne's reign, the
work strongly affirmed the idea that rich and poor, as well as master and slave, were "natural equals," but it in no way drew from this
the conclusion that slavery should be abolished or conditions made
more similar.[16] The point was to inspire respect and consideration
for others, to urge recognition of the unique value of every human
being, and to insist that everyone participate in the same economy
of salvation. In other words, what was supposed to follow from this
religious idea of equality was a morality of charity, not a political or
social model of any kind. Hence we need to distinguish what we
might call "human equality" and "social equality" in order to move
beyond vague suggestions of Christianity's role in the advent of the
modern spirit of equality.

The same can be said about the spirit of equality in America,
even though religious references were quite explicit there during
the revolutionary period. This is manifestly the case in the first of
the truths held to be "self-evident" in the Declaration of Independence (July 4, 1776): "All men are created equal."[17] It is also undeniable that the evangelical movements of the eighteenth century, superimposed on the original Puritan rootstock, found in Scripture

language and arguments that colonial militants drew on repeatedly as a ready source of authority. But from these biblical arguments they drew novel and radical consequences. Thus there was a sort of "subversion from within" of the religious message: despite the seeming continuity of the words, a profound rupture was in fact taking place.

The Ambiguities of Natural Equality

In addition to the Christian view of equality, legal and philosophical theories of natural equality also played a key role. These were influential throughout the eighteenth century. Although they retained a certain ambiguity, they contributed to an important rupture. This is clear from the tenor of the *Encyclopédie* article on the notion.[18] "Since human nature is the same in all human beings," the article states, "it is clear that each person must respect and treat others as individuals naturally equal to him- or herself, that is, as equally human." The article in no way challenged the existence of the nobility with all its attributes. For the author, the scope of natural equality was strictly limited to the moral dimension, implying nothing more than "duties of charity, humanity, and justice." This was quite a long way from the hidden power that the idea of an equality of similar individuals turned out to have in 1789, when it raised the prospect of limitless subversion of differences of every kind. The celebrated refrain that rebellious English peasants chanted in 1381, which they took from a sermon by John Ball—"When Adam delved and Eve span, who was then the gentleman?"—was already a good deal more radical. The starting point for Louis de Jaucourt/Sylvain Maréchal was also a stopping point, yet it was ambiguous enough to open the way to democratic equality. Indeed, democratic equality cannot be circumscribed or limited by any definition that would preclude the kinds of interrogation, controversy, and demands to which it gives rise. Conservatives, moreover, have persistently sought to impose such limits.

The Intellectual and Social Revolution of Similarity

In addition to the Christian legacy and the theories of natural right, two other factors contributed in the eighteenth century to the destabilization of early representations of the social bond, thus paving the way for the "revolution of similarity." The first of these factors was of an anthropological and biological order. It stemmed from the new conception of species made famous by the work of Georges-Louis Leclerc, Comte de Buffon. The second was sociological, associated with the advent of the individual.

It was in 1749 that Buffon inaugurated his *Histoire naturelle* with an essay "On the Nature of Man." In it, he described man as a unique and superior being totally distinct from all other animal species, owing to the nature of his understanding, the duration of his life and period of growth, and the existence of a "superior principle" that enabled him to expand his intellectual activity indefinitely, thereby increasing the distance between himself and other animals. Man was also malleable enough to thrive and multiply in all climates thanks to his ability to form complex and diverse societies with others like himself.[19] By thus showing that the identity of the human species was a material fact, Buffon changed the way in which it was perceived. This objectification altered understanding and provided a material basis for moral considerations of common dignity. Its tendency was in fact to minimize the differences between "civilized man" and "savage man," as well as between the inhabitants of different countries. In the concluding chapter of the essay, entitled "Varieties within the Human Species," Buffon explained that physical differences of appearance and skin color were simply the result of "external and accidental causes" and should be seen as subject to further evolution and even possible reversal.[20] For Buffon, then, the human race was originally one and its diversity was merely accidental, thus suggesting that the concept of "species" ought to be based on the notion of similarity. Therein lay the conceptual revolution. "All similar individuals existing on the surface of the earth are regarded as composing the species of such individuals."[21] *"Species,"* Buffon continued, "is an abstract and general word," because if it is to be used as a descriptive category, creatures must be considered in terms of their *essential qualities* and not their appearances. At this point in his argument, Buffon invoked Gottfried Wilhelm Leibniz's definition of similarity: things are similar if the only intrinsic difference between them is one of quantity. Identity of quantity implies equality, but identity of quality defines similarity.[22] This made it possible to rethink relations among human beings, although it would prove difficult to find suitable social terms in which to express this new definition: in both the United States and France, "equality" was the only generic term to convey the urgency of defining a new world of similar individuals.

The advent of the individual, the transition from *homo hierarchicus* to *homo aequalis,* to borrow Louis Dumont's categories, was also among the triggers that unleashed the modern demand for equality. This is not the place to treat this question systematically, and in any case, it is a question intimately bound up with the whole history of the social sciences. It is nevertheless worth noting that the advent of the individual cannot be understood as a simple process of disintegration of community in favor of the individuals comprised within it. Individuals had always existed, of course, and individual histories mattered long before the modern era began. The question should rather be approached in terms of the way in which the social bond is constituted. In so-called traditional societies, it was the identification with specific, highly structured subgroups that was essential. These societies were segmented (by castes, orders, estates, etc.), but these constituent subgroups were in many respects homogeneous. Distinguishing and identifying factors were thus fixed and embedded in society itself. Modernity changed this state of affairs for good by introducing complexity and diversity. As trade increased, populations became increasingly mobile, and as knowledge accumulated, societies became increasingly heterogeneous. "Individual variations," to borrow the language of the naturalist, seemed more palpable and marked.[23] The way in which individual identities and social relations were constructed was profoundly modified as a result. As we will see in what follows, authors such as Gabriel Tarde and Georg Simmel called attention to these changes at the turn of the twentieth century.

The Society of Independent Individuals

"In the formation of a society, we take it as a principle that all men who join that society are equals. This does not mean that they are all equal in height, talent, industry, or wealth, which would be absurd; but they are all *equals in liberty*." So said Jean-Paul Rabaut Saint-Étienne in the summer of 1789 in his *Idées sur les bases de toute constitution*.[24] Here, the idea of a society of equals refers to a form of social relation, a type of society, in which no person is subject to the will of any other person. Social equality is not an individual *attribute*. It makes sense only as a *social capacity*. To be autonomous is to be able to invent one's life, to exist as a subject responsible for oneself. Individual autonomy therefore implies a social guarantee: it can be deployed only in a society that banishes *all* forms of dependency. In a world of freedom, therefore, only a *society* of independent individuals makes sense. Autonomy necessarily finds its place in a framework of *active reciprocity*.

This understanding of equality lies at the heart of the Rousseauist ideal. In a letter that young Jean-Jacques sent to his father at the age of nineteen, he expressed his wish "to live without the help of others."[25] This is the reason for his praise, in *Émile,* of the figure of the artisan, "of all conditions the most independent of fortune and of men."[26] For Rousseau, this independence is the condition of a fully social existence. It allows each individual to establish a just relation to others, with mutual independence fostering positive exchange. To characterize the form of equality that Rousseau desired, one of his most profound commentators, Jean Starobinski, rightly spoke of "reciprocity of free consciousnesses."[27] This equality is associated with *human commerce* that is truly free. The prospect of such "equality as liberty" formed the historical matrix in which the modern aspiration to an emancipated existence developed. It therefore became identified with the fight against what appeared to be its radical negation: slavery. Slavery thus became the antithesis of political liberalism in the seventeenth and eighteenth centuries.

Slavery as the Archetype of Inequality

For us, the word "slavery" immediately evokes the horrors of the triangular trade and the situation of blacks in America before the

Civil War and in the Caribbean before emancipation. It merges in our minds with the history of colonization and of cotton and sugar plantations in the tropics. This was not the case in the seventeenth and eighteenth centuries. The word "slavery" was then used in a much broader sense to describe any ostensibly intolerable situation of dependence. The connotations of the word were primarily political and social, and only in a secondary sense was it used to denote a legal regime of economic servitude. In anti-absolutist literature, oppressed individuals and peoples subject to the whims of a despot who ignored their rights and denied their humanity were called "slaves." Just as the existence of privilege contradicted the idea that all men are similar, slavery radically negated the ideal of autonomy. At the end of the seventeenth century, for example, Pierre Jurieu, a leader of the Protestant resistance and one of Louis XIV's most celebrated adversaries, entitled his major work *Les soupirs de la France esclave qui aspire après la liberté* (The Sighs of Enslaved France, Which Aspires to Liberty).[28] At about the same time, in an England in the throes of revolution, Locke began his *Treatise on Civil Government* with a denunciation of slavery, and Algernon Sidney, the great theorist of English republicanism, entitled one of the first of his *Discourses Concerning Government* "To depend upon the Will of a Man is Slavery." In the eighteenth century, John Trenchard and Thomas Gordon wrote *Cato's Letters,* attacking the policies of the Walpole government and, in particular, the "condition of slavery" in which Englishmen lived. Accordingly, they compared their program of civil and political emancipation to abolition of this servile state. "Slavery is, to live at the mere mercy of another; and a life of slavery is, to those who can bear it, a continual state of uncertainty and wretchedness."[29]

Jaucourt, in long articles on "slavery" and "slave" written for the *Encyclopédie,* also dealt primarily with "political and civil slavery."

He described this in very general terms as a "violation of the principle of the natural equality of human beings" and associated it with situations in which an individual found himself deprived of dignity or autonomy. The word "slavery" stood for all that was most unbearable in the dependence of one person on another and of the difference in rank or status between individuals. When he wrote of slavery in the narrow sense, he referred only to ancient slavery, an artifact of archaic barbarity. Surprisingly for today's reader, he devoted only a brief passage at the end of the article to the situation of those whom he called "Negro slaves."

We find the same paradox in mid-eighteenth-century America. Political articles and pamphlets commonly denounced slavery there, and the depiction of Americans as slaves of the English was a central trope of independence rhetoric from 1750 to 1770. "We are the most abject of slaves," John Adams wrote.[30] Numerous other voices echoed the sentiment that because Americans paid taxes to which their representatives had not consented, they were slaves of the English. The servitude of the blacks who worked the plantations of the South figured much less prominently in this political literature, and when it was mentioned at all, it was only to be compared to the situation of the Americans vis-à-vis England or of Europeans living under despotic regimes! The slavery of the Negro was not considered to be more inhuman or degrading. American writers argued that if their "partial liberty" were to continue, they would end up no better than plantation slaves. Some went so far as to maintain that at least the Negroes elicited pity, whereas Americans were openly scorned by the colonial authorities. In both America and France, the force of the appeal for a society of autonomous individuals stemmed from the stigmatization of this kind of dependence.

The Issue of "Indentured Labor" in America

In colonial America, however, the concept of dependency included more than just this. For many Americans of humble station it also referred to direct experience or awareness of "indentured labor." In the seventeenth and eighteenth centuries, many immigrants could not afford to pay their own ways to America. Before the revolution in travel due to the advent of steam, maritime transportation was expensive and largely beyond the reach of people whose poverty might otherwise have encouraged them to take a chance on emigration. In many English and other European ports, ship captains or their agents would offer to provide transportation in exchange for a signature on a labor contract whose terms were highly unfavorable to the signer, who incurred an obligation to work for free for a period of five to seven years.[31] The system was also applied coercively to individuals sentenced for nonpayment of debt: the contract was a form of reimbursement. Delinquents could be deported, as could orphans whose parishes wished to get rid of them to reduce their assistance costs. The ship's captain or his agent would then sell the contract to an employer upon arrival, reimbursing himself for the cost of transportation plus a substantial profit. The employer paid the immigrant nothing for the specified duration of the contract, providing only room and board. In most cases a small severance payment was given at the expiration of the agreement. Indentured workers, generally called servants, were thus subjected for a fixed period to a form of servitude (sometimes known as "white servitude"), in the sense that they were legally bound to another individual. The law severely punished any indentured servant who attempted to quit his or her master. The servile character of the position was in many cases reinforced by harsh working conditions and treatment fit for a prisoner. In addition, the indenture could be resold before the contract lapsed, and the worker would then be transferred like movable property to another master.[32]

It has been estimated that as many as half of the immigrants to the thirteen colonies arrived on American shores as indentured servants. Hence experience of this type of dependency was widespread in the colonies, something that many Americans knew intimately in mind and body. Oppressive apprenticeship statutes established a similar type of dependency. Paradoxically, Americans were familiar with a wider range of servile statuses than existed in England. Thus many who wished to throw off the colonial yoke also aspired to establish themselves as independent workers. The term "independence" therefore acquired a double meaning. A republic could consist only of autonomous individuals (or "self-dependent" individuals, to use a term that was common at the time), men and women who were their own masters and in control of their own destinies, free of any type of personal dependence. The "social question" in America in the 1770s and 1780s was therefore not one of economic inequality between rich and poor: the fundamental divide was that which separated independence from dependence. Liberty was therefore intimately intertwined with equality. Individual autonomy was seen as essential to the regeneration of the social bond, which would be healthy again only when individuals ceased to be separated by barriers of any kind.

Market Equality

It was in this context that the formal idea of "market equality" emerged. To be equal to another individual meant to be capable of entering into free exchange in a reciprocal relationship: commutative equality, in other words. Reflecting this idea, the eighteenth-century meaning of the word "commerce" was more sociological than economic. It referred, in fact, to any peaceful and balanced relation between individuals. Hence it stood in contrast to a political order in which the masses were subject to the will of a few. Exchange substituted objective equivalence for the confrontation of wills and imbalance of power that existed in the political sphere. In the *Encyclopédie* article on "commerce," François Véron de Forbonnais wrote that "what we mean by this word in general is reciprocal communication. It applies more particularly to the communication between individuals of the products of their land and industry." In this connection, economic exchange constituted one of the *practical modes* of equality as relation. When individuals exchanged the fruits of their labor, they affirmed both their status as *independent equals* and their relationship as *interdependent equals*. In other words, people in the eighteenth century believed in the possibility of regenerative exchange. They spontaneously dreamed of ushering in a new world of a sort that Marcel Mauss would much later describe in his *Essai sur le don:* a world in which "the economy" is a process that mingles lives together with things, that recognizes the dignity of individuals while establishing equivalence through transactions.[33] One cannot understand the spirit of equality in the American and French Revolutions without recognizing this idea of the market as both an expression of liberty and a vector of equality. The market was seen as an institution of equality.[34] The eighteenth century thus theorized the *liberalism of reciprocity*.[35]

The emancipatory view of the market took a different form in Europe. In America, it was the *worker* who aspired to independence. In Europe, *work* was hamstrung by corporatist and regulatory restrictions that led to monopolies, which in turn resulted in inequalities and exclusions. In France, the abolition of guilds and closed corporations in 1790 symbolized this fight for market equality. In England, critics focused on apprenticeship rules, which Adam Smith discussed at length in *The Wealth of Nations*.[36] Classical political economy was thus intimately associated with the historical sociology of emancipation and independence, as Smith's work brilliantly attests. But Smith merely reflected the general tendency of the era. Before him, John Millar, a leading figure of the Scottish Enlightenment, whose work anticipated certain key themes of *The Wealth of Nations*, had already linked the market to the constitution of a society of equal and independent individuals. In his *Origin of the Distinction of Ranks*, he argued that the progress of civilization depended on the number of merchants and artisans with a direct interest in expanding their industry. Conversely, a society in which a large number of people live in a "state of dependency," tied to the soil and subject to their masters, tends to reproduce itself without change, since the means of subsistence come from submission to others rather than from one's own activity. For Millar, the emancipation of dominated social classes, be they servants, slaves, agricultural laborers, women, or children, was the vehicle of historic progress. "The influence of commerce and manufacturing seems to encourage liberty and tends toward a form of popular government."[37]

Thus, the idea of reciprocal utility was ready to replace that of hierarchical authority as a way of conceptualizing a properly functioning society, with equality and liberty marching shoulder to shoulder. For Millar, the advent of a republic of artisans coincided with the expansion of a market society.[38] In England in the second half of the eighteenth century, the language of economic liberalism was often tinged with neo-Harringtonian accents and filled with formulas drawn from civic republicanism and "country" ideology.[39] Later in the century, James Steuart would develop similar themes in his *Inquiry into the Principles of Political Economy*. He, too, argued that modern liberty was simply a consequence of economic independence. He developed an elaborate historical theory of the evolution of political regimes based on different types of social subordination. "All authority," he wrote, "is proportionate to dependence."[40] "The disadvantage, therefore, of the monarchical form, in point of trade and industry, does not proceed from the inequality it establishes among the citizens, *but from the consequence of this inequality,* which is very often accompanied with an arbitrary and indeterminate subordination between the individuals of the higher classes, and those of the lower; or between those vested with the execution of the laws and the body of the people associated with the advent of a society of autonomous individuals."[41] For Steuart, too, the market was thus associated with the advent of a society of autonomous individuals. It was possible for such a positive view of the market to take hold in the eighteenth century because the Industrial Revolution had yet to do its damage. The idea of an emancipatory and egalitarian liberalism therefore made perfectly good sense.

Optimistic Liberalism

"Anything that may establish the dependence of man on man should be proscribed in a republic."[42] These words of Bertrand Barère set the tone for the French Revolution's efforts to build a society of individuals. What the revolutionaries envisioned was not just a market society but a society in which each individual was master of his or her own fate and responsible for his or her own subsistence. The humiliating dependency of some on the assistance of the powerful was seen as a straightforward consequence of a more generalized dependency, a hypocritical and misleading extension of the subjugation on which the entire social order was based. The moral dignity of the individual was therefore inseparable from a capability of material independence. The idea of independence clearly indicated the advent of a new era in the history of humanity, the coming of which was greeted with extraordinary optimism.

Nicolas de Condorcet's *Esquisse d'un tableau historique des progrès de l'esprit humain* was a typical expression of this optimism. The philosopher identified the modern revolution with necessary progress toward equality. "Our hopes concerning the future of the human species can be summed up in three major points: an end to inequality among nations; progress toward equality within each people; and finally, real perfection of man."[43] Then would follow "actual equality, the ultimate goal of the social art, which, by diminishing even the effects of natural differences in the faculties, leaves standing only an inequality useful to the interest of all, because it will favor the progress of civilization, education, and industry without entailing dependency, humiliation, or impoverishment."[44] In describing the conditions under which progress toward this desirable state of affairs would occur, Condorcet identified three sources of difference among men: inequalities of wealth, inequalities of education, and inequalities stemming from the accidents of life. These three kinds of inequality were destined, he believed, "to diminish continually" (though never to disappear altogether). How? His arguments on the first point are particularly interesting to us. "It is easy to prove," he said, "that fortunes tend naturally toward equality, and that their excessive disproportion either could not exist or would cease promptly if civil laws did not establish artificial means of perpetuating and amassing them and if freedom of commerce and industry eliminated the advantage that every prohibitive law and fiscal privilege grants to acquired wealth."[45] This passage captures the economic optimism of the period.

In no sense, however, did Condorcet link this optimism, based on a general faith in the effects of progress, to the prospect of unlimited growth. On this point he was still a long way from Karl Marx. He shared the belief in moderating the passions and embedding economic activity in social relations. Although he denied advocating an "ill-conceived austerity," he nevertheless believed that "simplicity of manners" was necessary and that riches ought not to be "means of satisfying vanity and ambition."[46] These views, which might seem to be a legacy of the Jansenist philosophy of an earlier period, were still quite prevalent at the turn of the nineteenth century, during the course of which capitalism would impose laws of its own.

This persistence of faith in simplicity and moderation can be seen clearly in *Olbie*, the first published work of Jean-Baptiste Say. Published in 1799, this essay by the man who would become the indispensable economic thinker of the generation that witnessed the Industrial Revolution was in fact the work of a moralist. Indeed, its subtitle was "Essay on Ways of Improving a Nation's Morals." In a style deeply influenced by eighteenth-century utopian writers, Say describes the Olbians, the inhabitants of a country that has recently jettisoned its reactionary past (the fable is transparent). In order to establish a new administration and craft legislation tailored to the needs of a regenerated nation, a "good treatise on political economy" was deemed essential. But what the future economic educator gives us in this early text is not a preliminary draft of the work for which he would later become famous. In essence it is a lengthy exhortation to live soberly, to beware of excessive wealth, and to take care lest "the love of work be continually spurred by the desire for gain." In Olbie there was neither excessive opulence nor extreme indigence. Simplicity of taste was "a ground for preference and an object of consideration." If a man did his work badly—if he was, say, a merchant or artisan who abused the trust of his fellow citizens or an administrator who failed to render the services expected of him—then he should be declared a "useless person."[47] Thus the market would be regulated by morality and social pressure. Neither Malthusian pessimism nor the demons of large-scale industry had yet to darken this picture of the world.

The Republic of Modest Individuals

Optimistic liberalism and the idea of market equality lent intellectual credibility to the project of creating a society of independent individuals. Existing social structures were also important, however, especially in America. The disappearance of indentured labor, which was all but complete by 1790, had changed white society (we will see later how blacks were excluded from the collective imaginary). The young United States was at that time an essentially agricultural country of three million people (compared with twenty-five million in France). In England, 50 percent of the workforce was employed in agriculture, but in the United States 90 percent of the people were farmers, most of whom lived in small rural communities in which everyone knew everyone else. America was a land of smallholders, whereas in England four hundred families owned 20 percent of the land. American society was a society of face-to-face interaction and not yet a civil-commercial society of the sort that England and France were becoming. Trade in commodities was almost always enmeshed in neighborly social relations, and money played only a secondary role. In many instances, dealings with merchants and artisans involved an informal system of credit rather than direct cash payments.[48] Most Americans lived in a fairly homogeneous "society of trust," subject to strong social pressures, and in this context the idea of liberty was closely bound up with strong egalitarian sentiments. One might even speak of a veritable "culture of equality," an expression meant to capture the touchy pride of the mass of relatively independent artisans, merchants, and farmers.[49] To James Madison, it followed that the small independent farmer was the natural basis of republican liberty, an attitude that was in fact even more forcefully articulated in anti-federalist circles.[50] Although American society did evolve rapidly, this original spirit lived on, and the idea of equality remained firmly fixed in the myth of the independent individual, to whom any redistributive conception of society was alien.

Although the France of 1789 was quite different from the nascent United States, similar images of equality/liberty flourished there as well. The political ideal was the same. In France, however, these images were more remote from actual experience (even though the Revolution did have a significant effect on the distribution of landed property) and figured mainly in inspirational utopian literature or nostalgic tales. The French, like the Americans, dreamed of a republic of small farmers and artisans and would continue to do so for many years to come.[51]

The Community of Citizens

Citizenship is the third mode of expression of a society of equals. Equality is here expressed by way of inclusion or participation. The citizen is seen as both a subject, bearing specific rights, and as a member of a community. He is at once individual *and* people.[52] This figure of equality is in some ways a *measure* and in others a *relation,* and this dual nature accounts for the distinctiveness as well as the centrality of universal suffrage, which both recognizes *individual equality* (one man, one vote) and exhibits the *individual-in-community* (as a participant in the body politic).

The Individual Voter, or Radical Equality

One man, one vote: there is no simpler or more universally accepted notion of equality. If establishing equality in other areas remained problematic, in the political realm the solution seemed simple. When it comes to voting, no one would deny that equality in the most basic arithmetic sense is the only just way to allocate rights. This distinction—one might even call it an exception—deserves to be underlined. In no other type of resource do we find this coincidence of justice with equality. If individuals are "totally different and unequal," as Aristotle believed, then arithmetic equality and fairness are fundamentally separate concepts. Marx drove this point home, noting that in a world of diversity, arithmetic equality is inequality.[53] This led to his formulation of just distribution as *"to each according to his needs."* In voting, however, fairness and equality coincide perfectly.

The ballot homogenizes arguments and intentions and reduces them to a measurable, objective data point. It couches heterogeneous expressions in a common language and radically simplifies the social world. The ballot box reduces different reasons and passions to a uniform measure. Any hierarchy of knowledge or talent is set aside, and motives are not considered. In the end, the votes are simply counted, boiling the variety of individual preferences down to a clear, impersonal result. Equality thus arises from the fact that the votes are counted rather than weighed (the opposite of what suffrage, limited by property qualification, achieved). The citizen, endowed with one vote, is seen as a pure individual, symmetrical with all other individuals and stripped of all specific characteristics. "Citizens enjoy the right to be represented," Sieyès argued, "by virtue only of the qualities they share in common and not those which differentiate them."[54] To put it another way, the citizen symbolizes the generality that exists in each individual. He is identified, as Claude Lefort rightly observed, with a sort of "degree zero of sociality."[55] In exercising the right to vote, each individual is divested of his defining characteristics and associations. Abstraction is thus the quality that constitutes him socially and drives the development of the idea of political equality. That is why this form of equality is so radical and exemplary. It emancipates the individual from all the distinctions by which men are usually ordered and classified. From the learned scholar to the simplest spirit, from the richest man to the poorest of the poor—all are regarded as equally capable of thinking about the common good and drawing the dividing line between the just and the unjust.

Hence the advent of universal suffrage initiated a major revolution. It not only opened a new phase in the lengthy emancipation of humanity but also marked a crucial qualitative rupture. Some will judge this to have been a formal advance only and emphasize the manifold manipulations that followed. Nevertheless, it changed all previous understandings of the social bond. Indeed, universal suffrage establishes an order whose cohesiveness does not depend on the division of labor, collective belief, or assignment of each individual to a particular place in an organic whole. In other words, it is the order neither of market society nor of traditional hierarchical society. Universal suffrage opens up a new horizon for the collective imaginary: a horizon of radical, immaterial equivalence among men. It is a "constituent" right. *It produces society itself:* it is the equivalence among individuals that constitutes society. In this way, the right to vote achieves modernity, as the "democratic moment" that it symbolizes is superimposed on its "liberal moment," that of the autonomy of the subject.

The assertion that each individual counts as one and has a claim to an equal share of sovereignty, an identical capacity to offer an informed opinion about the organizing principles of life in common, goes much farther than a simple declaration of rights to free expression, dignity, security, and even subsistence. In this respect, one can even argue that the idea of democracy introduced a much more significant *intellectual* break in the concept of humanity than did the idea of socialism. In any case, the utopia of an economically egalitarian society was formulated long before the idea of political equality appeared. In the eighteenth century, for example, utopians such as Jean Meslier and Étienne-Gabriel Morelly boldly discussed ideas such as leveling disparities of wealth and common ownership of property yet did not for a moment consider the possibility that everyone might carry equal weight in political decision making. At its inception, socialism aimed to achieve a social community of brothers rather than a political society of equals. Although Charles Fourier, Pierre-Joseph Proudhon, and Marx had different ideas of the form such a community might take, all dreamed of reviving a mythical "primitive socialism," a form of organization *natural* to uncorrupted humanity. For them, the new society was but the resurrection and transformation of the world before the fall—a fall that they attributed to capitalism and individualism.

The Assembly of Citizens

The *right to vote* is not simply a personal attribute. It is also inseparable from the existence of a collectivity: the citizenry. Both elements—the possession of a personal right and the constitution of a community—clearly came together in the American and French Revolutions. That is why the notion of an *electoral college* took on central importance from the beginning. In the French case in particular, the right to vote was exercised in a physical setting of which we have lost all memory (although the term "college" has survived in law): a living gathering of citizens. The distance from contemporary practice is striking. Today, throughout the world, voting means entering a voting booth to fill out a secret ballot, which is then deposited in a ballot box. The whole operation takes no more than a few minutes. No words need be spoken. The ritual is solitary and silent. If a crowd gathers, it is only because people are forced to wait quietly in line for their turn to vote. No one would think of initiating an actual exchange of views. This is "seriality" in its purest form. For us, this scene is the very image of universal suffrage, but it was not always this way. In France, for instance, the voting booth was not introduced until 1913 and indeed was adopted in most places around the world in the early part of the twentieth century.[56] Originally, however, voting meant participating in lengthy meetings. The French case, which is particularly well documented, is instructive.[57] The material history of voting has long taken a back seat to legal and political histories of electoral laws, but it is essential for understanding how citizenship is exercised.

In 1789, the people voted in assemblies for the simple reason that no one had yet thought of any other way to do it.[58] Participating and meeting, like voting and deliberating, had never been regarded as separate activities. No one at the time would have interpreted "electoral participation" in the individualistic terms that seem natural today. The old "assemblies of inhabitants" were the inevitable starting point for everyone,[59] and the rules governing convocation of the Estates General "naturally" stipulated that deputies were to be elected in a complex process (involving several stages) based on votes expressed in large assemblies. The only difference—and it was an important one—was that after 1789 it was individual citizens who were summoned to meet rather than trade guilds, parishes, or some other form of constituted community. The rather awkward term for these meetings was "assemblies by individuals."[60] They were the very symbol of popular sovereignty.

The size of these *primary assemblies,* which met in each canton, varied with successive regulations but never exceeded nine hundred members. Beyond that number the body would be subdivided. In some rural areas, no more than four hundred members assembled, but this was still a large group. In the countryside, the only buildings large enough to receive this many people were churches. Elsewhere meetings were held in auditoriums or local government buildings. The procedure was complicated: verifying credentials, setting up an administrative office, calling voters by name to receive their ballots, and counting votes. Everything was slowed down by the fact that there were no official candidates, which meant many rounds of voting. Assemblies therefore took two or three long days to complete their work.[61] Participants truly felt themselves to be members of a group. They experienced citizenship as participation in an event no less than as an individual right. Many official texts used the term "members of primary assemblies" to refer to active citizens, thus implying that citizenship had a collective dimension.

These assemblies brought together men whom everything usually kept apart. Social horizons were broadened, as voters from different localities in the same canton gathered for the vote. Above all, the assemblies created a novel type of social relation between individuals of different conditions. Distinctions were effaced by proximity and hidden by the neutrality of alphabetical ordering. The experience gave the most modest of participants a sense of an expanded existence. Sieyès spoke of the "human assimilation" fostered by "the moral consciousness of the primariate [*sic*] to which one belongs."[62] The neologism "primariate" was meant to indicate that the primary assemblies represented a specific type of socialization. As one member of the Constituent Assembly explained,

> the ordinary man likes to find himself among his fellow citizens
> of all walks of life. If he encounters there one of those people who
> are so wealthy that in other circumstances they would scarcely pay
> attention to a citizen, he will approach him, because he knows
> that this man will not feel toward him the same disdain that he
> affects in the ordinary course of life. Here, all men draw closer
> together, equality breathes, and men of all walks of life, especially
> those who are not wealthy, like to participate in these
> assemblies.[63]

This is a good description of the type of social bond that was experienced in this setting. The right to vote, in the form of participation in primary assemblies, might thus be compared to a kind of sacrament of equality, of which it was an effective living symbol. Citizenship of this kind expanded the imagination and enabled people to envision novel relationships to others. As citizen, each individual experienced temporary relief from the pressures and influences that determined him (be they economic, social, or cultural). Significantly, contemporaries often used the phrase "moral electricity" to characterize this feeling of experiencing a previously unknown bond. One function of the assembly was thus to transfigure the quotidian in such a way as to signal the advent of a society of equals. This symbolic and moral effect of citizenship—one might almost call it utopian, so great was the abyss that it created between the old and the new—was often stressed by petitioners. For example, new voters petitioning the National Assembly noted "that we are changed."[64] In a petition drafted in April 1790 to mark the first communion of the children of a certain village, we find these words: "These are the premises of the glorious quality of citizen, which we owe to your labors and your virtues. . . . *We have become similar [semblables] to you,* members of the august body of Christian citizens."[65] Here, the idea of citizenship went together with the recognition of dignity. "Nothing does more honor to the justice of the legislator," another petition from the same era read, "than the determination he has enshrined in law to raise the humblest of citizens up from the contempt in which the insolence of our old institutions kept him in a degraded condition and to admit him to the noble title of activity, wherein he has contributed to the choice made by the representatives of the citizenry."[66] The ceremony that the comte de Mirabeau imagined for solemnly inscribing the names of youths who had reached the age of twenty-one on the official roll of citizens illustrates the symbolic character of the idea: "In patriotic and therefore religious ceremonies," he said, "everything shall speak of equality. All distinctions shall be effaced by the character of citizen."[67]

Thus, to be a citizen was to be granted a validating personal status as a member of a collectivity. Looking at American history in this light, Judith Shklar strongly stressed this aspect of the suffrage: "I know how illusory would be the belief that my vote determined anything; but nevertheless when I go to the polls, I have a satisfaction in the sense that we are all engaged in a common venture."[68] To have the right to vote is to count for something, to be someone important in the group, reflected in the fact that the candidates solicit your vote. During the campaign, at least, the voter sees people in power bowing down before him. Political science has long known, moreover, that voters are often less concerned with expressing a right than with asserting an identity or affiliation. This may help to explain a paradoxical fact that is particularly evident in the United States, namely, that people will fight passionately for the right to vote and then fail to make full use of it. Intense battles over voting rights have thus been followed by very low turnouts in elections. The same was true of France shortly after the Revolution, where very high abstention rates were observed.[69] "To be a voter," Shklar observes, "was as much a condition as a call to action."[70]

Civic Festivals and the Democratic Imagination

Elections were frequent during the French Revolution, and the procedures were often long and complicated. Despite the intensity of such moments, elections were in themselves insufficient to create a sense of community among citizens because of the extent to which they were hamstrung by procedural rules. Great importance was therefore attached to the organization of public festivals and other gatherings. Free of any institutional constraint, these were intended specifically to produce a palpable sense of community. In an age steeped in empiricist philosophy, people were convinced that the warmth of such gatherings and the influence of symbols would have tangible moral and sociological effects. The festivals offered an opportunity to "cast the nation in a mold," as one observer said.[71] Fabre d'Églantine summed up the political objectives in a speech to the Convention: "To seize people's imagination and govern them."[72] This imperative made it clear that no one was counting on institutions and laws alone to produce citizenship. Everyone knew that heads and hearts also mattered. Festivals were seen as a straightforward means of producing society. Indeed, the Constitution of 1791 recognized this role in Article I: "National festivals shall be established to preserve the memory of the French Revolution, promote fraternity among citizens, and foster devotion to the Constitution, the nation, and the law." Although the festivals of the revolutionary period had many immediate goals and a variety of contexts, all served to "gather people together in the one and indivisible space of civic ardor and transparency of the heart."[73] They made the social unit manifest and in a way demonstrated equality by merging the individual into an indistinguishable mass, a mere numerical constituent of a warmly emotional crowd. In this sense, they had two goals: to enable people to experience a transfigured, harmonious space and to dramatize the abolition of distinctions.

The first purpose of the revolutionary festivals was to allow participants to experience a truly public space. Festivals were organized as open assemblies, in contrast to earlier assemblies, which were compartmentalized and segregated by rank. In exemplary fashion, the Festival of the Federation, with its unified geometry, symbolized the advent of a horizontal world, plucking participants from their habitual constricted environments and proposing a veritable "dramaturgy of national unity," to borrow Mona Ozouf's excellent phrase.[74] The Champ de Mars therefore became the primary Parisian venue for large celebrations. Revolutionary processions headed there spontaneously, usually ignoring the capital's prominent places and thus demonstrating "that they were less concerned with a geographic center than with a metaphysical center."[75] The festivals sought to create moments of harmony, merging hearts and bodies in one unanimous whole. "The festivals impress a single, uniform character on the social mass," one commentator observed at the time, "and this creates a single, uniform spirit . . . which therefore molds all members of the state into a single, uniform whole."[76] It was expected that these events would instill a sense of the Republic as "one and indivisible" and effect a moral and social transformation of separate individuals into citizens. The real object of a festival was thus not its immediate pretext, such as the commemoration of an event, the celebration of an institution, or the honoring of an important principle: it was society itself. The festival was at once the symbol and school of the nation as a whole and of the civic community, beckoning each individual to transform himself or herself into a citizen.

The festival thus served as a propaedeutic for the learning of equality. It brought together people whom the circumstances of everyday life kept apart. Marching shoulder to shoulder, observing a spectacle, listening to a speech—these things were expected to efface the differences that people experienced in daily life. For a brief moment, it was as if a utopian city had come to life, enabling men and women to have their hopes and dreams come true. Festivals thus dramatized and therefore extended a variety of compensations for the differences that polite formalities were already putting back in place, as we shall see later on.

The Cement of Political Community

Americans did not need to spur their imaginations in order to flesh out the idea of a community of citizens. In order to break with the past, the French had created the nation as an abstract totality, independent of previous social and political identities, but postindependence American institutions were superimposed on communal realities that already existed. To be sure, independence had brought about a global political revolution, but it did not affect the way in which each American perceived his or her place in the community. Indeed, the sociological notion of community was much more immediately apparent in the United States than was the legal notion of citizenship.[77] Furthermore, the Americans did not divorce the procedures of shaping the general will from the existence of strong common sentiments. The groups with which individuals identified were in fact generally quite homogeneous, not only in religious terms (which were essential at the time) but also in social terms. A strong, immediate sense of equality as homogeneity prevailed.

Because this was not the case in France, there was a permanent need to flesh out the idea of the nation and the sentiment of equality among citizens. The dramaturgy of elections and festivals was not enough; the idea of a community of citizens had to be made real in everyday life. At first, many people counted on the schools to do this. From the middle of the eighteenth century on, education was therefore linked to political nation-building. The publication of Caradeuc de La Chalotais's *Essai d'éducation nationale* launched the debate in 1763.[78] A disciple of Locke and Condillac and zealous adversary of the Jesuits and their philosophy of education, Caradeuc proposed modern, secular teaching focused on useful knowledge.[79] But he went further, urging that schools be used as a means to build both the state and civil society. The revolutionaries radicalized and expanded this idea to propose a "pedagogical society" whose aim would be to teach liberty to the people and strengthen the feeling of equality. Mirabeau, in his *Travail sur l'éducation publique,* summed up this program by calling upon the state "to seize the imagination" of the people in order to transform them into citizens: "You seek ways to raise souls promptly to the level of your Constitution and to *bridge the immense gap* that it suddenly created between the new state of affairs and existing habits. The means you are seeking is none other than a good system of public education: it will make your edifice eternal."[80] After him, Talleyrand, Condorcet, Daunou, Lakanal, and many others would also look for ways to inculcate republican values and transform the French into a *new people* in realization of the revolutionary ambition to constitute a society of equals.

In the United States, equality as homogeneity had a basis that was essentially moral and cultural. The French took a much more voluntaristic and institutional view: the state sought to contribute to the construction of an egalitarian republic through policies of uniformization. In the French case, therefore, it is more correct to speak of equality as abstraction. Beyond the *commonality of participation* created by active citizenship, the state thus initiated a *commonality of ascription* to a shared norm or form. It is in this light, for example, that we should understand the decision taken in 1789 to establish new administrative divisions of the territory in order to destroy "the provincial spirit," which was seen as a destructive particularization of the spirit of equality. The revolutionary legislators' reverent attitude toward centralization reflected the same impulse. Although the purpose of centralization was to allow for more efficient management, it was more fundamentally linked to a certain vision of equality and production of the general interest. Language-unification and dialect-suppression policies had a similar purpose.[81] Equality was perceived as an attribute of indivisibility. The decision to standardize weights and measures was also part of an ideological struggle and sociological action of the same sort. The law of 18 Germinal, Year III, defining the decimal metric system, called upon citizens to "demonstrate their attachment to the unity and indivisibility of the Republic by making use of the new measures." By seeking to *uniformize* (the French word used at the time was "*uniformer*") words and things, the state sought to transform the nature of the social bond. It set itself the goal of establishing a new type of equivalence in relations between individuals. It explicitly attempted to fashion a nation of equals by liquidating apparent diversities wherever they occurred. In order to instill a sense of equality as belonging, it therefore attempted to influence everything that affected the social bond: the organization of space, the language, weights and measures, and even memory itself. This philosophy even influenced the role assigned to public monopolies, which were defended in France primarily as *guardians of the equality* that they were intended to maintain.[82]

To characterize all the various aspects of this process, Sieyès coined the word "adunation" to describe the movement whereby a group of individuals "make a nation," that is, achieve unity in equality. But he simultaneously used the word "assimilation," to which he imparted a then novel meaning.[83] He used the word to refer to "the condition of the social state" in which a uniform citizen spirit prevailed: citizenship "assimilated" men in such a way that their various differences came to seem relatively minor compared with the uniformity of their mores.[84] The importance that he attached to this is emphasized in his notes by the use of the term "ethnocracy," which he borrowed from the Baron d'Holbach.[85] If men were not assimilated, he warned, society could not endure, because the individuals who compose it would no longer be integrated into structuring organizations and would therefore be perpetually subject to dissociative forces. "How would you understand one another without a common reason, common sense, common belief, common god, or common territorial, intellectual, physical base, etc.? Without that, I cannot conceive of human assimilation."[86]

Diminishing the Importance of Differences

The revolutionary vision of a society of equals was organized around the three principles of similarity, independence, and citizenship. The idea of equality thus had more to do with the quality of the social bond than with the distribution of wealth. Still, the question of exactly what degree of economic difference would be deemed acceptable in the new society of semblables remained. Which differences might endanger the new society, and which were compatible with its basic principles? Tocqueville's phrase, "equality of conditions," encompassed a range of acceptable differences.[87] Yet he struggled to define the content of this concept: it was a kind of "imaginary equality," essentially social and qualitative, rather than a real, quantitative economic equality. "The general notion of similarity [semblable] is obscure," he concluded, leaving the reader unsatisfied.[88]

To elucidate this crucial point, we can begin with another formula of Sieyès's: "Inequalities of property and industry are like inequalities of age, sex, height, etc. They do not *denature* the equality of citizenship [*civisme*]."[89] Thus, for Sieyès, the problem was to ensure that subsisting differences among individuals did not establish an artificial order or *counternature* (as privilege did). Otherwise, distinctions would in effect become what Buffon called "essential qualities." But precisely where should the dividing line be drawn? When privilege was inscribed in law, the dividing line was clear. But then what? As we saw earlier, the term "privilege" was often understood in both France and the United States to denote unjustifiable differences. An essentialist definition of similarity proved to be an obstacle to progress. How, for instance, could one theoretically justify the difference between what Sieyès called "an absurd and chimerical superiority" and a simple "superiority of function"? A more dynamic definition was needed. Similarity had to be understood in terms of *living* as similar individuals (semblables). Equality could then be understood as a relation: as vitality of shared experience, as a quality of proximity, and as a facility of exchange. To think of equality as similarity thus meant deciding that in social life certain differences were of secondary importance. These differences were essentially of an economic order, since it was economic differences that most obviously threatened to produce a new inegalitarian order.

There were three ways of diminishing the importance of such differences: limitation, circulation, and correction. These defined three "strategies" for ensuring that economic differences did not become so dominant that they would threaten to reconstitute distinct types of humanity. In both America and France, the revolutionary spirit of equality availed itself of all three strategies.

Limiting Differences and the Precapitalist Vision of the Economy

What were the prospects for limiting social differences in the revolutionary period? In order to answer this question, we must consider the dominant economic representations of the period, which we discussed earlier. Consider, for instance, the debate about luxury, which persisted throughout the eighteenth century, focusing anxious attention on the relation between wealth and the social order. Political and moral ideas associated with the old civic humanism, transmitted indirectly through Jansenism, remained influential. Frugality and temperance were seen as crucial values, enabling individuals to master their passions and society to remain orderly. Writers since the seventeenth century had called for sumptuary laws, which would impose heavy taxes on luxury goods and thus limit man's subservience to wealth. Even Adam Smith shared this moralistic view, openly praising frugality even as he celebrated the virtues of the division of labor and increased trade. The founder of political economy was by no means an advocate of what we would nowadays call consumer society. "The capacity of [the rich man's] stomach bears no proportion to the immensity of his desires, and will receive no more than that of the meanest peasant."[90] For Smith, frugality was an instrument for moderating passions and regulating social life. With this concept he was able to develop his fundamental theory of the relative equalization of interests and needs, which he first published in *The Theory of Moral Sentiments.* In this respect, Smith remained under the influence of civic republicanism.

We can thus appreciate the importance of the eighteenth-century denunciation of luxury, which has rightly been characterized as "patriotic."[91] What is essential from our point of view is that this denunciation accompanied praise for a society from which excessive inequality would be eliminated and special interests would not soak up all the collective energy available. Abbé Coyer's *Dissertation sur le vieux mot de patrie* perfectly captured this widespread state of mind: "The homeland [*patrie*] is a mother who cherishes all her children and who is prepared to tolerate opulence and middling fortunes, but not paupers; greater and lesser individuals, but not oppressed ones; and who, even with this unequal division, preserves a kind of equality by opening the way for everyone to occupy the leading places.... If one sees two nations in one, the first replete with riches and pride, the second with misery and discontent, then the word *patrie* will not be heard."[92] This sensibility was shared at the time by writers who were very far from holding the same political and constitutional views as Coyer. In particular, both Montesquieu and Rousseau used similar terms to denounce luxury and the excessive social differences that it fostered. The former used the words "frugality" and "moderation" more than once and even discussed the "disorders of inequality,"[93] while the latter remarked that "the greatest harm has already occurred when there are paupers to defend and rich people to contain."[94] The idea expressed by all of these writers was thus one of *measure*. They sought not to validate any principle of economic egalitarianism but rather to preserve above all the possibility of political community. "With respect to equality," Rousseau wrote, "one should not understand the word to mean that the degrees of power and wealth are absolutely identical ... but that no citizen should be rich enough to buy another and none so poor as to be obliged to sell himself."[95] Even Meslier, a much more radical thinker, shared this view.[96]

We must keep this background in mind to understand the spirit of equality in the French Revolution. The majority of members of the Constituent Assembly were still steeped in a civic culture that reasoned in terms of balanced differences and moderation of inequalities. Consensus existed because this culture was forged in a precapitalist world, which had yet to experience the radical social upheavals of the Industrial Revolution. Economic inequality was of secondary importance because it was thought to be related to differences of *situation* that were not a priori associated with disparities of *condition*. That is why so little attention was paid to redistributive equality during the French Revolution. In 1791, Claude Fauchet stood alone when he proposed redistribution of property to the Confederation of the Friends of Truth.[97] To be sure, many other leveling projects were proposed. In 1793, for example, the idea of an "agrarian law" came up repeatedly. The passage of *le maximum,* or legal price controls, was followed by radical egalitarian proposals for the redistribution of wealth. Even in moments such as these, however, the *general* perspective was one of a "reasonable" distribution of wealth, with the proviso that it should be possible for anyone to accede to some kind of property. Although the famous *Manifesto of Equals,* which François-Noël (Gracchus) Babeuf's companion Sylvain Maréchal drafted in the waning days of the Revolution, later came to be seen as the founding text of modern socialism, owing to its call for collective ownership, it attracted no attention at the time, buried as it was in its author's personal papers.[98]

The American state of mind was not very different. In the 1770s and 1780s, Americans criticized luxury in much the same terms as Europeans, and the American ideal was one of a relatively homogeneous society in which economic inequalities were limited enough to avoid creating resentment or dividing society into alien and hostile groups. There is no better evidence of this than the writings of Benjamin Franklin, which aptly express what one might call the "American ideology" of the period. In *Avis à ceux qui voudraient s'établir en Amérique,* he expressed pleasure that "a happy and general mediocrity" prevailed in the United States, which at the time lacked both the offensive wealth and grinding poverty found in Europe.[99] In *Poor Richard's Almanac,* a cheap edition of which could be found in almost every home in America, Franklin called upon his fellow citizens to display the wisdom and moderation necessary to maintain this ideal.[100] For him, the history of the United States and the virtues of its inhabitants would establish a stable society in which inequality would be relatively unimportant. Many Americans of the colonial period conceived of their future as a "Christian Sparta" rather than a land of triumphant capitalism.[101]

The Spirit of Equality and the Circulation of Differences

Privilege was not defined solely by material distinction and impressive symbolism. It was also a function of time: in essence, privilege inscribed difference in time, giving permanence to hierarchy. To justify this immobility, privilege claimed to be owed the interest on some ancient debt, or else it invoked some primordial distinction, the memory of which it sought to keep alive. Hence it was inextricably linked to a worldview in which the past took precedence over the present. Because privilege was permanent, it instituted an intolerable counternature. The spirit of equality attacked claims of this sort and insisted on the rights of the present. Thus equality of conditions was understood as implying a necessary *mobility* of conditions. It was judged in terms of circulation as well as distribution. Eighteenth-century political economy, which saw the modern economy in terms of circulation, partook of this same revolution of ideas. Unlike the stagnant economies of old, based on ground rents, the modern commercial economy was based on the incessant flow of merchandise, with men following in the wake of goods. The market economy was consequently seen as the scourge of the society of orders. It sapped the very foundations of the old distinctions of rank. For a time, money was therefore seen as "the great leveler." Until it was accumulated in such colossal amounts as to constitute "a new feudalism," lucre did indeed help to undermine old hierarchies.

Circulation thus equalized differences, but its leveling effect also had a more durable psychological source. If liberty is the defining characteristic of the individual, then each man defines his identity in terms of his ability to project himself in time and refuse to be confined to a designated place or preordained estate. This freedom defines what I call *imaginary equality,* which refers not to a mental representation or specific future state but rather to the possibility of a change of situation. It is the idea of possibility, in its very indeterminacy, which is essential. "All estates are practically undifferentiated in themselves, provided that one can escape from them if one wishes," as Rousseau observed.[102] In this sense, a society of semblables, or similar individuals, is defined as one in which each individual can imagine himself in the condition of every other individual. This fluidity includes not only the hope of improvement but also the fear of degradation, yielding equilibrium between envy and compassion. Similarity is established by psychological comparison with other individuals. Each person learns to identify with or even appropriate other people's stories. Proximity is not a fixed property defined by one's situation but a variable defined by one's capacity for projection. Sieyès used the striking phrase "equality of expectation [*espérance*]" to describe the temporal construction of the perceived egalitarian relation.[103] It was here that the notion of equality of opportunity originated.[104] Hence perpetuity in all its forms was as much of a threat to equality as monopoly and privilege: this was one of the leitmotifs of both American and French revolutionaries.

The Correction of Differences through the Quality of the Social Bond

In *La Nouvelle Héloïse,* Rousseau speaks of the special atmosphere surrounding the grape harvest. "In the evening, everyone joyfully returns home together. The workers are fed and housed throughout the harvest, and even on Sundays, after the evening service, the people join with them in dancing until supper. On other days, everyone also sticks together after returning to the dormitory.... Everyone sits down to dinner together: masters, day laborers, and servants. Each serves without distinction of rank, without exclusion or preference."[105] For days or weeks, the vine grower and harvesters thus form a distinctive society. Normally individuals in cities and towns live apart, each in his own world, wedded to his own habits, defined by his estate, but at harvest time these usual distinctions are suspended. Everyone mingles in the warmth of evening gatherings and shared meals. The harvest metaphor shows how the spirit of equality could accommodate certain forms of economic inequality. Unequal situations were counterbalanced by strict equality of rights, and civility became another way of expressing egalitarian sentiments.

Rabaut Saint-Étienne described the operation of this egalitarian economy quite well by showing how a form of *moral equality* could reduce the perception of material inequality. In his eyes, moral equality was "the surest, truest, and most durable" form of equality, and he described it as follows: "By this I mean a state of society in which all men live as brothers, so that inequality of wealth and conditions disappears before the feeling of fraternity and concord that dominates and covers everything."[106] In a democracy, moral equality was therefore supposed to serve as a corrective to economic inequality, tempering its perception. For Rabaut Saint-Étienne, this was all the more necessary because "you will never be able to eliminate all inequality of wealth." He therefore conflated the "politics of equality" with the need to promote "equality of affections," which was but another name for fraternal feeling. As a model for this view he proposed the Quakers, whose attitude toward equality he described as follows: "They live as brothers, though they are not all equal in wealth. Yet the rich man's pride and insulting vanity are absolutely foreign to them. . . . They have grasped the true spirit of society, which is fraternity, so that a man who is not very wealthy can live in society with a man of great fortune."[107] For Rabaut Saint-Étienne, to live in the same society was the meaning of moral equality, which used proximity as a corrective for the tendency of economic distinctions to lead inevitably to social segregation.

This view of inequality explains why fraternity played such a central role in the French Revolution. Jurists and philosophers have nevertheless found it difficult to integrate fraternity into their theories, because they see it as no more than a fleeting sentiment.[108] Historians since Jules Michelet have explained the frequent recourse to both the language and imagery of fraternity as an expression of national cultural unity. Indeed, the idea of fraternity came to life in the vast gathering known as the Festival of the Federation (1790).[109] For Michelet, the Revolution was "the unanimous epoch, the holy epoch in which the entire nation, still largely innocent of class conflict, marched beneath a fraternal banner." Fraternity was both a quality and a metaphor for union and the nation. The sense of proximity engendered by fraternal feeling compensated for the highly abstract nature of concepts such as the general will and *"le Tout,"* or totality of the citizenry. But the importance of fraternity can also be analyzed in another way, in terms of a general economy of equality. To evoke family ties among citizens was to invite them to look at one another with fresh eyes, to incite them to see one another as semblables, abstracting from those qualities that might alienate, divide, or differentiate. Fraternity thus served as an emotional corrective to the functional distances of everyday life. It was a way of "refusing to confine the individual within the concrete conditions of his existence."[110]

Another corrective to material inequalities could be found in the civilities of everyday life. As we will see later, these played a central role in establishing democracy in America. But they also played a key role in France: a revolution in civility was a major feature of the new spirit of equality. The date June 19, 1790, means nothing today, whereas "the Night of August 4" has become a symbolic phrase. Yet the decree of June 19, which abolished titles of nobility (and prohibited their use) and also banned coats of arms and liveries, was of equal symbolic importance.[111] From that day on, it became illegal to claim any noble title. Individuals were to be identified by their family names only, not just in daily life but also in government documents and on official occasions. The revolution in civility thus completed the revolution in law. Its material consequences were much less significant than those attending the abolition of privileges. In practical terms, it was enough to remove the coats of arms from residential facades and to cease requiring one's servants to wear liveries in order to comply with the law. Although this decree was adopted at an advanced stage of the revolutionary process, it nevertheless unleashed a torrent of indignation, in marked contrast to the unanimous outpouring of enthusiasm that greeted the abolition of privileges on the Night of August 4. One hundred thirty-eight deputies—more than half of those who remained in the Constituent Assembly—signed and published an angry protest against the decree.[112] Why this difference? The reason is easy to discern: August 4 merely affected interests, whereas June 19 struck at the symbolic heart of aristocracy. The very identity of the nobility, its own idea of its distinction, was the target. Furthermore, the protestors did not fail to invoke the vast sacrifices to which they had assented in 1789, the justice of which they readily acknowledged, yet they vehemently rejected what they saw as a purely formal measure. Indeed, the problem in their eyes was that the symbolism of distinction was essential. For instance, one of them contrasted equality before the law, which he recognized as necessary, with "equality of conditions" (a formula used by speakers on all sides), which was deemed to be a "philosophical chimera."[113] With the revolution in civility, a crucial barrier was wiped away, so that the definition of equality would now remain permanently open. The question of *republican civility* thus became inseparable from a consideration of the ways in which a society of equals might be constituted.[114] This revolution in civility played an important part in establishing a complex economy of equality in which the form of the emotional bond among individuals modified their perception of the material differences between them. The imagination of equality thus took on new force and meaning. People began to imagine a society in which the differences among individual situations would be blurred by a powerful sense of communal existence, as if inequalities of wealth were in a sense "privatized."

The rules of politeness were simultaneously redefined to facilitate a new style of personal relations. For instance, the title "citizen" became an obligatory form of address in the spring of 1792: the expression of proximity marked a new step toward equality. "When the Revolution in material things is complete, it will still need to be achieved in words," as one member of the Convention said. that body decided to address all its future proclamations to "French citizens." The most significant change in the realm of civility was even more radical: the progressive spread of *tutoiement* (that is, the use of the informal form of the second-person pronoun, *tu*, rather than the formal *vous*). This was seen as a move toward "the pure and simple language of nature" and as a means of "restoring equality."[115] The usage spread in late 1792 among members of clubs and fraternal societies. Arguing that "the word *vous* was incompatible with the law of equality," the general assembly of the *sans-culottes* of Paris decided in December 1792 to ban this "relic of feudalism" and to demand the use of *tu* "as the word worthy of free men."[116] From that time forward, *tutoiement* became a sign of fraternity in the sections. A petition to the Convention on 10 Brumaire, Year II, called for making this custom official, arguing that when *tu* was used, relations between individuals exhibited "less pride, less distinction, less hatred, more apparent familiarity, a greater penchant for fraternity, and consequently more equality."[117] The obligatory use of *tu* proved ephemeral, however. It disappeared after the Ninth of Thermidor and the *journées* of Prairial. It nevertheless underscored the importance of *lived equality*. Civility was for that reason an essential aspect of the social bond, which it helped to construct by establishing norms of respect and attention. The very formalism of the rules that governed the use of *tu* after it became a mere form of politeness reminded everyone of his or her status. Its significance was therefore both political and sociological.[118]

Civil spaces were therefore seen as crucial elements in the constitution of a society of semblables. Sieyès was a pioneer in pointing out how public spaces could bring men together and thus play a key role in a democratic society. "Public properties," he wrote, "are friends of equality.... They are entirely in keeping with the spirit of equality and for the benefit of the poor, on whom they bestow an infinite variety of actual and relative pleasures that would otherwise be granted exclusively to a few of the wealthy. Hence we must have sidewalks, streetlamps, gardens, porticos, public holidays, etc. Let the public spirit tend toward the level of equality, while personal industry, aiming to achieve inequality, enriches society and thus works to the benefit of all."[119] Sieyès hoped for a convergence of public spirit with personal industry, but at the same time he suggested that the vigor of the former could compensate for differences caused by the latter.

Accomplishments and Unfinished Business

The Continuous Revolution of Civility in America

Although Americans proudly affirmed that "all men are created equal," the country was strongly influenced by the thinking of the distinguished men who met in Philadelphia in 1787 to draft the

Constitution. Their concept of representative government was to entrust the reins of government to a natural aristocracy legitimated by the ballot box. The word "democracy"—fraught with ambiguity and danger—was obviously not a part of their vocabulary. When they asserted that the people ought to be "the fountain of power," they had no intention of inviting the masses to intervene directly in politics or decide the direction in which the country ought to head. In America, as in England, the formula was interpreted in an essentially "liberal" sense. To speak of popular sovereignty in what might be characterized as the old sense of the term was primarily a negative strategy, intended to remind the royal government that it was the servant and not the master of the people and that its authority was strictly limited by its moral obligations and responsibility to society. Representative government and democracy were definitely not seen as synonymous. In the minds of the founding fathers, democracy evoked images of anarchy, violence, instability, and disorder. It was associated with the rule of demagogues, who appealed to the basest instincts of the dregs of society. After the Terror in France, Jacobinism was demonized and added to this repertoire of negative democratic images. To the respectable elite, a regime in which ordinary people spoke out on public issues and debated affairs of state was frankly unthinkable, and they never imagined that the idea of equality as they conceived it could lead to such a thing.

Ultimately, the American Founding Fathers believed that the limits of the revolution would be defined by the moral and constitutional principles that had triggered it. What happened proved otherwise, however, and in this respect American history is very different from French history. In France, Napoleon put the Revolution on hold in 1800, and the enthusiasm it had elicited in key moments dissipated. To be sure, feelings of bitterness and impotence ensued, as Terror gave way to a depressing era of bourgeois mediocrity and limited suffrage. The early years of constitutional monarchy in France were a time of disillusionment. Americans also experienced disillusionment in the early 1800s, but for precisely the opposite reasons. What alarmed them was not the end of revolution but its continuation.[120] In America one can speak of a *continuous revolution*. The thirty years between the presidencies of George Washington and Andrew Jackson were notable for a steady rise of the egalitarian ethos. Federalist ideas gradually receded, while "republican" ideas gained strength.

One important sign of this change was the increasingly frequent use of the words "aristocrat" and "aristocracy" with a critical edge. It almost seems as if the struggle against aristocracy did not really begin in America until after 1800. The Jacksonians made the anti-aristocratic animus a key component of their political identity. The word "democracy" took on a positive connotation as the opposite of "aristocracy," which became broadly pejorative.[121] Profiteers, stock-jobbers, cynical industrialists—all were indiscriminately lumped together as aristocrats.[122] Democracy therefore came to be seen increasingly as a *form of society* and not just a political regime (in contrast to representative government for some, to despotism and tyranny for others). Furthermore, democracy was a social form in which the primary concern was with ordinary people. The political language of the Federalists, steeped in references to Antiquity and the old European civic humanism, thus began to give way to a new and much more concrete vocabulary. For Jackson and his supporters, the people were no longer the abstract political subjects of sovereignty, a mere inscription on the facades of public buildings. They addressed their speeches to palpable social and occupational groups: working men, honest laborers, poor farmers, and simple folk. The "great mass of the people" was made flesh, as it were. This marked the political ascension, the coronation, so to speak, of "the common man"—a development with which Jackson's name would forever be associated. It was in America that the "society of semblables" gained a face.

To take the measure of the march toward equality in the United States, there are no better guides than the Europeans who crossed the Atlantic in the 1830s. Of these, Tocqueville was the most celebrated. But he was not alone.[123] His traveling companion Gustave de Beaumont also published an account of his impressions entitled *Marie, ou l'Esclavage aux États-Unis* (1835). Michel Chevalier, having only recently turned his back on Saint-Simonism, also crossed the ocean to produce two volumes of *Lettres sur l'Amérique du Nord* (1836). In 1827 Stendhal's friend Victor Jacquemont published his observations of the "democratic mores" of the Americans, which were widely read (he was the first to use the term "democratic mores").[124] In England, Mrs. Frances Trollope published *Domestic Manners of the Americans* in 1832, which was widely read and commented on, while Harriet Martineau published *Society in America* in 1837. Each of these books added a distinctive touch to the portrait of Jacksonian America. Hence the public had already begun to read about what Achille Murat was the first to call "equality of conditions" several years before Tocqueville's book appeared.[125] It would be futile to attempt to summarize these thousands of pages in a few paragraphs, but it is worth pausing to mention a few points that are especially relevant to the subject that concerns us here: on the one hand, the sense of similarity and forms of democratic civility, and on the other, the perception of the variability of wealth.

Chevalier reported being struck by *democratic sameness:* the fact that no one seemed to deserve special distinction or to attract particular notice. "In public places and while traveling," he wrote, "no man is the object of special attention, no matter what his talents or what services he has rendered. He is shown no special consideration, nor is he treated with any particular politeness: all men are equal."[126] Beaumont was also struck by everyday social forms: "In this country there exists neither aristocratic pride nor popular insolence," he wrote. To this Norman country squire, it seemed that no *economy of distinction* regulated relations between individuals, unlike in Europe,[127] where "it is so depressing to run the constant risk of being classed too high or too low, of encountering the disdain of some and the envy of others." For him, the directness and roughness of interpersonal contact in America seemed to express the sense of American equality. "To please the American people," he wrote, "one must be plain to the point of crudeness.... The reason why Americans are so eminently sociable is perhaps also what prevents them from being polite: there are no privileges to arouse envy, but there is also no upper class whose elegance can serve as a model to others."[128] All of the travelers agreed that the most striking thing about America was that democracy was reflected first of all in manners and that Americans especially prized their democratic attitudes toward one another. Indeed, for Americans themselves, these everyday expressions of mutual respect, ease of contact, absence of condescension in discussion, and naturalness and simplicity of manners were the most immediate consequences of the idea of equality. People spoke more and more of "democratic society" and a "democratic way of life," and the phrase "democratic individual" was in common use to denote a person whose manners reflected this ideal.

This *democracy of consideration* was reflected in a series of flattering terms of address. All women were entitled to be treated as "ladies" and all men as "gentlemen." The polite formula "sir" also became commonplace in 1830s America. The spirit of equality was thus reflected in a general ennoblement of sorts.[129] By contrast, it was also common to openly mock people whose lifestyle, attitude, or language indicated some claim to distinction. For instance, the ironic epithet "Brahmin" was attached to old New England families. Anyone who affected "aristocratic airs" was mocked, and people laughed at those "who ate with their pinkies raised." Such people were more likely to be the butt of sarcasm than the object of envy.

In regard to labor, European travelers were struck by the separation of status from function. For instance, the educated did not condescend to working men engaged in manual trades. Michel Chevalier was especially struck by the personal dignity he observed in people of modest station: "The American worker is filled with self-respect."[130] By way of example, he noted that American workers, unlike their European counterparts, were extremely reluctant to use the word "master" and preferred neutral words such as "employer." A wage worker or self-employed artisan always took care to avoid doing anything that might lead to confusion of his condition with the disdained status of the domestic servant. To illustrate this concern to avoid reproducing the hierarchical relations of old, Chevalier mentioned that shoemakers and tailors almost always refused to measure their customers at home, insisting instead that clients come into their shops. It should come as no surprise that, for these European travelers, the relation between masters and servants was such a key indicator of American social life.

Consider, to begin with, an important statistic: there were far fewer domestic servants in the United States than in Europe. There is abundant evidence that wealthy people found it difficult to hire servants in America. In France in 1800, servants accounted for 10 percent of the active population. The percentage in Britain was even higher. When Friedrich Engels wrote *The Situation of the Working Class in England,* he remarked that servants there outnumbered workers. There was nothing shocking about the term *domestique* in early nineteenth-century France (it was not until much later that the term "household employee" came into common use). In America, by contrast, the term "servant" had humiliating connotations, since it was associated with harsher forms of dependence such as indentured servitude and even slavery. Trollope remarked that to refer to a free citizen as a "servant" was seen as an affront to republican principles. The term "master" was similarly avoided in favor of the more generic "boss."[131] Those employed as servants did not see their position as defining a social status. Tocqueville was struck by how vigorously servants insisted on this distinction. His chapter on the question is among the most remarkable of the second volume of *Democracy in America.* It was in his discussion of the master-servant relationship that he most clearly revealed what the idea of equality of conditions meant in the United States. "Under democracy, there is nothing degrading about the estate of domestic service because it is freely chosen and temporarily adopted and because it is not stigmatized by public opinion and creates no permanent inequality between servant and master."[132] What might have seemed to be a social relation as far removed as possible from equality was thus in fact taken as a prime example of democratic equality, abstracting from the most glaring of differences. In

America, the functionality of the hierarchical bond did not alter the fundamental sense of equality.

Money as Leveler

The egalitarian civility that prevailed in 1830s America had not yet been affected by economic transformation. Still, Jacksonian America was no longer the fundamentally agricultural country of the revolutionary era. Cities and transportation networks had developed along with industry, and the westward movement of the frontier was part of a dynamic process that created new wealth and growing inequalities. Although the earlier celebration of frugality and of the beneficial effects of modest wealth persisted in the thinking of some, a different sort of society was beginning to emerge. People had also begun to treat the contrast between the rich and the poor as a new structural fact about society, as distinct from the 1820s, during which the distinction between "democrats" and "aristocrats" still dominated the scene.[133] These new voices were still few in number. The feeling that wealth was the legitimate fruit of individual effort was still widely shared. The "self-made man" was seen as a true national hero, the embodiment of American values.[134] The average man thus saw the newly rich more as a projection of his own aspirations than as an affront to his modest station in life. Above all, most people still believed in a high degree of social mobility: the rich had yet to become a caste or a class. Wealth was still a characteristic of *individual situations* rather than a true social condition.

To illustrate this distinction, Mrs. Trollope reported the following bromide: "If a man grows rich, let us take care that his grandson be poor, and then we shall all keep equal."[135] Wealth was indeed precarious, as reflected in the large number of bankruptcies. Beaumont was struck by the fact that an American who was about to introduce him to a group of friends advised him not to be critical of bankrupts, as there were several in the group. In castigating the immobility of the upper classes in Europe, whose wealth depended in his view on "caste monopolies," Murat, in exile in the United States, spoke of the "universal balance wheel" that kept society running smoothly and observed that it was "as laudable to go bust there as to make a fortune." He summed up the essence of the spirit of equality as follows: "There is a rising current in every well-organized society. It consists of those who improve their social position. . . . There is also a descending current. It comprises those who by chance find themselves placed above the social rank to which their industry and talents assign them, cannot hold on to it, and fall. . . . It is in the interest of society that both currents be allowed to run freely."[136] This passage sums up the way in which Americans understood the equality of conditions, with economic distinctions reduced to secondary importance owing to the mobility of wealth and individualistic factors of economic success. Under these conditions, existing inequalities were not a source of anxiety or instability.[137] The contemporary American idea that money was the "great leveler" or even the "great apostle of equality"[138] should be understood in the same light: the rapid circulation of money meant that temporary inequalities did not congeal into privileges, monopolies, or perpetual advantages.

The feeling of equality of conditions also stemmed from pride in being able to lead an independent existence. Although the number of people who could in fact live independently decreased in the

1830s, the idea of independence as a possibility or promise continued to shape representations of self and society. It remained a central feature of the democratic imagination, as attested by the cult status that Ralph Waldo Emerson's essay *Self-Reliance* has enjoyed since it was first published in 1841. In this vibrant ode to individualism and autonomy, Emerson pointed the way to *equality as singularity*, treating nonconformity as the essential condition of a true society of equals. In calling upon his fellow citizens to insist on their radical incommensurability, he suggested that every American could live with his head held high and felt himself to be the equal of everyone else.

The Ambiguities of Political Equality

Although the egalitarian revolution in American mores may have seemed complete by 1840, egalitarianism in the political realm was much more ambiguous. Independence had not led to a decisive rupture in the rules governing electoral participation. Americans had in fact voted while still under English rule, but mainly in local communities to choose aldermen or to decide local policy as a group, as in New England town meetings. The purpose of such elections was not to choose representatives of the people. Voting had no political dimension. It was not a vote of sovereignty but rather an exercise of basic management functions. Hence the term "citizen" was not used. The royal charters that governed the right to vote varied from one colony and locality to another, but in all cases it was linked to the ownership of property.[139] It was deemed natural that only those directly affected by public policies, specifically as taxpayers, should be considered full-fledged members of the community (the term "stakeholders" was already used). The rules were drawn in such a way as to exclude new arrivals and temporary visitors. In some places, religious affiliation was also important. During the colonial period, Catholics were excluded from voting in five states and Jews in four. Although the suffrage was much broader than in England, it was far from "universal." It has been estimated that fewer than 60 percent of adult white males met the voting requirements.[140]

The American Revolution yielded changes in the voting rules but did not alter the basic framework of the system. For example, restrictions concerning Jews and Catholics were lifted (although the constitution of South Carolina maintained "recognition of the existence of God" as a condition of voting). Property and tax qualifications were reduced in a number of states (with Pennsylvania taking the boldest steps), yet one-third of the states left colonial restrictions untouched. In some places militiamen were automatically registered to vote. But the philosophical basis of citizenship generally remained that of the citizen as property owner or taxpayer rather than "the individual" as such. All the Founding Fathers agreed on this point. All were wary of the risks of extending the suffrage too broadly, especially in the cities. For instance, Gouverneur Morris argued that only landowning citizens could be counted on to "safeguard liberty" while expressing fear that wealthy individuals might manipulate urban workers. James Madison went so far as to say that the corruption of the English parliament was due to an overly broad suffrage in cities and towns.[141] Hence it is not surprising to learn that in 1780, only one state, Vermont, had granted the right to vote to all adult males. Significantly, moreover, no one campaigned for uniform voting rules. That each state was allowed to legislate its own voting rules shows that the right to vote was not considered to be a fundamental political right.

The right to vote was only very gradually extended in the United States.[142] In 1855, property or tax qualifications still existed in seven of thirty states. What is more, the expansion of the vote in other states came only after numerous obstacles had been surmounted and many reverses overcome. When Massachusetts ended property qualifications for voting, for example, violent protests ensued.[143] New, more insidious (because less overtly discriminatory) restrictions appeared in the 1850s, with the shift in the social structure owing to the arrival of immigrants in large numbers and the emergence of an urban working class. For example, literacy tests and education tests were introduced. Even before their use to prevent blacks from voting in the post-Civil War South, such tests were deployed to prevent Irish Catholics and other immigrants from voting in Connecticut and Massachusetts, and many other northern and western states followed suit in the 1870s. Stricter residence requirements were also established to prevent "vagrant" populations from voting. Voting rules still varied widely at the end of the nineteenth century, and these differences would persist for many years to come. By the mid-1920s, there were still thirteen northern and western states that banned illiterate citizens from the polls, and it was not until the Voting Rights Act of 1965 that the southern states were prohibited from using literacy tests and grandfather clauses to prevent blacks from voting.

In America, then, progress toward universal suffrage was slow, and there was no sharp repudiation of the restrictive practices that had prevailed during the colonial period. The country became fully "democratic" in small steps. Among many factors driving this evolution, two played a major role. The first was the pressure exerted by the advance of the frontier. The new states had no colonial past, the people who lived in them had easy access to land, and the egalitarian impetus was strong. Even more important was the transformation of the nation's social structure.[144] The proportion of landowners decreased, as more and more farmers rented their land or owned only very small amounts of property, while the growth of the urban population tended to decrease the proportion of the population that met property qualifications. Literacy tests and restrictive residence conditions were one response to this, but the restrictive impulse was countered by a shift from a functional conception of voting to a concept of voting as a right.

The details of this history point to the power of latent resistance to full political equality and reveal some persistent blind spots. For instance, the idea of giving women the right to vote did not emerge in the United States until quite late in the century, to say nothing of the even more persistent exclusion of blacks and Native Americans. In this respect, the history of equality is inseparable from a historical anthropology of individuality. It must also take account of the prejudices and reactions that define the horizon of similarity at any given point in time. In this respect, the United States can serve as a laboratory for the study of democratic equality. It exemplifies the most audacious advances as well as the most troubling reverses and most odious prevarications, exhibiting as much sincerity as hypocrisy in meeting the challenges it set for itself.

The French Paradox

The postrevolutionary history of equality in France consists of a series of advances and retreats. Napoleon reinterpreted the French

Revolution in an authoritarian spirit, which combined a merito-cratic idea of equality with a Caesarism tinged with what would today be called populism. The parliamentary monarchy represented a new beginning, symbolized by the introduction of property-qualified voting *(le régime censitaire)*. Although some of the essential achievements of 1789 were preserved, such as equal rights and the principles of representative government, the ideas of political equality and active citizenship receded into the background. Res-toration liberals sought to bring the revolutionary process to an end. Although they celebrated 1789, they feared the rising tide of political and social demands that the Revolution had brought in its train and were therefore obsessed with imposing a minimalist interpretation on revolutionary ideals. François Guizot, for in-stance, spoke of "purging the principles of 1789 of any anarchical admixture."[145] Liberals saw universal suffrage as the most terrible of threats and sought to dash egalitarian aspirations. As we will see in what follows, the conservative-liberal ideology aimed to im-pose this degraded vision of democratic modernity.

In reaction to the limited suffrage enacted by the July Monarchy, universal suffrage became a major issue for the regime's oppo-nents. If America brought the idea of equality down to earth by embedding it in social life, the French projected it into the political sphere throughout the nineteenth century. The influence of this political vision was increased by the fact that French society con-tinued to resist the emergence of any intermediary bodies, so that the essence of the social was itself understood in political terms. The struggle for universal suffrage actually coincided with in-creased expectations of equality in the early 1830s.[146] This explains why the proclamation of universal suffrage in 1848 aroused such immense hopes. People truly believed that the provisional government's action would transform society from top to bottom. This explains the unprecedented outpouring of lyrical statements, joyful demonstrations, and expressions of fraternal enthusiasm in the spring of 1848. This state of mind was reflected in the government's extraordinary declaration: "Henceforth, elections are the property of all, without exception. *As of the date of this law, there are no longer any proletarians in France.*"[147] At the time, the word "proletarian" did not mean simply "exploited worker." It connoted the idea of general exclusion by evoking the Roman *proles,* or nonpropertied citizens. Thus universal suffrage was expected to resolve the social question and mark the beginning of full equality.[148] Many songs spoke of freed slaves and "holy equality" in the same breath. As the first elections of April 1848 approached, the *Bulletin de la République* observed that "the Republic, which excludes none of its sons, summons all of you to political life. This will be *for you a new birth, a baptism, a regeneration.*"[149] In one of his earliest poems, Eugène Pottier, the future author of the *Internationale,* wrote:

> Tout français est électeur,
> Quel bonheur! Moi tailleur,
> Toi doreur, lui paveur,
> Nous v'là z'au rang d'homme.[150]

[Every Frenchman is a voter. What joy! I, the tailor, you, the gilder, he, the paver—there we are, ranked as men.]

The year 1848 did indeed mark the anointment of the citizen. The enthusiasm quickly faded, to be sure, and the June Days and the confrontation of Reds and Whites in 1849 served as reminders that social differences had not been erased. Yet the brief but happy interlude of fraternal republican utopia illustrated the fact that in France, the anticipation of equality was associated above all with an idealization of politics.

2

THE PATHOLOGIES OF EQUALITY

Divided Society

In the history of equality we find a constant tension between achieved forms of equality and resistance to the egalitarian idea. The ambiguity of that idea was partly responsible for this, as were the political battles and social demands connected with it. The Industrial Revolution and the advent of capitalism decisively inflected this tension, however. These developments ended the hope of minimizing the importance of economic differences and imposing social limits on the market—a hope that had played a central role in shaping the revolutionary idea of equality in both France and America. The prospect of a society of equals, which had been linked to a precapitalist vision of the economy, now had to be rethought. By the mid-nineteenth century, the transformation of the mode of production imposed a whole new set of laws of production and exchange. Enormous economic inequalities developed, leading to important social exclusions and divisions that radically transformed the whole notion of equality, initiating a new round of revolutionary and reactionary responses.

Two Classes and Two Nations

The work of Jean de Sismondi is a good indicator of how this turning point was perceived. In 1803, he published his first book on economics, *De la richesse commerciale*.[1] This was the very same year in which Jean-Baptiste Say published the first edition of his great *Traité*.[2] Sismondi ringingly endorsed economic freedom in all its aspects. None of this would be worthy of special note had he not published in 1819 his *Nouveaux principes d'économie politique*, which completely contradicted his earlier position. The book's subtitle, "On Wealth in Relation to the Population," hints at the nature of the change: Sismondi was now interested in people and not just in the general mechanisms of exchange and production of wealth as such. Why this revision? As he explained in his introduction, observing "the cruel suffering inflicted on factory workers" had opened his eyes.[3] His book painted a searing portrait of the misery engendered by the new regime of free competition associated with the spread of the factory system. Sismondi was the first to point out that labor and capital were destined to become permanently warring powers. "The most fatal change in the condition of the laborer," he wrote, "is that the worker is now born a worker and will die the same, whereas in the past the condition of worker was merely a preparation, a stepping-stone on the way to a higher station."[4] Manufacturing, far from being a boon to modern society, was thus *the* social problem in Sismondi's eyes. "If it creates an indigent population uncertain of the future, anxious about its existence, and discontented with the present order of things; if, in other words, it creates proletarians, then what we call prosperity is on the contrary a national calamity," he memorably wrote.[5]

At the time, England was seen as a laboratory that had created a monstrous version of modernity. Indeed, it was in English factories that the ravages of modernity first appeared—ravages to which the French attached the label "pauperism." Books describing and denouncing the new scourge were plentiful in the 1830s. Alban de Villeneuve-Bargemont and Charles de Coux, representing what would later be known as the Christian school of political economy, were among the most critical writers on the subject. They called for a revival of the old artisanal system and a more localized economy, as well as a return to the soil. Statistical studies also began to appear, initially in England with the famous series of "Blue Books" commissioned by Parliament.[6] French writers closely followed the situation from the other side of the Channel. For instance, Baron d'Haussez published *La Grande-Bretagne en mil huit cent trente-trois*,[7] and in the same year (1833) Maurice Rubichon published a thick volume entitled *Du mécanisme de la société en France et en Angleterre*. These works described in detail a population "packed by myriads" into factories and "forced into labor more relentless and humiliating than that of galley slaves" while reduced to "food, clothing, and housing so wretched, indeed so precarious, that each day doubts whether the next will come."[8] Somewhat later, in 1840, Eugène Buret, with the support of Louis René Villermé, produced the definitive work on the subject, *De la misère des classes laborieuses en France et en Angleterre*, which received a prize from the Académie des Sciences Morales et Politiques for its distressingly dark portrait of English factories and the proletarians they employed. "England, the land of big industry, is also the land of social warfare," in his incisive description.[9] In Europe and throughout the world, the name "Manchester" became synonymous with hell on earth.

Books about the ravages of the factory system were not limited to recounting the misery of the workers. Anger was directed not just at hunger, destitution, and crowded hovels but also at the sudden and radical undermining of the old vision of a society of equals. The new proletariat revived the specter of a fourth order driven outside the gates of the city and even excluded from the human community.[10] With the rise of new industry, society once again found itself radically divided. "At the time of this writing," Buret observed, "the two English classes, workers and capitalists, are as disaffected with each other and as divided as they can possibly be. It is a veritable secession, something resembling a preparation for civil war."[11] This was the central leitmotif of his study. He repeatedly used phrases such as "absolute separation," "growing separation," and "division into two hostile classes." Although Buret's immediate target was England, he saw the problem in more general terms as the sign of a redoubtable contradiction: "Just as inequality was eliminated from the political and civil order," he wrote, "it was reborn in fact and in law with greater force than ever before in the industrial order."[12] Although Buret spoke bluntly, he was by no means a dangerous revolutionary. His work was awarded a prize by a group that included Guizot and Tocqueville as well as Villermé and Charles Dunoyer. To be sure, not all readers reacted to his words in the same way. If some were spurred to revolt, the upper classes were simply gripped by the fear that vengeful violence might erupt—a fear heightened by memories of the convulsions that had marked the early years of the July Monarchy. The revolt of the Canuts in Lyon in 1831 had caused the first alarm to be sounded. In an article published in the very sober pages of the *Journal des débats*, Saint-Marc Girardin caused a sensation with an analysis that combined cynicism with terror: "The sedition in Lyon," he wrote, "revealed a grave secret—the secret of an intestine struggle in society between the propertied class and the unpropertied class. Our commercial and industrial society has an open wound, as all societies do, and that wound is its workers."[13] The proletarian? For Girardin, he was the enemy, the barbarian, the incarnation of the insurrectionary menace. His words would leave a lasting imprint on many minds. He even dared to write that "every manufacturer inhabits his factory as planters inhabit the colonies, one against a hundred, and the sedition in Lyon was an insurrection akin to the uprising in Santo Domingo." Indeed, "the barbarians who threaten society do not live in the Caucasus or the Tartar steppes. They are in the suburbs of our manufacturing cities."

The article was shocking, but it revealed conservative fantasies even as it acknowledged the reality of the new social division. How could anyone remain faithful to the spirit of 1789, even reduced to its most minimal terms, if there was no longer a single nation but in fact two distinct societies? This was the question that was coming to dominate people's minds. In his *Lettre aux prolétaires* of 1833, Albert Laponneraye, one of the leading figures of the Société des Droits de l'Homme et du Citoyen and the author of the first history of the French Revolution intended for workers, made this stark observation: "The 33 million individuals who populate France are divided into two nations, whose interests are quite distinct and separate: a nation of the privileged and a nation of the unprivileged, or proletarians."[14] The problem was therefore not just a question of *inequalities*. It was deeper than that, and it struck at the very idea of a common society. The word "helot" began to be used to characterize those who were seen as having been cast out. The revival of "proletarian" was similar, it being another word borrowed from Antiquity to evoke a casting out, an insuperable rejection. For Lamartine it was a "filthy, insulting, pagan" word, which reinforced the feeling of repulsion inspired by the reality it named.[15] Militant workers claimed the designation as their own for that very reason, because they wanted to call attention to the stigmata of their condition in order to make an impression. The proletarian was an individual "who stayed outside," in Auguste Blanqui's famous formulation.[16] What Laponneraye was attacking was therefore in the first instance a situation of exclusion. Although he was one of the most radical of the working-class agitators of the early July Monarchy, he did not favor communal ownership (it was not until the 1840s that Étienne Cabet and the neo-Babouvists took this turn). Although he spoke of a "leveling of conditions," he simply meant that everyone should be subject to the same rules in a common society. The existence of a certain inequality of wealth did not shock him.[17] He rebelled, however, against the division of society into two hostile blocs. In his history of the revolution of 1848, Daniel Stern remarks that a substantial segment of the popular classes "had begun to stand apart as a separate class, a nation within the nation to which people began to apply a new name: the industrial proletariat."[18] A few years later, Benjamin Disraeli used almost identical language in his novel *Sybil, or the Two Nations* (1845). He, too, spoke of rich and poor as two alien nations that shared nothing in common, as if they were "living on different planets."[19]

The Exclusion of the Proletarian

As noted earlier, the invention of the term "pauperism" in the early 1830s reflected this new perception of social distinctions. Alban de Villeneuve-Bargemont observed that "indigence, under the new and sadly energetic name 'pauperism,' has invaded the working classes of the population. It is no longer an accident but a condition forced upon a substantial number of members of society."[20] The new "misery" inherent in the worker's condition was of course reflected in specific deprivations, such as wretched housing, patched clothing, and hunger. These things aroused anger, but it is important to note that there was more to the idea of pauperism, which also referred to the social consequences of exclusion. This was the real scandal. "Extreme misery casts the afflicted populations out into a savage existence," Buret wrote. "Pauperism is tantamount to a veritable social ban: these wretched people live outside of society, as 'outlaws.'"[21] This theme was central to the working-class literature of the period. "We are not like other men," thundered one of labor's most widely heeded spokesmen,[22] while the first French newspaper specifically aimed at workers, *L'Artisan, journal de la classe ouvrière,* published the following warning in 1830: "O! bourgeois nobles! Stop driving us from your midst, for we, too, are men and not machines."[23] Popular songs spoke of workers as "separate from the human race."[24] The people, Proudhon remarked, are "cut off from humanity by misery."[25] These quotations could be multiplied endlessly. The birth of the industrial proletariat and the reality of social separation thus revived words and expressions that had served forty-one years earlier to express the people's relation to the world of the privileged. With workers "isolated from the nation, expelled from the social and political community, left alone with their needs and their miseries," as Buret put it, the project of building a society of semblables had lost all meaning.[26] The starkest of differences had imposed its law. Hence throughout the 1830s and 1840s the advent of a "new feudalism" was constantly denounced. The phrase was common to working-class writers, official investigators, and even legitimists, who were quick to insist that bourgeois industrialism marked a regression from the good old days of "happy dependency."[27]

The most famous political manifestos of the nineteenth century denounced this segregation and called for a restoration of the egalitarian ideal. One such was Sylvain Maréchal's *Manifeste des égaux,* whose original publication in 1828 marked the birth of socialism. Another was the *People's Charter* in Britain (1839). Victor Considérant's *Manifeste de la démcoratie au XIXe siècle* (1847) and Marx and Engels' *Communist Manifesto* (1848) also denounced the new division of society into classes, as did the Proudhon-inspired *Manifeste des Soixante* (1864).

The Return of Slavery

The new proletarian condition was also seen as incompatible with the ideal of independence. Buret was one of many who contrasted the artisan, who was a citizen and counted for something in the nation and enjoyed "relations of service and fraternity" with the other classes, with the industrial proletarian.[28] The confrontation with the new social economy of dependency was a central element of working-class thinking in this period. "Association" became a watchword for those interested in reviving the old ideal of autonomous, emancipated labor, but rather now in a collective mode. Some explored the possibility of "new guilds" capable of organizing to protect labor.[29] Everyone felt that the proclamation of the freedom of labor and the elimination of the old system of guilds had led to a novel form of dependence under the factory system. The first word that came to mind to describe the new system was, significantly, "slavery." But it was no longer the "civil and political slavery" of which people spoke in the seventeenth and eighteenth centuries. The slavery to which the condition of the proletarian was now compared was plantation slavery. "Slavery is still alive among us," as one Saint-Simonian put it, and these words described industrial society as many people experienced or perceived it.[30] Songs of the period often compared poor working men to "white Negroes" or "white slaves," and Spartacus was revived as a symbol of emancipation.[31] The dehumanization of the proletarian was thus linked to his radical dependency on the capitalist. Although the word "slavery" seemed an obvious one to use to describe the situation in the factories, everyone recognized that it posed a problem for liberal political regimes. Hence the comparison of the two forms of slavery was significant both intellectually and socially.

Clearly, the legal status of the proletarian was different from that of the plantation slave (or of the domestic slave in Antiquity).[32] It was attractive, however, to consider the distinctiveness of the new proletarian condition in the framework of a general economy of misfortune, that is, of dependency and exploitation. The problem had already drawn the attention of Charles Comte, whose *Traité de législation* (1826) devoted an entire volume to the question.[33] Baron d'Haussez, one of the first French observers of working conditions in English factories, raised a troubling question: "These Negroes whose fate inspires so much pity—are they as unfortunate on their plantations in the colonies as the Whites confined in the filthy workshops of Manchester and Birmingham?"[34] Allowing for the obvious objection that the proletarians were at least free, d'Haussez's response typified the opinion of many:

> No, their lot differs from that of the Negroes only with respect to the way in which individuals are sold. Negroes are simply bought

and paid for in a single payment. Whites receive a small interest on the capital that they are supposed to represent. Slaves are dependent on masters interested in their preservation. Workers can die, and self-interest devoid of humanity will not speak up for them. Both are slaves, attached to the soil that sustains them. The Blacks work in the open air, the Whites in a pestilential atmosphere. The former are bought, the latter hired. It is difficult to distinguish between them.[35]

Like d'Haussez, a majority of workers saw the proletarian condition as an aggravated form of slavery. The way in which Félicité de Lamennais summed up the question in *Le Livre du peuple* (1838) fixed certain words and images in people's minds. Speaking of the modern worker, he wrote: "He would have been better off with total slavery, because the master at least feeds, houses, and clothes his slave and cares for him when he is sick because it is in his interest to keep him alive. But the worker belongs to no one. He is used as long as there is profit to be made from him, and then he is tossed aside."[36] Lamennais would continue to hammer on these same themes in *De l'esclavage moderne* (1839). There was nothing scandalous about the comparison at the time, because it merely underscored the degree to which the dependence of the proletarian was seen as the most awful imaginable betrayal of the old ideal of a society of equals.[37] Remember that only thirty or forty years separated these statements from 1789.

America and the Market Revolution

America in the 1830s and 1840s cannot be described in the same terms as England and France. Manufacturing developed more slowly in the United States. One did not see the factories filled with women and children that observers in Europe described. Self-employed labor was far more common, and it shaped the way that most Americans imagined their society. To be sure, the "market revolution"[38] had begun to have an effect, and Jacksonian ideology can be understood as a critical reaction to this as well as a continuation of revolutionary ideals. But in America the Industrial Revolution was far from complete. To the question "What is American labor?" Daniel Webster, one of the leaders of the Whig opposition to the Democrats, responded in 1840 that "the best way to describe it is to say that *it is not* European labor."[39] He based this assertion on an estimate that 90 percent of American workers, including small farmers, artisans, and merchants, were still self-employed. This estimate was actually much too high (it reflected conditions at the beginning of the nineteenth century), but it did accurately reflect the way in which many people still viewed the society.[40] To be sure, voices on the Democratic side had begun to complain about the destructive effects of nascent capitalism. These contrasting representations arose within a single political culture, however. They differed only in their judgment of reality, which one side saw as conforming to the shared ideal and the other as contradicting it.[41]

The American culture of individual autonomy remained so powerful, moreover, that the emergence, however limited, of a new group of wage workers was seen as a problem and a threat. No one expressed the fear that America would be undermined by this new contradiction better than Orestes Brownson in his famous 1840 essay "The Laboring Classes."[42] The fiery pamphleteer saw the decline of independent labor as the beginning of a new America defined by the clash between man and money and condemned to give up its original ideals. For him, wage labor could only be a form of slave labor, opposed to free labor. Wage labor, he argued, was a "trick of the devil," which offered employers all the benefits of the slave system without any of the drawbacks, in addition to which it was in no way an object of opprobrium, as slavery was. Although Brownson recognized that the factories of New England could not be compared to those of Birmingham or Manchester, he did not hesitate to say that "we regard the slave system as decidedly preferable to the system at wages."[43] Brownson's views on the matter were no different from Lamennais's. A "hard money Democrat," he voiced the fear of early factory workers that they would one day end up no better off than southern slaves.

Thus the rise of capitalism led to a break with revolutionary ideals on both sides of the Atlantic, with varying consequences. Impatience for change increased, and new expectations arose. New utopian ideas emerged, and conservatism was redefined. The "first globalization" of the late nineteenth century would exacerbate the social and political consequences of capitalism. Between the advent of capitalism in the early part of the century and the first globalization toward the end, the egalitarian ideal was revised in four main ways:

1. The conservative-liberal ideology of the 1820s and 1830s was based on a minimalist legal reinterpretation of the egalitarian revolution. Its goal was to legitimate existing inequalities by linking them to the immorality of the proletariat or by naturalizing them.
2. Conversely, communism, which made its appearance in the 1840s, proposed a new rationalized communitarian society based on the elimination of competition, which was blamed

for everything that had gone wrong. Communists understood equality as an instrument for building a unified,
harmonious society.

3. The advent of the first globalization in the 1890s complicated
   matters. Protectionist nationalism emerged, pitting a definition of equality as homogeneity, based on xenophobia and
   defense of the nation, against the earlier revolutionary ideal
   of equality as a relation between individuals.

4. In America the idea of equality was radicalized in the form of
   racism, rejecting nonwhites from society in order to establish
   an imaginary equality among those who remained.

Thus, the idea of democratic equality was perverted in four distinct ways, each of which represented a radical reinterpretation of
the egalitarian principle. These pathologies would persist until the
advent of the redistributive welfare state.

The Conservative-Liberal Ideology

American and French revolutionaries enshrined equality of *conditions* as their credo. To be sure, the society of *semblables* that
stemmed from this principle in no way implied an equality of *situations,* but situational differences were justifiable only if they had no
inherently social character. Acceptable inequalities were defined by
two qualities: virtue and talent. Article VI of the Declaration of the
Rights of Man and the Citizen (1789) stipulated that "all citizens,
being equal [in the eyes of the law], are equally eligible for all public
ranks, positions, and employments in accordance with their capability and without distinction except in regard to their virtues and
talents." The Declaration of Rights of 1793 repeated the same

words. Virtue and talent: individual behavior on the one hand and natural endowment on the other. Throughout the nineteenth century, conservative-liberal ideology justified itself on the basis of an extremely broad interpretation of these themes. By maximally extending the realm of individual responsibility (in the interpretation of virtue) and insisting on the importance of inherited characteristics (for the judgment of talent), conservatives reduced the social determinants of inequality to the bare minimum. The very idea of democratic society was subverted by this endlessly repeated semantic device.[44] The idea of similarity was therefore divorced from questions about the precise basis of comparison. It was whittled down to mere equality of rights.

The Stigmatization of the Worker

The most important social fact in 1830s France was the explosion of inequality due to the rise of capitalism. Paradoxically, however, it was the wretched workers themselves who would be put in the dock by conservatives, who argued that working people had only themselves to blame for their distressing situations. Even extreme inequalities could thus be made to seem morally justifiable. To gauge the degree to which such arguments soothed the conscience of the bourgeoisie, one has only to read some of the period's major social surveys. Writers such as Adolphe Blanqui, Louis Reybaud, and Louis René Villermé did yeoman service in revealing the condition of the working class. They visited hovels, followed workers to the cabaret, visited stifling, filthy shop floors, and published statistics about wages, accidents in the workplace, and the ages of children employed as machine operators. They investigated details of daily life such as clothing, diet, drink, gambling, and sexual behavior. Villermé in particular made an impression with his *Tableau de l'état physique et moral des ouvriers* (1840). To be sure, he offered a terrifying account of the lives of the men and women who worked in the cotton, wool, and silk factories that he visited in Lille, Rouen, and Mulhouse. But what he saw did not make him pessimistic or critical of modern industry. Indeed, he pointed out areas in which it seemed to him that workers' lives were improving in small ways, and countered pessimists of all stripes with the observation that "it is good that workers know that their condition today is better than it has ever been."[45] Although Villermé did not deny the effects of competition on wages, he argued that "except in times of crisis, the vast majority of hard-working, sober, thrifty, and provident workers can sustain themselves and their families, even if they cannot put anything aside."[46] This was the core of his position: misery was ultimately caused by improvidence, corruption, debauchery, and drunkenness. Strictly economic and industrial factors played a part in determining the working man's condition, but for Villermé the essential point was that workers failed to understand that "the remedy for their poverty lay in their good behavior."[47] Wage increases would therefore do no good if "habits of debauchery and disorder" persisted.

The denunciation of working-class vices as the principal causes of worker misery and therefore of intolerable inequalities became the leitmotif of any number of critiques. Take Buret, for example. No one painted a darker picture of the condition of French and British workers, yet he was ferocious in linking misery to vice. His social criticism never transcended a pervasive moralism. After pitilessly describing the "wretched neighborhoods" in which industrial workers lived and observing men, women, and children who had "lapsed into a savage existence," he concluded that "you see such horrifying misery that it inspires disgust rather than pity, and you are tempted to see it as just punishment for a crime."[48] If Buret "succumbed" to the temptation to stigmatize the proletariat, many other commentators had no such scruples and simply excoriated workers without compunction. The effect was a veritable ideological bombardment. Saint-Marc Girardin, who distinguished himself in 1831 by characterizing the *canuts,* or silk workers of Lyon, as "barbarians," led the offensive, whose ultimate goal was to salve the conscience of the bourgeoisie. "History teaches us that misery is the punishment for laziness and debauchery," he coldly observed in 1832 from his lectern at the Sorbonne.[49] Cartloads of books and articles rang the changes on this theme throughout the July Monarchy. In a compendious volume devoted to the "dangerous classes" and considered authoritative at the time, Honoré Antoine Frégier went even further. He transformed workers into criminals by adding the adjective "dangerous" to "poor" and "vicious" in characterizing the working class. It was no longer enough, he argued, to see the proletarian as miserable and depraved; the worker was also a threat of the most serious kind.[50]

If individual vices were the true sources of misery, then the only way to deal with the problem was to improve the morality of the working class. Joseph-Marie de Gérando, a leading philanthropist of the time, maintained that "virtue is the true guardian of man's well-being."[51] Most social investigators came to the same conclusion: the best way to improve the worker's lot was to promote morality. In Gérando's pompous formulation: "Virtue, which brings benefits to all human conditions, offers special help to each of them, and it comes with a sort of predilection for wrapping the working class in its salutary protection."[52] The solution, repeated ad nauseam by the literature on pauperism, was therefore "providential virtue" rather than the welfare state or the regulation of capitalism. According to Gérando, the practice of such virtue would not only prove beneficial to individuals directly but would also have a specific *political effect:* by teaching each person "to be content with his fate," it would lead people generally "to consider others in apparently happier situations without envy" and thus spare them the ill effects of "impatience and bitterness."[53]

We have thus far been concentrating on the French case, but there is an equivalent literature from the other side of the Channel. The major parliamentary surveys of pauperism converged toward a similar solution: a call for the moral improvement of the working class. We see this in the conclusion of the first and most celebrated of those surveys, the one completed in 1834. Its seven impressive folio volumes contained a wealth of damning details, statistics, and direct observations (on which Marx would draw extensively in writing *Das Kapital*). The royal commissioners concluded their work with the following lines: "The commissioners recognize and affirm that we must count not so much on any sort of economic arrangement as on the influence of moral and religious education."[54] Thus moral improvement was proposed as a remedy in England as well as France.[55] Since workers were responsible for their own condition, there were no grounds for speaking of injustice.

Conservative-liberal governments responded to this call for proletarian virtue and responsibility by taking steps to develop it.[56] Their "egalitarian policy" was thus reduced to institutionalizing various ways of providing for future eventualities. The first workers' mutual associations and savings banks arose in this context. French governments did not go beyond this, but their English counterparts went further. A veritable moral-improvement state took shape in England with the establishment of workhouses, the razing of slums, and the passage of a whole arsenal of laws (to prohibit sexual relations before marriage and to combat obscenity, for example). The government was assisted by powerful leagues for the promotion of virtue and philanthropic societies such as the London City Mission, the Charity Organisation Society, the Salvation Army, the London Bible Women and Nurses Mission, and the Moral Reform Union, to name only the best known and most active of them.[57] Their very existence helped to accredit the idea that the most glaring inequalities were entirely consequences of vice and impiety.

The Industrial Regime and Necessary Inequality

As we have seen, conservative liberalism constantly sought to reduce the scope of the notion of social inequality while at the same time expanding the influence of individual responsibility and natural inequalities. In this spirit, the shape of the new capitalist economy was presented as an objective justification of the role of natural inequalities in the functioning of society. Dunoyer, one of the leading ideologues of the July Monarchy, developed this point at length. He devoted several sections of his principal economic work, *De la liberté du travail,* to the question of inequality of conditions in the industrial regime.[58] "The effect of the industrial regime," he wrote, "is to destroy factitious inequalities, but this only brings out natural inequalities all the more."[59] In his view, modern industry allowed natural inequalities to be expressed to the fullest rather than masked by the advantages of birth and other socially instituted differences. Thus, everything began with differences in physical, intellectual, and moral capacities, which supposedly defined the laws of the human race. The effect of the industrial regime "is therefore not so much to eliminate inequalities among men as to classify them in a different way."[60] In other words, the industrial regime is purely natural! This was the heart of the new conservative-liberal ideology that took hold in Europe in the 1830s and 1840s. The new ideology also moralized nature by refusing to distinguish between natural faculties and behavior and by assimilating intelligence to virtue and talent to good behavior, thus transforming natural differences into moral distinctions. Another consequence was the abandonment of an idea that had been prominent during the Revolution, according to which the law could be viewed as a benevolent second nature. The idea that men could be regenerated and thus saved from circumstances that seemed to define them also disappeared. In the end, nature was simply identified with the existing order of things.[61]

Dunoyer did not leave it at that, however. "Having said that equality of conditions is not possible in the industrial regime," he continued, "I make bold to add that it is desirable."[62] In a growing, innovative economy, "superior abilities . . . are the source of everything that is great and useful. . . . Reduce everything to equality and you will bring everything to a standstill." Social inequalities were therefore a functional necessity, he believed. They were the basis of the necessary division of labor and a motive for emulation. "The development of industry would quite simply be impossible if all men were equally happy," he concluded. Inequality thus produced creative tensions, and in Dunoyer's eyes even the depths of misery had a role to play: "It is a good thing that society provides inferior stations into which families that behave badly may fall and from which they may not rise unless they behave well. Misery is that awesome hell. It is an inevitable abyss, situated alongside the mad, the dissolute, the debauched, and all the other species of vicious men, to keep them under control."[63] For all these reasons, inequality could therefore be seen as the law of the world, at once natural, moral, social, and psychological. In the nineteenth century, the *laws* of the liberal economy were also natural laws hostile to equality. This way of looking at things allowed conservative-liberal ideology to combine the most aristocratic and reactionary concepts of inequality and portray them as a positive and essential driving force of social life. This was the context in which the contradiction between liberty and equality was analyzed theoretically.

Equality versus Liberty

Jacques Necker was the first to touch on this opposition in his *Réflexions philosophiques sur l'égalité.*[64] Published in 1793 as the fourth volume of his *Révolution française,* this work may be seen as the first comprehensive conservative interpretation of the revolutionary phenomenon, a French counterpart to the work of Edmund Burke. But whereas Burke mainly attacked what he saw as the illiberal political ideal of the Revolution, Necker proposed a more social critique, anticipating some of the major themes of later liberal works on the irresistible progress of equality. He accepted the idea of natural equality as well as equality of rights but condemned what he saw as a deviation from these principles. In his eyes, the problem was that the destruction of unjustified distinctions (primarily those based on birth) led to an attack on social differences in general: "War is made on all superior qualities, on wealth, on talent, on benefits, on reputations, on fleeting authorities. No one wanted anything that stood out once political equality became the token by which all other equalities were measured."[65] Hence for him the most urgent task was to break the chain and the spell. How? By declaring equality to be the enemy of the social order whenever it spilled over its strict original boundaries. "Harmonized inequality is the universal watchword," he argued. Nineteenth-century conservatives would take this critique a step further by establishing a strict hierarchy between the values of liberty and equality. Liberty should take priority, they believed, because it could be universalized, whereas equality, which required a transfer of wealth, was accused of "partiality" and linked to the idea of social division. In short, it implied class warfare. In practice, equality meant expansion of coercive government power, without which, conservatives argued, it could not be achieved. The theme of "liberticide equality" was central to conservative-liberal ideology, justifying the social status quo and resistance to reformist ideas.

An attack was launched at the same time on similarity, which was also suspected of being turned against the original ideals of the Revolution. Tocqueville of course paid close attention to what he considered the most worrisome tendency of democratic society. Although he recognized similarity as the "generative principle" of democracy as a social form, he also warned against the possibility that it would lead to a society governed by conformism and mediocrity. The society of semblables might then depressingly resemble a "common mass," "an innumerable host of men, all alike and equal, endlessly hastening after petty and vulgar pleasures."[66] Friedrich Nietzsche later voiced the most radical version of this critique with his obsessive scorn for "the human herd." This was a second way to dismiss the egalitarian ideal. The offensive would proceed relentlessly on both fronts, liberty and distinction, as the fear of property owners was linked to aristocratic contempt for the plebs.[67] Nikolai Berdyaev's early twentieth-century masterwork *The Philosophy of Inequality* offered a striking synthesis of both themes.[68] The very idea of a general reduction of inequalities obviously made no sense in this context, in which the value of equality was so depreciated. Belief in the principles of 1789 was maintained by interpreting them in the most minimalist sense possible.

The Naturalization of Inequality

The invocation of talent also played a central role in the legitimation of inequalities, though a certain distortion of the notion of talent was required. Even before it was consecrated by the Declaration of the Rights of Man and the Citizen, the term was widely used, and used in particular by Rousseau and Thomas Paine, as a way of explaining and justifying differences. It was not rigorously defined, however. Consulting contemporary dictionaries reveals clearly that the word was associated with the natural order. "Talent," we read in the *Encyclopedia,* "is a natural disposition, an aptitude in a mechanical or liberal art. . . . Talent of all sorts is not within our power and should not therefore inspire pride in ourselves or contempt for others." The 1786 edition of the *Dictionnaire de l'Académie française* gave this definition of talent: "Gift of nature, natural disposition and aptitude for certain things, capacity, [and] ability." The term implicitly referred to eminent qualities, to exceptional capabilities. Talents were in a sense always special, particular. If they were not equally distributed by nature, they could nevertheless be seen as being to everyone's benefit. Talent distinguished certain individuals, but it was a friend to humanity in general, because nature (everyone believed) is benevolent. In the eighteenth century it was to nature that people turned to legitimate their projects of emancipation or to seek models of a just order. It was on the side of the good, the just, and equality. To speak of natural equality seemed obvious, and utopians presented themselves as faithful observers of nature. In 1755, Morelly was thus able to entitle the work in which he first formulated the communist ideal *Le code de la nature*.

In the nineteenth century, the perception of nature "changed sides," if I may put it that way. It was invoked more often to explain what divided men rather than what brought them together, and what constrained rather than what liberated them. In the process, one went from justifying the distinction of a few to justifying a generalized system of inequality and a social hierarchy. This change was the great achievement of conservative-liberal ideology, of which Guizot's work offers an excellent illustration. Guizot made free use of revolutionary rhetoric to denounce the idea of privilege, but whereas the revolutionaries of 1789 challenged privilege in the name of a principle of *social equality*, Guizot contrasted it with a principle of *natural inequality*. For him, privilege was a pathological form of inequality rather than an affront to equality. It is therefore worth taking the trouble to follow his reasoning step by step. "Men," he wrote, "are all of the same nature and therefore fully similar [semblables], but the forces with which this nature is endowed are not distributed to all in the same proportion, and in this respect, men really are unequal."[69] Natural inequalities are therefore a fact, based on forms of superiority or distinction likely to be considered "objective." What was unacceptable to Guizot was simply the transformation of these natural inequalities into *social inequalities* narrowly defined in terms of privilege. As he saw it, this transformation took place in two stages. First came an extension of natural inequality beyond its original province, as, for example, when physically superior men attempted to assert general power, repressing people with different kinds of talent, or when people endowed with a certain type of superiority prevented others from acquiring the capabilities from which they derived their strength. Natural inequalities became social when those who possessed them sought to exclude other, equally natural inequalities that might rival or claim a share of their power. "For instance," Guizot explained,

> those who rule by superiority of arms tried to prevent their subjects from acquiring skill in arms, no matter what propensity they may have had to become strong in turn. Those who owed their power to superior intellect sought to stifle the development of the mind. The rich were afraid to see the poor become rich. Every inequality originally derived from the influence of certain forms of natural superiority declared war on the very same forms of natural superiority that gave them their titles and might give those same titles to others, thereby creating rivals for themselves.[70]

The second way in which natural inequalities became social inequalities, according to Guizot, was that those endowed with natural superiority sought to perpetuate their advantage by passing it on from one generation to the next. An individual superiority was thereby transformed into something almost genetic. This was the history of the nobility, which sought to derive exorbitant privileges from hypothetical great deeds in the past.

For Guizot, these two types of claims were the basis of privilege. "What constitutes privilege," he wrote, "is the fraudulent and illegitimate extension in space or time of the real superiority that gave rise to it. From its inception, privilege renounces its origin and combats its principle. It declares itself to be the enemy of natural inequality, which was its source, and the protector of a factitious inequality whose artificiality it seeks to attenuate by opposing the free development of the true inequality that would shatter it."[71] What Guizot rejected in privilege was not inequality as such but the fact that privilege upset and destroyed the order of natural superiorities. "The essence of modern (democratic) society," he explained, "is to reject any *factitious inequality* and to give free rein to natural inequalities."[72] In other words, privilege disrupted the proper relationship between unequal and equal: it introduced inequality where equality ought to predominate, and it destroyed inequality where it should have been able to assert itself. Hence it was a twofold perversion of inequality.

Inequalities were thus perfectly acceptable if strictly linked to *individuals* and *situations,* intertwining natural qualities with characteristics of personal activity. Guizot summed it up this way:

No artifice should impede the ascent or fall of individuals in the social order. Natural superiority and social pre-eminence should not receive any factitious support from the law. Citizens should be left to their own merits and strengths. Each person must be able on his own to become all that he can be and must not confront any institutional impediment to his rise, if he is capable of it, nor should he receive any assistance to remain in a superior situation, if he cannot maintain himself there on his own. I do not hesitate to make this assertion. When it comes to equality, this is the full extent of public philosophy. It goes this far and no farther.[73]

These theories, formulated at the height of the struggle between liberals and ultra-royalists in the early 1820s, did not accurately predict the practice of the July Monarchy, which was obsessed with fears of a new social revolution. Nevertheless, Guizot's reductionist version of both equality and inequality would remain influential for quite some time, despite biases and prejudices that limited the scope and circumscribed the interpretation of his theories.

The Science of Inequality

Guizot's idea of natural inequality became influential because it claimed to be based on incontrovertible scientific findings. Veritable "sciences of inequality" emerged in the nineteenth century. In this respect, the break with the Age of Enlightenment was striking. Buffon's mid-eighteenth-century natural science had contributed to the rise of an egalitarian imaginary. By contrast, in the nineteenth century, sciences that claimed to demonstrate a physiological basis of inequality drew considerable public attention and were everywhere in the limelight.[74] Phrenology is a case in point. It began with the work of a German physician, Franz Joseph Gall, who developed a revolutionary method of brain dissection at the end of the eighteenth century. Gall's method completely revolutionized the anatomy of the brain by revealing the previously unnoticed importance of the cortex and the central nervous system.[75] This work marked an epochal advance in neuroanatomy, still recognized to this day. But Gall pursued his observations further still and formulated the totally revolutionary hypothesis that different areas of the cortex are linked to various human faculties. He located twenty-seven "cerebral organs" and drew a functional map of the cortex (later extended to include thirty-six functions). Gall distinguished areas associated with the various senses, language aptitude, and memory as well as feelings and proclivities (love, ambition, perseverance, compassion, violence, etc.), in addition to a range of capabilities. For instance, he distinguished a capacity for abstraction, poetic ability, and mechanical skill. He then argued that the intensity of each of these functions was directly proportional to the volume of the relevant area of the brain, which could be measured directly on the surface of the skull by the presence or absence of visible protuberances.[76] Phrenology ("the science of the mind") was born. Gall set forth the goals of the new science in a work published in French in 1809, *Recherches sur le système nerveux en général et celui du cerveau en particulier*. This work "naturalized" virtues (and vices) as well as talents, the two variables that served to justify inequality.[77]

Although scientific research had discredited phrenology by the late 1830s, it continued to enjoy extraordinary public success. Its audience expanded as its content grew increasingly vague. Some philosophers saw it as a vindication of materialism. Fourierists, for example, related their theory of passions to Gall's theory of functions. Gall's work also became almost fashionable, eliciting enthusiasm even in high society circles, as Mesmer's theory of animal magnetism had done in the late eighteenth century. Honoré de Balzac was a booster among many others, and visitors flocked to the Musée Phrénologique, which opened its doors in Paris in 1837.[78] Pierre Leroux, exiled to Jersey, gave a course in phrenology in 1853, which Victor Hugo eagerly attended.[79] Phrenology also seemed capable of opening new avenues to social reform. For instance, Félix Voisin persuaded the Ministry of Justice that it might be useful for preventing juvenile delinquency by allowing early detection of criminal proclivities, which could then be countered by appropriate education.[80] An "Orthophrenic Institute" was established for the purpose in 1834. Rather more vaguely, socialists and republicans saw phrenology as the possible basis of a progressive social physiology (subsequently adapted to hygienist-eugenicist purposes). The *Almanach de la communauté pour 1843,* published by Théodor Dézamy, one of the pioneers of French communism, praised it in this light.[81]

It is striking to note that phrenology enjoyed its greatest and most lasting social success in the United States. The Fowler brothers were intimately associated with its good fortune. In the 1830s and 1840s, they crisscrossed the country giving phrenological consultations to guide their clients in their matrimonial and professional choices and advise them on child rearing. They sold small earthenware heads on which the various areas of brain function were marked out. Later, they established offices in New York, Boston, and Philadelphia to advise firms in selecting job candidates based solely on photographs of their heads. Like related specialties such as graphology, astrology, and numerology, phrenology gained a solid foothold in nineteenth-century America. Edgar Allan Poe, Herman Melville, and Henry David Thoreau all referred to it, and Walt Whitman sought an examination by the Fowler brothers. Such an enthusiastic reception cannot be put down to popular credulity alone. Why were Americans so receptive to the phrenological idea (its content was so vague that it can hardly be called a theory)?

Faith in science was no doubt part of the answer, along with the hope that science might lead to a reliable method of human improvement. But the more important reason was that phrenology provided an easy and intellectually acceptable way to reconcile the egalitarian imperative with the existence of fully "naturalized" inequalities. That is why André Siegried said that in order to understand America at the turn of the twentieth century, one needed to study two books: the Bible and a manual of phrenology! When the scientific shortcomings of phrenology became too glaring and the practice began to fade from fashion, another way of "naturalizing inequality" took its place in the United States: intelligence testing. "What craniometry was to the nineteenth century, intelligence testing has been to the twentieth," observed the great naturalist Stephen Jay Gould.[82]

Intelligence testing originated in 1857 with a French psychologist, Alfred Binet, a disciple of Théodule Ribot and Jean-Martin Charcot at the Salpêtrière.[83] Interestingly, Binet was first attracted by craniometry, which had already begun to fade, before turning to psychology in the belief that a new method was needed to measure the intelligence of schoolchildren. A study commissioned in 1904 by the Ministry of Public Education gave him the opportunity to develop his first metric.[84] With the help of his collaborator Théodore Simon, Binet produced a diverse battery of tests to determine a student's general intellectual level, independent of any specific knowledge or scholastic competence (such as the ability to read or do sums). The goal was to measure formal intellectual abilities: capacity to reason, aptitude in making correlations, understanding statements, creative potential, etc. A "mental age" was assigned for each test, and this made it possible to determine an overall mental age for the student. By comparing this with the student's biological age, it was possible to identify children in danger of scholastic failure. Later, this measurement was standardized in the form of an intelligence quotient (IQ).[85]

Although Binet had perfected his technique for the very pragmatic purpose of helping pupils in difficulty, many others seized on it in a very different spirit. It was used to classify, order, and assign individuals to fixed categories. After Binet died in 1911, Simon also turned in this direction, as can be seen from the preface he wrote for a reprint of their collaborative work. The IQ test, Simon wrote, "is the first example of a direct measure of an individual's psychological worth. It placed the idea of human inequality on a basis other than vague sentiment. It made it possible to demonstrate the universal role of inequality and even to measure it."[86] It was in this spirit that IQ measurement spread in America. The army was the first to make extensive use of it in World War I, examining and testing nearly two million soldiers. Enthusiasm spread rapidly. The United States became the land of testing. The movement had its high priests, who sustained the common faith, and even its central administration: the Educational Testing Service was established in 1947 to administer the famous Scholastic Aptitude Test (SAT), which has ever since decided the fate of young Americans applying to college. To be sure, these methods were severely criticized on both methodological and substantive grounds.[87] The passion for the tests was only marginally affected, however. Tests continue to influence collective representations of the social, and most people have come to accept their role in this regard.

The American cult of testing, succeeding the cult of phrenology, clearly exposes the central contradiction underlying the history of liberal capitalist democracies: the coexistence of an egalitarian founding philosophy with a social reality marked by substantial inequalities. Because this tension has been greatest in the United States, the temptation to naturalize inequality has also been most obvious there.[88] Thus "desocialized," inequality was able to prosper in a society viscerally attached to the idea that all men are created equal. Inequality was legitimated, moreover, by being linked to individual merit and inherited talent alone. To be sure, this broad portrait needs to be filled in with finer detail. There were many ways to naturalize inequality in America. The more extreme efforts, exemplified by a controversial work entitled *The Bell Curve,* were worlds apart from the routine administration of the SAT.[89] What is common to all, however, is a refusal to think about social inequality in its own terms.

The time has come to say a word or two about conservative interpretations of Charles Darwin in America and Europe. Many works on both sides of the Atlantic extrapolated a "social Darwinian" account of social inequality as a consequence of the principle of natural selection and survival of the fittest. Deterministic Darwinian theories of inequality were often linked to nationalist or racist views (of which Arthur Gobineau's *Essai sur l'inégalité des races humaines* was an early example). Such erroneous interpretations of Darwin's ideas were enormously influential in the late nineteenth century because they offered a naturalistic justification of inequality.[90]

Limited Equality of Opportunity

Conservative-liberal ideology also featured a very restrictive interpretation of the idea of equality of opportunity, especially in the French context. In principle, careers were open to virtue and talent, but conservatives were obsessed with protecting existing social hierarchies. The schools were caught up in this contradiction: they were supposed to give everyone a chance (democratic-liberal principle) while at the same time assigning each individual to his or her proper place (conservative principle). The existence of an inherent tension between the ideal of universal education and the realities of the social hierarchy with its radically different occupations was of course not a new discovery at the turn of the nineteenth century. It had already occupied social theorists in the century before. Even the boldest reformers confessed to fears that ambitions would grow out of control if education were too widely disseminated.

Consider, for example, the way in which Louis-René de Caradeuc de La Chalotais and Denis Diderot approached the question. La Chalotais's *Essai d'éducation nationale* is particularly worthy of attention. It was a pioneering work that in many respects anticipated the public and secular educational philosophy of the founding fathers of the French Third Republic. A tireless scourge of Jesuits, La Chalotais was nevertheless alarmed at the sight of farmers and artisans who sent their children to small-town schools.[91] Faced with the threat of what would today be called diploma inflation, La Chalotais sounded the alarm: "For the good of society, the people's knowledge must not extend beyond its occupations." He consequently lashed out at the Christian Brothers, whom he accused of creating too many schools. "They came and ruined everything," he wrote. "They teach people to read and write who should have been taught only to work with planes and files but no longer care to do so." For him it was quite plain that "any man who looks beyond his tedious occupation will lack the courage and patience to do what must be done." His fear that the schools would disturb the established social order and occupational hierarchy ultimately came into conflict with his reformist ambitions.

We find the same contradiction in Diderot. In his *Plan d'une université*, the philosopher called for elementary schools whose doors would be "open *without distinction* to all the nation's children." He insisted on the importance of not discriminating against anyone because he considered it absurd to condemn "the subaltern conditions of society" to ignorance. In subsequent chapters, however, he sounds a very different note. His generous egalitarian pronouncements give way to much less expansive statements about the need for individuals to remain in their places. He railed against "false learning that makes people stubborn," blasted "the foolish ambition of parents determined to save their children from their subaltern occupations," and bluntly concluded that "nothing is more harmful to society than fathers disdainful of their occupations and senseless migrations from one estate to another."[92] It would be wrong to view these words of Diderot and La Chalotais as mere survivals of past attitudes, as accidental revivals of old prejudices in an otherwise progressive analysis. On the contrary, they were fully modern, anticipating a *future problem*. In the old society of orders, no confusion of estates or ranks was possible. Everyone knew that he occupied a definite place. The tension between conditions and ambitions—a tension centered on the schools—would develop fully only with the advent of democratic liberal society in the nineteenth century. One early consequence of this was a call for separate schools for the "working class" and the "educated class." As the French educational system took shape under the July Monarchy, countless voices warned against "malicious popular instruction" and the danger of creating large numbers of ungrateful, frustrated, unhappy people by opening the doors of the schools too wide.[93]

The meritocratic ideal, though continually proclaimed, was restricted in this context to elite recruitment. Conservative-liberal ideology merely continued the work of revolutionary reformers in this respect. To be sure, those reformers were less obsessed with the need to ensure reproduction of the social order. But they were steeped in a very French culture of political rationalism, in which the idea of good government was limited to placing enlightened leadership at the summit of society.[94] Democratization of elites was therefore the key question in their eyes. This view was widely shared in France, as is evident from a petition submitted to the Convention on September 15, 1793, by the *département* of Paris.[95] It is symptomatic of a progressive approach to education that was entirely "democratic-hierarchical." The petition reflected an obsession with scouring the society to identify what one might call its "hidden geniuses." Interestingly, it received direct support from popular sections and societies, despite an abundance of other issues that these groups would presumably have judged more urgent at the time. This shows that the subject was seen as essential. At the heart of the text was the following statement: "When a child is born in the midst of twenty-five million citizens, it is more than likely that it will turn out to be an ordinary person, but there is also a chance that nature will have endowed it with eminent qualities. If the nation attends to its interests and seeks to profit from all its advantages, it must not lose sight of that child, wherever it happens to be born." As an example, the petition proposed a highly intelligent child born to modest shepherds on the Lozère plateau, whose talents would remain underexploited if the child were not rescued from its less-than-stimulating surroundings. Failure to do so would be a waste, not only for the individual but above all for the nation, to which a superior mind might have contributed something of value. In this instance, in other words, equality was understood as a willingness to search *everywhere* for talent rather than provide equal education for all or hold out the possibility of general social advancement. Using vivid imagery, the petition spoke of searching cellars and attics inhabited by the poorest of citizens in the hope of finding a hidden Newton. It was in this link between *highest and lowest* that people saw the essence of equality and the opportunity to apply the principle that all careers are open to talent. It was the fate of the *genius* (the embodiment of absolute talent) rather than of the ordinary person that was taken as the measure of equality. One might call this *summit meritocracy*.

A permanent consensus developed around this view in nineteenth-century France. It became the least common denominator around which conservatives and progressives could coalesce. Conservatives, as we have seen, continued to fear the effects of ill-conceived educational reform, which they believed would spur impossible ambitions and lead to widespread frustration. Yet they also continued to trumpet "the sacred rights of the talented poor," to whom a hand should be extended, they argued, wherever talent happened to be found.[96] Equality was thus defined by the (theoretical) possibility that anyone might join the elite rather than by any index of progress for the average person. This justified focusing attention mainly on the apex of the pyramid, the so-called Grandes Écoles. From the Revolution onward, the primary criterion was therefore that anyone, no matter how humble, should be allowed to compete in the entrance examinations. For instance, one of the great reformers of the Directory and Consulate periods, the chemist Antoine-François Fourcroy, who along with the mathematician Gaspard Monge played a key role in establishing the École Polytechnique, proposed selecting a few thousand "national students" in every *département* to provide a pool of candidates for recruitment by the Grandes Écoles.[97] What were the actual consequences of this meritocratic vision? A certain skepticism is in order. For example, a parliamentary report from the early years of the July Monarchy shows that in 1833 there were only 1,674 scholarship students in all the *collèges royaux* (the equivalent of today's lycées), and only 251 new scholarships were awarded (scholarships ran for seven years, the entire period of study).[98] In other words, there was a wide gap between theory and practice. This, however, did not prevent the flourishing of a veritable *meritocratic ideology,* which the conservative regimes of the period used to justify themselves.

Standing atop the knowledge pyramid and serving as a gateway to the most prestigious public jobs, the École Polytechnique was at the heart of this ideology. In 1848, Hippolyte Carnot, the minister of public instruction, suggested a surprising method for "expanding this school's recruitment to all the people": all elementary school students should be made familiar with the subjects included in the school's entrance examination, and the secondary schools *(collèges)* should then prepare students for the exams for free.[99] This was an extreme but not atypical view of democratization as a question of organizing a vast pyramid—a vision of the educational system as a *social distillery.*

Note that none of these projects, nor those proposed during the revolutionary period, made room for the idea of the university as it was then understood in Germany and England. What the French wanted was not an institution of research, scholarship, and learning but rather a mechanism for classifying individuals grafted onto a system of instruction in applied knowledge. The sociological function was more important than the intellectual function. Few in France spoke out against this concept of education. The vast majority of conservatives and republicans shared the same cult of competitive examinations and the same vision of democratization, although some would prove bolder in their thinking in an area dominated by narrow views. During the Restoration, for example, Joseph Jacotot was isolated for refusing to believe in the unequal distribution of intelligence or the justice of a society based on a supposedly "objective" hierarchy.[100] At the end of the century, Jean-Gustave Courcelle-Seneuil was similarly ignored after he launched a brilliantly astute attack on the rigidities of the Grande École system and the perverse effects it engendered in his *Étude sur le mandarinat français*. He accused the schools of creating new forms of privilege and new castes, their democratic claims notwithstanding.[101] In republican educational circles, Henri Marion was virtually the only authority to denounce what he saw as his compatriots' "rage for classification and comparison."[102]

In France, this meritocratic legitimation of inequality gave rise to a *meritocratic classification model*. Guizot used the phrase "mobile aristocracy of equality"[103] to characterize what would become a vital feature of French political culture. From the July Monarchy to the Third Republic, *republican elitism*, a product of this model, grew stronger and stronger to the point where it eliminated all other definitions of equality. The principle of limited equality of opportunity at the top of society has masked the overwhelming reproduction of the existing hierarchy at lower levels.[104] The essential function of ideology is to distort reality in this way, masking it behind principles that no one would think of challenging.

Utopian Communism

Critique of Individualism and Competition

The specter of social dissolution haunted many minds in the early nineteenth century, especially in France. Leroux put it bluntly: "Society is nothing but a mass of egotisms. It is no longer a body. There is only a corpse with its several limbs."[105] To be sure, lapidary formulas such as these, repeated a thousand times over, resonated in a variety of ways. For some, they reflected aristocratic nostalgia for a society that revolved around the "great eminences" that supposedly defined its essence. For others, they evoked worries of a more "spiritual" kind, having to do with the simultaneous decomposition of the moral and social order. Many were troubled by the disappearance of corporatist solidarities among working men and the emergence of a new industrial regime.

All of these anxieties were fueled by a simple sociological fact: the advent of a society that was both atomized and divided. This was the context in which the word *"individualisme"* first appeared in French. The word emphasized the stark contrast with the old order. One reformer spoke of "the dreadful sentiment that the language has thought useful to dignify with the blunt appellation 'individualism.'"[106] Another spoke of "individualism, terrifying, somber, and menacing."[107] Saint-Simonians began to use the word systematically in the mid-1820s. Leroux, Prosper Enfantin, and Laurent de l'Ardèche all used it in the columns of *Le Producteur* to denounce the emergence of a fragmented society of clashing wills and anarchic special interests. The principal Saint-Simonian journal of the period criticized "the hostile spirit inherent in the reign of individualism."[108] The use of the word "individualism" in these contexts established a link between the moral concept of selfishness and the economic concept of competition. Working men and socialists seized on the latter term to characterize modernity's harsh and painful impact on the working class.

In the 1820s, the Saint-Simonians were the first to sound the alarm about the ravages of competition, which they saw as the source of all hostility and all inequality. In both theoretical works and more popular tracts, they portrayed competition as the cause of social suffering. In opposition to the "economic sect," which presented competition as a necessary condition of progress, Saint-Simonians argued that it was in fact the cause of pauperism and the growth of the proletariat.[109] Across the Channel, Robert Owen, the period's great reformer, proposed an identical analysis. One chapter of his manifesto was entitled "On Competition." "Competition," he wrote, "creates a covered civil warfare between individuals. . . . It is productive of evils of every description."[110] Fourier used similar language. In his writing, the words most frequently associated with competition were anarchy, waste, oppression, and war.[111] The denunciation of competition was a rallying point for all socialists in this period. Though divided among a host of rival factions, they came together to condemn competition. In this respect, moreover, they were merely following popular sentiment.

In France, it was Louis Blanc who made an indelible impression on collective memory with his comments on competition in *l'Organisation du travail*. Along with Lamennais's *Livre du peuple*, this pamphlet served as a breviary for an entire generation. "Competition is a system for the extermination of the people," Blanc wrote. "It is an industrial process by means of which proletarians are forced to exterminate one another."[112] "With competition," he continued, "there is no liberty, because it prevents the weakest from developing their abilities and delivers them into the hands of the strongest. With competition, there is no equality, because it is nothing but inequality in motion. With competition, there is no fraternity, because it is a form of combat."[113] In this and other texts, Blanc arraigned competition as the absolute enemy of the human race. It was an "abominable system," a "mysterious tyranny," and a "source of all the people's suffering" and would lead to an "inevitable worldwide conflagration." What could be done to stop such an evil? One word served as an inspiration to all: "association." Fourierists, Saint-Simonians, and rebellious workers all rallied around this banner despite different definitions of the concept. The word was often tainted with nostalgia for corporatism, often rooted in an unduly rosy view of the old world of guilds and their fraternal spirit. Many "craftsmen" in both England and France joined together in the early 1830s to establish the first workers' cooperatives. They also organized embryonic trade unions, which attempted to negotiate with employers over rates.[114] Blanc went further, outlining an alternative mode of economic regulation managed by a "protective state" that would actively and authoritatively intervene to harmonize the production of state-organized "social workshops."[115]

Subsequently amended and elaborated, this Jacobin reformism was destined for a bright future in France. It would suffer a major reverse in the spring of 1848, when an experiment with "national workshops" ended in failure, but even before that, throughout the 1840s, it drew fire from two directions. To workers steeped in a culture that idealized autonomy and self-organization, it seemed too state-centered, while to early exponents of the communist ideal it seemed insufficiently radical. The prospect of "absolute equality" of wages inspired doubts of two kinds. For workers who read the newspaper *L'Atelier*, the idea was unrealistic. They believed that work incentives were inevitable and frankly expressed fear of any measure that might lead to "exploitation of the hard worker by the slacker."[116] The equal-wage system, which was adopted in 1848 by a number of workers' associations backed by Blanc, soon had to be suspended, moreover.[117] It did not appeal to those who embraced the formula "From each according to his abilities, to each according to his needs." Indeed, Marx used these words in one of his earliest texts to criticize the demand for equal wages. In Marx's view, this idea merely transposed into the economic sphere the abstract vision of social relations underlying the notion of human rights.[118] He would continue to insist on this point as late as his famous *Critique of the Gotha Program* (1875). There, the author of *Capital* showed that rights, which exist only as "equal rights," are always in essence bourgeois rights. The "system of liberty and equality" is nothing but market society, which is governed by exchange value, since in a market society one value is always exchanged for another "equal" value. In the context of labor, an "equal right" could only be an unequal right for unequal work. Marx thus warned German socialists that they were on the wrong track: their demand for a "fair division of the product of labor" did not transcend the bourgeois idea of rights but fell squarely within its limits. To transcend this circumscribed notion of rights, he proposed a radically new principle: "From each according to his abilities, to each according to his needs." Similarly, early advocates of egalitarian community also believed that a fairer system of remuneration would not by itself lead to the emancipation of labor. They looked to a more radical idea: the abolition of competition.

Utopian Socialism

At this critical juncture, a number of writers produced accounts of utopian communities. Rejecting what they believed to be a selfish and divided society, Owen, Saint-Simon, Fourier, Cabet, and the followers of Babeuf all called for a new social order. Using words such as "association" and "organization," they conjured up a world from which competition would be banished. To be sure, their "systems" differed in many important respects. Fourier sought to harmonize differences by harnessing the passions in all their variety, while Owen and Saint-Simon looked to scientific organization as the key to social unity. To read their innumerable works today can be rather disconcerting, for they are full of bizarre ideas. Contemporaries understood, however, that these theories could not be dismissed simply because they seemed strange. Utopian thought exerted a powerful attraction that was impervious to the condescending and sarcastic jibes of those in power. Indeed, utopian writers prided themselves on their claims to scientific knowledge. Owen was an important industrialist, recognized and respected for his achievements, and *polytechniciens,* militant proponents of a rational order, were numerous among the Fourierists and Saint-Simonians. Above all, utopian thinkers responded not only to immediate social suffering but even more to the diffuse anxieties of the age. They also echoed in a rather confused way key Christian values. All this explains why utopian thought flourished when it did. Recall, for example, that 100,000 enthusiastic Cabet supporters flocked to the docks of Le Havre to bid farewell to disciples of his who left France in 1849 to found the utopian community of Icaria in Texas, or that some years earlier, thousands of people turned out in the French provinces to hear the preaching of Saint-Simonian missionaries.[119]

Rational organization was the hallmark of all proposed utopian communities. Owen was the first to offer the blueprint of such a community. He had meditated on the idea while managing his huge factory at New Lanark, which was taken as a model of its kind. He also participated in innovative experiments in education and the organization of work and in 1819 worked to pass the first law in England limiting the working hours of women and children. He was therefore seen as a leading figure in British philanthropy. His industrial experience radicalized him, however. He came up with the idea of "industrial villages," whose goal would be to reconcile harmony with abundance. Conceived as communities of 1,200 people living on 750 hectares of land, these were to be places in which all aspects of daily life would be collectivized, including cooking, washing, leisure, education, and health—all were to be organized, while industrial and agricultural production would be carefully planned and regulated. Within the community, everyone's needs would be satisfied, and solidarity would emerge naturally from the organization of communal life.[120]

Utopian socialism mingled enthusiasm for the idea of rationally organized community with assurances that such a thing was possible. The proliferation of settlements in America based on communal property seemed to validate the notion. Engels wrote a thorough study of these experiments, which he characterized as "successful."[121] He saw them as proof that a harmonious society without competition was possible. Indeed, he believed that it would be "infinitely easier to administer a communist society than a competitive one."[122] In a rational world, Engels wrote, everything would be simple: no more waste, no speculation, no paralyzing rivalries. The word "communism" gained popularity as a way of designating and radicalizing the idea of a communal society free of competition.

The Communist Idea

It was Cabet who popularized the term. He used it in the first edition of his *Voyage en Icarie* (1839). He also included it in the titles of two pamphlets that he published in the 1840s: *Credo communiste* and *Pourquoi je suis communiste*. In doing so, he was reviving an old word from the economic and legal lexicon of the eighteenth century. For instance, Mirabeau had used "communists" in a treatise on agricultural economics to characterize the members of religious communities (subject to *mainmorte*).[123] In the 1840s, the term began to be flaunted as a banner by those who made communal ownership the centerpiece of their vision of an ideal society (a choice that distinguished them from those who thought exclusively in terms of rational organization, sometimes linked, as in the case of the Saint-Simonians, to a hierarchical or meritocratic form of organization). Indeed, 1840 marked an intellectual turning point. In addition to Cabet's publications, Morelly's *Code de la nature* was reprinted that year. Morelly was seen as an important precursor. Another set of pamphlets became a rallying point for the movement known as "neo-Babouvism."[124] Shortly thereafter, Théodore Dézamy's *Code de la communauté* became a key reference. Marx read these texts, and in doing so his thinking matured; he paid homage to them in *The Holy Family*.[125] To understand the philosophical foundations of the communist idea of equality, one must begin here.

Two endlessly repeated words characterized the new order of things to which the pioneers of the communist-communitarian idea aspired: "unity" and "fraternity." "My principle is fraternity. My theory is fraternity. My system is fraternity. My science is fraternity," trumpeted Cabet, whose intention was to radicalize the Jacobin idea of unity and indivisibility.[126] In his *Code de la communauté*, Dézamy proposed definitions of these terms to which all "communitarians" subscribed. "Fraternity," he wrote, "is the sublime sentiment that leads men to live as members of a single family, to fuse all their various desires and all their individual power into one unique interest."[127] As for unity, "it is the indissoluble identification of all interests and all wills." Seen in this light, equality was not simply a means of distributing wealth or a principle of justice. It was above all a structural property of the social order. Dézamy characterized it in terms of *harmony* and *perfect equilibrium*. In other words, equality was achieved by including individuals in a unified society *(un monde Un)*. There was nothing merely numerical about it. It was rather a *collective equality*. That is why all writers in this tradition referred repeatedly to family structure as an allegorical image of the communitarian ideal. In a community, as in a family, the abolition of inequalities of wealth and condition was in fact a straightforward *consequence* of a bond considered to be organic. Equality stemmed from the fact that everyone belonged to an overarching protective order. Competition was impossible, because in such a framework there were, strictly speaking, no autonomous individuals. The individual did not exist as a distinct interest or particular will: he manifested himself only as part of a whole. Thus it was a *simplification* of the organization of the human race on which communitarians ultimately counted to abolish the reign of competition. Unity implied suppression of antagonisms, irrelevance of differences, a total absence of distinctions.

"From each according to his abilities, to each according to his needs" was therefore not a principle establishing *individual rights*. The possibility of awarding different goods to different people was not understood as a consequence of free choice by the "consumer" or of individual preferences. It was seen as a socially determined and objectifiable outcome. For instance, it was because something like "communal child rearing" was envisioned that each family was entitled to a share of resources proportional to its size.[128] Because the "palaces of equality" (in Dézamy's phrase) were conceived in terms of a totally communal existence, the range of human needs was understood as a purely social fact. It derived from the psychological, physiological, and sociological characteristics of a totality. By the same token, different abilities were seen as parts of a system. The goal was to construct a radically *deindividualized* society. Cabet thus waxed enthusiastic about the workshops of Icarie, which formed "but a single vast machine, each cog of which smoothly fulfilled its function."[129]

The associated idea of *fraternity* also had a direct sociological interpretation. It meant that all the inhabitants of a community were supposed to consider themselves members of the same family, joined together by natural bonds that were not of a contractual order. This was a very different approach from the one that had prevailed in the revolutionary period. Fraternity had then been invoked because institutional reform had seemed insufficient to usher in a new society. Fraternity had been seen as a compensatory emotion, a corrective virtue to mollify the individualist principles that the revolutionaries had adopted. It pointed toward a sort of *sentimental contract* that could help to implant the social contract. It underscored the need to link politics and virtue, to balance the predilection of revolutionary political culture for an absolute and abstract interpretation of the general interest by introducing a practical civility based on kindness and attention to others. Fraternity was in the nature of a moral obligation intended to broaden the application of legal obligations. The "fraternal socialists" of the 1830s and 1840s still saw fraternity in these terms. Leroux, who sought to "put fraternity in the center" of his work, illustrates this to perfection.[130] Faithful to the revolutionary heritage, he tried to construct a fraternal bridge between liberty and equality. For Leroux, the sentiment of fraternity made it possible to "fill the immense gulf that political institutions and religions have thus far allowed to subsist between man's love of himself, or egoism, and love of humanity in general, or charity."[131] He therefore saw fraternity as the active principle of a new secular religion, which democratic society needed to function properly. (For many republicans, this way of thinking about what *bound* men together beyond the formalisms of exchange and political contract would prove essential. Writers from Edgar Quinet to Ferdinand Buisson would dedicate themselves to bringing some form of secular spirituality to life.)

Nothing comparable existed among proponents of communal ownership. In their model, the elimination of private property would suffice to bring mores in line with institutions. In their view, man is immediately and exclusively social. In a society of radical equality, therefore, there would be no need to rely on sentiments as a crutch to help bring individuals together. Equality rested on the twin pillars of deindividualization and homogenization of society.

The Extinction of the Political, the Economic, and the Psychological

Equality, whether understood as a relationship or a mode of redistribution, can only be envisioned as an ongoing project and permanent effort. It is never at rest; it is always a struggle. It advances in the face of injustice, whenever illegitimate distinctions or exclusions are identified. It is rooted in the heterogeneity of human beings, in social division and conflict, and in claims of superiority. Therein lies the difference between the idea of a community of equals and that of a society of equals. The latter defines a horizon; it is an objective, a goal whose precise contest is continually subject to public debate and criticism. It is part of a permanent democratic debate concerning the notions of justice and equality. By contrast, the communist community, as it was conceived in the 1840s, assumed a world in which anything that might fuel discord, domination, and exploitation had been eradicated. It was a world based on unanimity (in the political order), abundance (in the economic order), and the elimination of envy and selfishness (in the order of individual relations)—in other words, a world from which the political, the economic, and the psychological had all been banished.

For a Cabet or a Dézamy, there was no place for conflict or deliberation. The society they aspired to create was radically apolitical, in the image of eighteenth-century utopias. Broadly speaking, their projects extended Morelly's vision in the *Code de la nature*. An audacious precursor of communist thinking, Morelly gave no thought to establishing a representative government or mobilizing the people to create new social institutions. In Britain, Owen vigorously opposed Chartist demands for universal suffrage, which he scornfully dismissed as a "popular hobbyhorse."[132] In *Voyage en Icarie,* Cabet argued that the new social and political order he hoped to bring about would have no need of a pluralist press, because grounds for anxiety and opposition would have disappeared. There would be no need for more than "one local newspaper for each village, one provincial newspaper for each province, and one national newspaper for the nation."[133] It is worth noting that he proposed to entrust the task of publishing the news "to public officials elected by the people or their representatives," arguing that newspapers "would be nothing more than the minutes of meetings and would contain only narratives and facts without any commentary by journalists."[134]

In each case the goal was to replace the government of men by the administration of things, according to the Saint-Simonian slogan that Marx would later make his own. One sign of this antipolitical worldview was the extreme precision with which organizational forms and modes of life were described and prescribed.[135] For Morelly, people's lives were already regulated with mechanical precision. Morelly anticipated and codified everything: work requirements, the minimum marriage age, the color and fabric of clothing to be worn in different circumstances, the suckling of infants, the schedule of holidays, the architecture of buildings, and the arrangement of living quarters.[136] Owen, Cabet, and Dézamy were equally precise and peremptory, each in his own way. Since self-management was inconceivable, everything had to be thought out in advance and set in rationally planned stone. The second characteristic of these utopian visions was authoritarianism. In one of his projects for a planned economy, Babeuf imagined that the "working members" of the national community could be moved about from village to village by the "supreme administration," in accordance with the needs of the community, and he did not shrink from envisioning a sentence of perpetual slavery for those found guilty of fraud.[137] This is a crucial point. In an apolitical society, there was no place for discordant voices or deviant behavior. There was no possible median position between adherence to the system and exclusion. One had to be either inside and obedient or else be banished from the community. In his *République de Dieu*, Constantin Pecqueur warned that "systematic infraction of the fundamental law leads to exclusion" and urged "voluntary and meritorious respect for the law of fraternity, or else positive sanction in the form of excommunication or expulsion from the union."[138] By contrast, the essence of democracy is the belief that opposition is essential to its operation and that no one can be expelled from the body politic.

In the antipolitical community, equality was thus a consequence of joint dependency and submission. It was as *subjects of rational organization* that men and women were alike and not as autonomous individuals dealing with one another.

The champions of communitarian order did not rely solely on good organization to encourage individuals to merge with the community. They also believed in the possibility of a society from which envy, the source of the desire for distinction, would be banished. Selfishness and envy were seen as structural impediments to equality, since they led individuals to look for ways to appropriate the property of others, as well as to complacency about other people's disadvantages, attitudes that could lead to permanent discrimination and alienation. Communitarian socialists initially approached the issue in an anthropological perspective. Like many of their contemporaries, they also believed in the regenerative virtues of education. Cabet, for instance, looked upon education and culture as "all-powerful and almost creative divinities,"[139] and argued that a new human species could be developed in the same way that novel varieties of plants and animals were bred.[140] He was convinced that an appropriately educated generation of workers and citizens would "become accustomed to taking reason as their guide and practice all the virtues of fraternity." Then, he maintained, there would be "no more rivalry or competition or antagonism or exploitation or even hatred or discord, but everywhere fraternity, union, and peace." In the same vein, Owen subtitled his major work, *A New View of Society,* "Essays on the principle of the formation of the human character. Preparatory to the development of a plan for gradually ameliorating the condition of mankind," and that education was always central to his vision of reform.

For the communitarians, however, the economy could also change man, in two ways. One was to eliminate private property, and the other was to usher in an era of plenty. The elimination of private property was at the heart of the revolution of equality as conceived by Cabet and Dézamy. Babeuf was the first to theorize it. Without private property, he argued, it would be impossible to accumulate wealth or power.[141] If each person received what he needed from the collectivity, then he would become "independent of good or bad fortune." Without fear of the future or hope of riches, the individual's relationship to time would be altered. Everyone could then live entirely in the present thanks to the elimination of property, thus putting an end to the "fatal folly of distinctions," which always stemmed in one way or another from the need for self-protection. For Babeuf, in other words, the elimination of private property was not limited to property in the means of production. It was the very idea of personal possession, that is, of an individual connection to durable goods, that he sought to eradicate in order to eliminate envy at the source. The utopians hoped to eliminate society's work on itself, the always open and problematic relationship that the members of society entertain with the conflicting representations they have of their relations. Hence they wanted nothing to do with "imaginary equality." The members of utopian communities did not dream and did not compare themselves to one another. Fundamentally, they were indifferent to each other: their relations were strictly functional. They were merely cogs in a machine.

Another way to think about the eradication of envy and egoism was to contemplate the prospect of a society of abundance. In capitalist society, Owen argued, everyone is rightly afraid of being cheated and deprived of his means of subsistence if he does not carefully attend to his own interests. This would no longer be the case in a communitarian society, he explained, because "all the natural wants of human nature may be abundantly supplied; and the principle of selfishness will cease to exist for want of an adequate motive to produce it."[142] And what was the recipe for achieving such abundance? For an industrialist like Owen, it was one of the expected benefits of rational organization and technological progress, but, even more importantly, it would come from the revision of aspirations that would follow the elimination of private property. In such a setting, production would be limited to a small number of basic consumer goods, since it would no longer be possible to save or acquire production goods or real estate. Abundance, frugality, and productivity were thus linked for Owen: in a frugal modern society, he argued, "every individual may be trained to produce far more than he can consume."[143] This structural link between abundance and the realization of communism would prove central to the Marxist worldview.

By transcending capitalist market society, communism would eliminate the social relations mediated by interests on which that society was based. Only then could one imagine the possibility of transforming human relations into "pure commerce." Communism thus rested on the extinction of economics, defined as the science of the production and distribution of wealth in a world of scarcity. Indeed, Marx explicitly identified capitalism with market society and, more profoundly, with the economy as such. His work is incomprehensible without his philosophical critique of political economy. Communism was inconceivable without a society of abundance. Only in such a society would "economics" be abolished, because scarcity would no longer exist.[144] Otherwise, he wrote in *The German Ideology*, "penury would become general, along with need, the struggle for the necessary would begin again, and society would inevitably find itself in the same quandary as before."[145] Communist society thus aimed to achieve *natural harmony among men.* In this way, Marx became the heir of the optimistic material- ist philosophy of the eighteenth century. In the *1844 Manuscripts,* he defined communism as a perfected form of naturalism. "When one studies materialist teachings about man's original goodness and equal intellectual endowments, about the omnipotence of experi- ence, habit, education, and the influence of external circumstances, the great importance of industry, the legitimacy of pleasure, etc., no great sagacity is needed to discover the links between these things and communism and socialism."[146] Whereas Adam Smith had con- ceived of economics as the realization of eighteenth-century phi- losophy, Marx imagined the elimination of the economic sphere altogether. In other words, he imagined the fruition of eighteenth- century materialism.

Communism was rooted in the idea of a pure social bond, of a society in which relations among men would not be mediated by economics or politics. But how could one conceive of society in a way that made sense without mediation of any kind? Marx recog- nized this difficulty and dealt with it explicitly in the *Grundrisse.*

"Mediation is of course necessary," he wrote. "In the first case [market society], one begins with the autonomous production of private individuals, which is determined and modified *post festum* by complex relations: the mediation is effected by commodity exchange, value, and money, all of which are expressions of the same relation. In the second case [communist society], *it is the presupposition itself that serves as mediation.* In other words, the presupposition is a collective production, the community being the basis of production. From the beginning, individual labor is there posited to be social labor."[147]

This text is crucial. It shows that for Marx it was the assumption that society is a totality, a rational order, that established the possibility of a social bond. The elimination of political and economic mediation was therefore justified by the fact that all individuals derive their identity from being members of the same social body. Communism as a society of pure commerce among men thus paralleled the liberal utopia based on a diametrically opposite mode of organization. Man was compelled to achieve a universality that could only be attained by way of an external force that was all the more elusive because it presented itself as nothing other than man himself. The individual was thus immediately part of the community, universality epitomized.

Deindividualization, Indistinction, and Similarity

Across all its various expressions, the communist idea was based on what we may call a deindividualization of society. This was a necessary condition for imagining a society from which competition had been radically banished. Equality under such conditions resembled homogeneity or identity. It is crucial to understand the extent of this deindividualization. It was more than just an assertion of the preeminence of the collective. Underlying deindividualization was an anthropology of *indistinction,* which led to a literal interpretation of the idea of similarity. The work of Dom Deschamps, a Benedictine atheist whose powerful and original work Diderot admired, is useful for assessing this aspect of utopian communism.[148] A contemporary of Morelly, Deschamps went further than any other eighteenth-century thinker in exploring the anthropological and moral implications of an ideal communitarian order.

In *Observations morales* (1770),[149] Deschamps impressively described the type of equality that a society governed by a "spirit of disappropriation" would presumably usher in.[150] The ensuing identity of mores would, Deschamps believed, result in a true society of semblables: individuals who would be differentiated only by sex. "The same mores," he wrote, "would as it were turn men and women into one identical man and woman."[151] For him, then, similarity meant indistinction or nondifferentiation. He meant this literally: "In the long run, we would resemble one another more than the most similar animals of the same species." Furthermore, faces "would nearly all have the same shape," and tastes and temperaments would also be similar. Distrust and rivalry would no longer be possible in a society in which everyone was identical, because there would no longer be any difference between "mine" and "thine," nor would there exist anything that might spur envy or incite a desire for superiority. There would be no rivalry over women, because all women would be the same: in fact, women would form a community unto themselves and become a common possession of all men. There would be no differences of rank of any kind. History, too, would disappear, since similarity would mean endless repetition of the same social acts: nothing could change. "Every day would resemble the next," Deschamps concluded.[152] Worry and anxiety would therefore vanish from this immutable world: men and women "would rise and retire in tranquility, always content with themselves and those like them, and always satisfied with their condition."

The concept of equality as indistinction was frequently borrowed by nineteenth-century utopian theorists. Fourierists and Saint-Simonians imagined a world made totally homogeneous by the mixing of human groups. The work of Victor Courtet de l'Isle is typical of this way of conceiving progress toward democratic equality.[153] Courtet belonged to a generation that was passionate about physiology and phrenology and hoped to see the advent of a positive politics based on the science of man. The young Saint-Simonian was an active member of the Paris Ethnological Society, founded in 1839, where he sat alongside Michel Chevalier, Gustave d'Eichtal, Adolphe Guéroult, and Olinde Rodrigues, who numbered among the principal lieutenants of Prosper Enfantin. He set forth his views on progress toward equality in a book that would make him famous, *La Science politique fondée sur la science de l'homme, ou étude des races humaines sous le rapport philosophique, historique et social* (1838).

Drawing upon works considered to be scientific at the time, such as those of physiologist William Frédéric Edwards, Johann Friedrich Blumenbach, and Georges Cuvier, Courtet acknowledged inequality among the races of man, but unlike many others, he drew no "racist" consequences from this observation. Whereas Gobineau, starting from the same premise a few years later, concluded that the superior white race must be preserved from "unfortunate admixtures," Courtet championed racial mixing. For him, a policy of racial fusion was the cornerstone of democratic anthropology. "If we assume a people consisting of a single unmixed race, we can predict that it will passionately adore equality," he wrote.[154] If France was animated by the spirit of equality, he argued, it was because its mix of populations was older and more permanent than elsewhere. "Do you want a society based on the most perfect equality?" he asked in his conclusion.

Then bring together individuals born of the same stock, of the same families, and rendered as identical as possible to one another through constant cross-breeding. No one in such a society will resign himself to a subaltern position. Everyone will wish to rule. Those who are on top one day will be brought down the next, honored and reviled by turns. Those at the bottom will be consumed by jealousy until their turn comes to be raised up and arouse jealousy in others. It is impossible for order to prevail in such a society, but what will prevail is an absolute leveling of conditions and powers.[155]

Courtet did not share the irenic views of Deschamps. For Courtet, homogeneity would not lead naturally to social peace. He thought of it rather as a sociological device for regulating the psychological propensity to dominate others. Deschamps believed that indistinction would end competition in all its forms, whereas Courtet believed that it would bridle competition by preventing it from establishing lasting political and social differentiation. Yet both thinkers shared a common view of equality as indistinction.

A Second Look at the Question of Competition

In communist circles, the vision of an eradication of competition was thus interpreted at once juridically (elimination of property), sociologically and economically (substitution of communitarian order for conflicting interests), anthropologically and morally (eradication of selfishness and envy), and even ontologically, if we follow Deschamps's radical argument. The spirit of this radical critique was broadly if loosely shared by workers in France and Britain in the 1830s and 1840s, although achieving universal suffrage also came to be seen as a top priority in the march toward social emancipation. The sectarianism of the leading communist theo-rists, along with their miscellaneous obsessions, gave many pause, however. Yet few asked what the deeper philosophical meaning of the denunciation of competition might be. Recurrent use of the adjective "unlimited" made it possible to attack both the principle of competition itself and its abusive excesses, blurring the distinc-tion between a mode of economic regulation and the broader issue of competition as a social form. Critics were thus able to get away with expressing very general indignation in the face of the misfor-tunes of the proletariat. The communist critique drew mockery from some while terrifying others, but it was never seriously ques-tioned.[156] Real debate among socialists would have to await the decline of Chartism in Britain and the failure of the revolution of 1848 in France. The way this debate was conducted in the columns of *L'Atelier* is of particular interest in this connection.

In a substantial article, Anthime Corbon, the author of a cult book entitled *Le Secret du peuple de Paris* (1863), tackled the issue head on.[157] He, too, looked upon competition as a "powerful cause of disorder and misery." But he also questioned what its complete suppression would mean and whether it was even possible, given that competition merely reflected "the diversity of interests." For Corbon, competition was intimately associated with the advent of a society of individuals and, as such, was nothing other than the "exercise of freedom." In other words, its source was modernity it-self, and the increasing social heterogeneity that modernity im-plied, hence it was to some extent "indestructible." Competition had "its necessary side and its detestable side." How could this con-tradiction be overcome? According to Corbon, the answer lay in regulating and reforming the "detestable" side of competition: first, by encouraging the development of workers' associations, which would organize and regulate the labor market, and second, by the influence of the law, which would punish abuses and unfair competition. In short, the goal was to work toward a "social appropriation" of the market.

This was also Proudhon's approach. In his *Système des contradictions économiques,* he vigorously attacked Cabet, dismissing both the indulgent celebration of the market by liberal economists and Cabet's view of the market as catastrophe. Proudhon agreed with Corbon that it was a delusion to think that competition could be abolished. "One might as well ask whether personality, liberty, and individual responsibility can be eliminated," he wrote. Competition was "the mode in which collective activity manifests and exercises itself, the expression of social spontaneity, the emblem of democracy and equality."[158] Yet he also denounced competition's anarchical excesses when "left to itself and deprived of guidance by a superior and efficacious principle." The remedy was "regulation" *(police)* of the labor market, and Proudhon's book was devoted to a consideration of how that could be done. Like Corbon, he believed in the virtues of mutuality and association, as well as in the possibility of inventing modernized forms of corporatism. Following this suggestion, his disciples would lead the way in the development of syndicalism in the 1860s. But Proudhon also sought to reverse the balance of power between capital and labor by organizing and broadening the issuance of credit.[159] He therefore proposed a "People's Bank," where workers could borrow capital rather than be forced to sell their labor. Proudhon's influence among workers was considerable. He inspired any number of reform projects. Yet the social philosophy that it expressed was overshadowed in France by other critiques of capitalism. The demonization of competition and the exaltation of equality as identity retained their underground influence.

National Protectionism

Protectionist ideology soon became the matrix for another form of equality as identity, in which the nation would be extolled as a homogeneous entity. I use the word "ideology" advisedly to mark the difference between protectionism as economic policy and protectionism as social philosophy. In 1848, when Friedrich List published his *National System of Political Economy*, he proposed a *Zollverein*, or customs union, as a means of unifying Germany by "assisting the economic development of the nation."[160] He sought to identify conditions likely to promote the "industrial education of the country."[161] In his lexicon, "tariff protection" was all but synonymous with entrepreneurial spirit, prosperity, and growth. When the United States restricted imports in the final decades of the nineteenth century, it relied on identical arguments. Economic strategy and dynamism were central to the American case. But the protectionism advocated by conservative liberals in France was of an entirely different order.

National Labor: First Formulations

Anti–Corn Law agitation reached its height in Great Britain in the early 1840s, but free-trade advocates in July Monarchy France were far less successful. Businessmen in great commercial cities such as Bordeaux and Marseille did pressure the government, but they failed to persuade the general public, and their lobbying of parliament went nowhere. In short, they lost the battle of ideas. Even their most eloquent advocates, such as Frédéric Bastiat and Henri Fonfrède, elicited only modest enthusiasm compared with Richard

Cobden in England. The strong men of the government, such as Adolphe Thiers and Guizot, stood at the other extreme from Robert Peel across the Channel: "On the question of industry, we are conservatives; we are protectionists," Guizot insisted.[162] In fact, he showed little interest in economic and industrial issues and had no a priori position on them. His embrace of protectionism was purely political, determined entirely by his concern with social stability. For him, the terms "conservative" and "protectionist" overlapped completely. His primary concern was that free trade would lead to "an abrupt, sudden, and general disturbance of the established order," and he therefore aimed primarily "to spare industry and other major interests from any unexpected disruption or alteration."[163] But the French preference for protectionism in the 1830s and 1840s had deeper roots. It was also a response to the social question. Indeed, protectionism claimed to offer an alternative to the growing inequality that accompanied the growth of the new industrial proletariat. It sought to construct a "national labor force," supposedly unified in its opposition to the centrifugal forces of the market. This approach established a connection between equality and the critique of competition.

The idea that protectionism could be an egalitarian and unifying force held great appeal for conservatives in the July Monarchy.[164] Conservative spokesmen saw protectionism as a way of playing down class tensions by introducing a new calculus of collective identity and homogeneity. Charles Dupin, one of the regime's leading thinkers, said that customs barriers would replace the image of the proletariat with one of workers grouped together "in glorious equality beneath the tricolor flag."[165] A figure of inclusion thus supplanted the specter of exclusion. "If we wish to speak the truth," he insisted, "let us speak of French workers and not of proletarians."[166]

The problem was thus no longer capitalist exploitation. It was "cosmopolitan competition," which was accused of posing "the gravest danger to the working class." This would become the regime's official ideological mantra. The phrase "national worker"[167] was preferred to the threatening term "proletarian," and the principles of a "patriotic economics" suggested a structural community of interests between industrialists and wage earners.[168] In a sign of the times, the first organization of French industrialists, the remote ancestor of today's employer associations, called itself the Association for the Defense of National Labor.[169]

At the time, national protectionism was also defined in sociological terms by way of a contrast between consumers and producers. Proponents of free trade logically emphasized the interests of the consumer, whom they portrayed as the obvious beneficiary of lower tariffs on imported goods. Champions of protectionism rejected this argument on the grounds that the consumer was an abstraction that reduced humanity to a mere accounting of costs and benefits. For instance, Mathieu de Dombasle described the consumer as "a dummy behind which some people hide interests of a very different sort."[170] It therefore came as no surprise that a "cosmopolitan minority" rushed to the consumer's defense. The producer was the opposite, Dombasle argued, a much more concrete figure, whose interests, which were structurally linked to the interests of many other people through a chain of dependencies and solidarities, were rooted in the nation's soil. Producers therefore naturally formed a body, a coherent and enduring social order. It was only logical for them to adopt a "patriotic point of view." Conversely, consumers were pure, de-territorialized individuals motivated by nothing but the "liberal spirit."[171] To be sure, England contradicted this view, because there the popular classes were fully identified with the Anti–Corn Law movement in the 1840s.[172] But this was seen as an exception, due to the social gulf that (ostensibly, in the French caricature) separated the landed aristocracy, which reaped the benefits of high prices for corn, from the great mass of the people. France, Thiers and Guizot argued, knew no such division. Its land was much more broadly divided among many smallholders, and in general interests were not as violently opposed as they were in England.[173] Protectionism, Dupin insisted, meant the France of small businessmen, craftsmen, and landowners united—the "organized fatherland" against the foreign competitor. "The point of maintaining customs barriers," he concluded, "is therefore to protect, defend, and save all of society, which is threatened in its very foundations."[174] Meanwhile, the founder of the Association pour la Defense du Travail National never tired of repeating that "protection is instituted for the benefit not of a few privileged interests but primarily for the workers and ultimately for the nation as a whole."[175]

The opposition between a protectionist France and a free-trade Britain in the late 1840s is a good indicator of the differences between the two political cultures. Structural differences in the distribution of land have already been noted, but beyond that we see two different conceptions of the social bond and two ways of constituting a nation. France envisioned social cohesion as stemming from a central principle, the source of national identity. It treated the political sphere as the matrix of collective membership. In Britain, civil society was paramount, or at any rate became paramount after the Chartists failed to achieve universal suffrage. Hence in Britain the figure of the consumer was central, the consumer being the immediate symbol of people's everyday lives. In other words, the consumer was not a disembodied abstraction there. What John

Atkinson Hobson called "civic consumers" formed a palpable social bond. In a sense, they created the nation from below. In very practical terms they produced the common society, whereas in France the nation was created from above, in an identity-defining communion. It was therefore quite logical that syndicalism long preceded the formation of left-wing political parties in Britain, in stark contrast to France.[176] Furthermore, consumer cooperatives in England played a key role in organizing a popular movement, led by the Rochdale Society of Equitable Pioneers in 1844. The celebrated Free Trade Union rode the crest of a major social movement in England, a movement that incidentally involved large numbers of women, who were thus brought into the public sphere much earlier than in France.

Still, national protectionism was only an emergent ideology in France in the 1830s and 1840s (debate became polarized in 1846 after the repeal of the Corn Laws in England). Forged in employer and government circles, the ideology made little headway in the popular classes. Indeed, workers began to identify with the figure of the proletarian, which was precisely what the proponents of the "national labor" discourse hoped to prevent. Leading popular spokesmen did not advocate free trade but were frequently critical of the illusions peddled by the protectionists. For example, Blanc insisted that working conditions would be improved not by protectionist measures but by the organization of labor. Meanwhile, workers associated with *L'Atelier* were critical of industrialists who championed national labor, accusing them of being concerned mainly with "preserving the big profits that the protectionist system assures them of earning."[177] In a celebrated speech "On the Question of Free Trade" in 1848, Marx naturally denounced the "freedom of capital" but also attacked protectionism as conservative.[178] In fact,

French workers generally rejected both free trade and protectionism, regarding both doctrines as irrelevant to the solution of their problems.[179] The free-trade association thus failed in its efforts to sustain a popular movement based on the English model. Nor did the conservative-liberal position arouse any enthusiasm, especially since it was promoted by those who obstinately defended property-qualified voting and rejected universal suffrage, which the lower classes saw as the solution to all their woes.

The Golden Age of National Protectionism

It was with the coming of the Third Republic that national protectionism was finally able to leave its mark on France. The economic situation proved crucial, since the advent of the Third Republic coincided with the beginning of the great depression of the late nineteenth century, together with the upheaval caused by the first globalization. But changing perceptions of the internal economic situation also played a role in the rise of protectionist culture. It is fair to speak of this period as a time of true "nationalization" of social representations of French territory. Historians have long emphasized certain material and cultural features of this transformation, such as the construction of a railway network that facilitated the circulation of men and goods; the rise of primary education; and the generalization of conscription, which forced many young Frenchmen to leave their immediate environments. These factors contributed greatly to the modernization of rural France in particular, but they also deeply affected the working class. Until 1848, most workers perceived economic reality in terms of its effects on particular trades and local economic conditions. Conflicts were not seen solely in terms of antagonism between employers and employees.

For instance, the term "competition" referred to tensions between different crafts and guilds as well as to hostility between workers in different localities. Agricol Perdiguier gave a colorful account of sometimes violent confrontations between workers of different towns in his book *Livre du compagnonnage* (1839). In another great classic of working-class literature, *Léonard, maçon de la Creuse,* Martin Nadaud also told of hostility between different groups of craftsmen and rivalries between different cantons and villages.[180] He recounted in detail competition in the workplace and friction between Parisians and seasonal workers from the Creuse. Toward the middle of the nineteenth century, workers continued to see disputes between "villages" or "guilds" (*corporations,* a word that was still in common use) as key factors in the organization of economic life. An important parliamentary report of 1884, dealing with the social effects of the economic crisis of the time, still treated what it called "the three types of competition" as more or less equivalent: competition between crafts and individual craftsmen, competition between the provinces and Paris, and competition between France and other countries.[181] The "nationalized" picture of the economic order only began to come into focus in the 1880s, as foreign competition came to be seen as the decisive factor. This change was crucial to making the working class more receptive to protectionist discourse.[182]

In France and elsewhere in Europe, with the exception of Great Britain, tariffs were consequently increased in this period. In France, the protectionist reaction was plain to see by the early 1880s, with the suspension of the Anglo-French Treaty of 1860. It would reach its apogee in 1892 with the adoption of the celebrated Méline tariff (named for Jules Méline, a republican minister and close colleague of Jules Ferry, who sponsored the bill). What distinguished France from other countries, however, was that protectionism developed into a full-blown political culture. The movement had its newspapers, such as *Le Protectionniste* (1879) and *Le Travail national* (1884), and its champions. It became a central issue of political debate in the period. In the legislative elections of 1889, strengthening tariff protections proved to be a winning theme, along with revision of the constitution.[183] Quite logically, the new chamber enthusiastically passed the Méline tariff. The Third Republic consolidated its base by defending protectionism, transforming it into a "popular movement," as Ferry put it.[184] In his view, tariffs "protected the worker's wage" while also protecting the interests of farmers. Indeed, tariffs helped to win rural support for the new regime. "Today's protectionist movement has its roots in the democracy that cultivates grapes and wheat. That is why it has succeeded," Ferry opined.[185] But the tariff measures also had a larger goal, which was to establish a national identity that would compensate for social divisions. For instance, an article in *Le travail national* proposed that the split between capital and labor be replaced by a new idea of collective solidarity against a foreign threat.[186] Democratic equality began to understand itself in terms of membership in a distinctive protective community. This gave rise to an image of society in which the economic sphere was incorporated into a political vision of egalitarian citizenship and national unity.

Conservatism and Colonialism

In France, the political culture of protectionism was initially linked to a conservative and fundamentally anti-economic vision. It incorporated an exacerbated version of the old agrarianism of the eighteenth century, which rejected industry and dreamed of a static rural society. In an essay that became a bestseller, *Le Retour à la terre et la surproduction industrielle* (1905), Méline envisioned an urban exodus to follow the rural exodus, as a static agricultural economy put an end to the disruptions due to "industrial engorgement." The idea was well received, especially by the large number of small farmers who worshipped stability above all. Traditionalists and Catholics were also enthusiastic, having been persistent critics throughout the nineteenth century of an industrial system that was corroding what they took to be the natural bases of social existence. More broadly, Méline's book was hailed by all who rejected the first globalization as a source of heightened competition. Tinged with nostalgia, the political culture of national protectionism defined a broad consensus, which enabled the republican regime to win over the French heartland in the 1890s.

This consensus was reinforced by colonial and imperialist ventures that coincided with the raising of customs barriers in France and elsewhere. Imperialism offered an alternative to the stagnation that Méline feared. Economically, it was seen as a complement to protectionism: "The protective system is a steam engine without a safety valve, unless it is supplemented and corrected by a sound and serious colonial policy," observed Ferry, the first to theorize the economic function of colonization.[187] Republicans in government also expected that their colonial policy would bolster France's power and restore the nation's pride after the humiliating defeat of 1870 and the loss of Alsace and Lorraine. Protectionism thus served the simple political function of restoring a positive collective image, and it was hoped that this would also help to answer the social question. Much has been said about Cecil Rhodes's celebrated remark: "He who would avoid civil war must be an imperialist."[188] But the economic calculation that underpinned this idea illuminated only one aspect of the policy of colonial expansion. In France especially, colonialism was only one aspect of an ideological offensive, a way of promoting collective satisfaction in conquest and demonstrating joint superiority over the peoples one claimed to be civilizing. The orchestration of this shared sense of superiority also helped to alleviate class tensions.[189] Colonialism thus counterbalanced and camouflaged domestic inequalities by depicting the nation as a community in confrontation with the rest of the world. In other words, a negative form of equality replaced the positive equality of the democratic project.

Intellectual and Political Rearrangements

The formation of this protectionist political culture contributed a great deal to transforming the late nineteenth-century French ideological landscape. National protectionism was able to present itself as an alternative to socialism. The evolution of a writer like Maurice Barrès illustrates the possibility of a shift from one to the other. In 1892, he was the first to use the word "nationalism" to denote a type of *domestic politics,* hence a view that had nothing to do with Michelet's or Ernest Renan's understanding of nationalism. For Barrès, nationalism was capable of fully achieving the ideal of "worker protectionism" (to use a phrase that was common at the time), whereas socialism would inevitably fail. Indeed, national protectionism promised an immediately comprehensible efficacy.[190] By treating foreigners and nationals unequally, protectionism gave a negative but palpable meaning to a certain idea of equality, whereas socialism proposed a more exacting but also far more problematic definition of equality, whose achievement was to be deferred until after some hypothetical revolution.

The year 1890 proved to be a pivotal time, as political ideas accommodated themselves in various ways to the new constellation of nationalism, socialism, and protectionism. It was undoubtedly the protectionist idea, moreover, that occupied the central place in the ensuing transformation of images of equality. The national protectionism of the governing republicans was the dominant mode, but other, more radical configurations also emerged. Barrès's "reinvention" of nationalism has already been mentioned, but there were even more extreme variants. In Blanquist circles, often characterized as neo-Hébertiste, national protectionism took on a "social chauvinist" character that was violently xenophobic and anti-Semitic. The transition from revolutionary radicalism to ultranationalism was one of the period's most striking examples of ideological and political reclassification. For example, it was former Blanquists who organized the League for the Defense of National Labor in 1894 and published a xenophobic newspaper, *L'Idée nationale,* which made a fetish of slogans such as "France for the French," "France invaded by foreigners," and "nationalist socialism." Yet they remained socialist, because they portrayed themselves not only as xenophobes but as "proponents of the most absolute social equality."[191] How can one explain the fact that ardent admirers of Louise Michel were able first to support General Boulanger and then move to such an extreme antiforeigner position yet still believe in absolute egalitarianism? The only possible interpretation is that a former ideal was somehow *perversely reconstituted* rather than rejected. Recognizing that their plans for revolution and insurrection could never succeed, these erstwhile leftist radicals transposed their demand for equality into a new key.[192]

Working-Class Protectionism and Xenophobia

These new commitments influenced public opinion and social movements. As resistance to foreign imports developed, so did sentiment in favor of protecting "national labor" against immigrant workers in France. The idea of taxing employers who used foreign labor found support in the Chamber of Deputies, and many bills along these lines were filed. The phrase "worker protectionism" gained currency, expanding the original idea of tariff protection.[193] The issue figured in the legislative elections of 1893 despite the fact that tariffs had already been revised a year earlier. Thirty newly elected deputies had run on platforms advocating either a special residence tax on foreigners or banning foreign workers from employment in public works projects, and forty bills dealing with the issue were filed during the legislative session.[194] It was during this campaign that Barrès gained notoriety with an incendiary pamphlet entitled *Contres les étrangers,* "Against Foreigners."[195] The text, a veritable political manifesto, was a synthesis of the main themes of xenophobic protectionism: a special tax on employers using foreign workers; expulsion of foreigners who relied on public assistance; and systematic national preference in hiring. Interestingly, Barrès linked these views directly to a philosophy of solidarity and equality. For him, the idea of the fatherland completely reframed the social question. It was by turning the socialism of his youth inward that he became one of the principal exponents of nationalism in these years. Here is important evidence that the protectionist idea had transcended the realm of political economy to take on comprehensive social and political significance.

In addition to this broadening and proliferation of meanings of protectionism, a new xenophobic political vocabulary emerged. It was no longer surprising to find the most violent and enraged language in the writing of overheated, hate-filled authors of the new extreme right. The pamphlets published by the League for the Protection of National Labor are a fine example of this tendency.[196] Page after page was devoted to the theme of "invasion," "incursion," and "infiltration." Foreign workers were depicted as criminals and troublemakers. In what critics called the "rising tide of naturalizations" they saw "unnatural acts" and a threat that "the French race will surely be overwhelmed before long." But the tone of some prominent republicans was not very different. A report presented to the very academic Lyon Society for Political Economy denounced an "invasion which, though peaceful, is nevertheless still an invasion."[197] Foreigners were accused of coming to France "to steal jobs and prosperity from our workers" and treating the country as a 'milk cow.'" Again, the tone of the republican left was similar. One republican, Christophe Pradon, reporting to the Chamber on various national labor protection bills, also used the word "invasion" and spoke contemptuously of foreigners.[198] For instance, German workers were the same people "who had served as scouts for the Prussian army," while others were "shady characters." Paris was described as receiving the "social rubbish of two continents" along with a "shadowy society of exotic adventurers with dubious occupations." Although the government ultimately rejected proposed laws drafted in this spirit, it did so primarily because it feared international retaliation (as Méline among others argued). But this did not halt the rise of xenophobic sentiments, as the language of the deputies revealed.

Street demonstrations against foreign workers consequently multiplied in the 1890s. To be sure, these were not entirely a new phenomenon. There had been antiforeigner social movements during the Restoration and July Monarchy, although these movements were often directed as much against rival occupational groups as against natives of other regions.[199] Hostility was even stronger after 1848, owing to disillusionment stemming from the failure of universal suffrage to resolve the social question. Only toward the end of the nineteenth century, however, did the movement assume its full proportions with a large number of xenophobic incidents.[200] Some of these were bloody, like the extremely violent attack on Italian workers at Aigues-Mortes in 1893, which left fifty dead.[201] In addition, there were numerous attacks on Belgians in the Nord region. The unions and various socialist parties opposed these reactions but could not control them. These, too, were savage affirmations of a kind of corporatist equality. Significantly, xenophobia was most virulent among the least skilled and most vulnerable workers, who chose a negative way of expressing their desire for a status and integration they had been unable to achieve through work.

A Negative Equality as Identity

National protectionism was sustained by a purely negative vision of equality. Proximity was defined by community membership and refusal of alienation. Barrès put it bluntly: "The idea of 'fatherland' implies a kind of inequality, but to the detriment of foreigners."[202] In other words, the goal was to bring (some) people closer together by exploiting a relationship of inequality. This negative equality in relation to outsiders was reinforced in Barrès's mind by the desire to organize another community of the rejected, this one internal rather than external: namely, "the crowd of little people," humble capitalists and workers united in opposition to the "big barons" and "feudal lords." Indeed, Barrès sometimes superimposed both the internal and external dimensions by attacking a "redoubtable plutocracy of exotics."[203] This extreme position shows clearly that the concepts of identity and equality always refer to a complex interplay of proximity and distance, individuality and collectivity, and class and nation.

What was distinctive about national protectionism was that it represented an extreme case, the result of a radical polarization of both identity and equality. It also simplified the social to the utmost and thereby reduced the idea of equality to the single dimension of community membership, which itself was reduced to a negative definition ("not foreign"). The first reduction abstracted both interaction between individuals and class relations. The second recognized only the collective dimension of identity. The function of distance was of course fundamental. On this score, recall the splendid words of Michelet: "The conflict with England did France an immense service," he wrote. "It confirmed and defined its nationhood. By uniting against the enemy, the provinces discovered that they were a people. Seeing the English up close, they felt French. Nations are like individuals: they come to know their own personalities by resisting what they are not. They identify the self by recognizing the non-self."[204]

Indeed, the constitution of an identity always needs a demarcation, a separation, a mirroring effect of some sort. Biologists have noted the way in which the self is constituted by recognition of the non-self. Immunology studies the mechanisms by which this occurs.[205] But identity must be linked to a properly positive idea of shared existence to produce a democratic sentiment of membership. This is what distinguished the revolutionary nation of 1789 from the nationalist nation of the late nineteenth century. The former was associated with the formation of a society of equals, but the latter conceived of integration solely in the nonpolitical mode of fusion of individuals to form a bloc.

Constituent Racism

The distinction between "them" and "us," which is related to the representation of equality as identity, did not exist exclusively in the form of an opposition between inside and outside, as in the case of the nation. Anthropologists and sociologists have for many years been aware that such a distinction plays a crucial role in the constitution of smaller groups. "Presumably most groups gain some of their strength from exclusiveness," as Richard Hoggart notes in a justly celebrated remark, "from a sense of people outside who are not 'Us.' "[206] Literature and social science continue to explore this "economy of distinction" in its manifold daily manifestations, and especially in the form cultural differences. But more radical forms of difference have existed: for example, strict racial segregation has sometimes served as a source of collective identity. Segregation goes beyond relative differentiation in a context in which certain common characteristics are acknowledged. Under segregation, the very idea of commonness is subsumed and transformed by the fact of segregation. A polarization takes place, and this gives rise to a radically undemocratic view of equality. A prime example of this extreme form of equality as identity can be found, sadly, in the history of the United States. To gauge the significance and extent of American segregation, we must turn to history and ask, first of all, why segregation did not begin until twenty years after slavery had been abolished. The puzzling fact that segregation was not a survival of the old slave system in the post–Civil War era but rather a creation of the period known as Reconstruction must be explained.

The Invention of Segregation in the United States

When the Civil War ended in 1865, the Thirteenth Amendment abolished slavery, but the southern states were unwilling to see their entire social order dismantled as a result. Several of them immediately adopted "black codes" for the purpose of limiting the economic and social consequences of emancipation. For instance, an ordinance passed in one Louisiana town stipulated that every black person had to be in service to a white person or former landowner. The goal was to preserve the old forms of dependence within the new, externally imposed legal framework of wage labor. Black codes therefore sought to keep black workers tied to their jobs, limit their geographic mobility, and subject them to strict contractual obligations. Other legislation restricted their civil rights in various ways, such as making it difficult for them to acquire land. Blacks were thus legally emancipated but remained second-class citizens and in some cases virtual forced laborers. In response to these difficulties, the Civil Rights Act of 1866 made it clear that freed slaves were full-fledged American citizens. Establishing the priority of federal over state citizenship, this legislation hampered the southern states' ability to turn back the clock. A few years later, in 1869, the Fifteenth Amendment sought to end Reconstruction by granting blacks the right to vote. Legally, blacks and whites were now fully equal. It was in this context that the process leading to segregation began.

Having failed to establish a post-slavery legal order capable of ensuring white domination, the South turned to violence. Whites treated blacks harshly. The Ku Klux Klan, founded in 1866, fought to keep former slaves out of politics. Unwilling to countenance equality with former slaves, many whites adopted extraordinarily brutal methods.[207] Beatings for minor infractions and even lynchings became common.[208] Substantial numbers of whites were especially disturbed by the black exercise of the right to vote—a concrete symbol of equality. The line at the ballot box was a palpable representation of a new nonhierarchical social order in which the color of one's skin did not determine one's place. In North Carolina, so-called fusionist coalitions emerged in a context of universal (male) suffrage. In the 1870s and 1880s, several southern states witnessed the formation of "interracial" coalitions of workers and farmers around "populist" platforms. Whites in power realized that maintaining their control depended crucially on their ability to limit the right to vote; if blacks continued to make gains in this area, the white elite saw revolutionary change ahead. But how could black voting rights be limited when the Fifteenth Amendment prevented state legislatures from excluding blacks from the polls? An indirect attack was called for.[209]

From the late 1870s on, conditions were therefore imposed on the right to vote, conditions which, though not explicitly discriminatory against blacks, in practice kept them away from the polls. Various "techniques" were used. Some states imposed a poll tax, which few blacks could afford to pay. There were also tests of a prospective voter's ability to understand the Constitution, which uneducated blacks inevitably failed. There were also literacy tests, which illiterate whites were able to avoid, owing to "grandfather clauses" that exempted anyone who had voted before 1867 or who descended from someone who had, which of course meant only whites. Technical procedures such as the use of voting booths and multiple ballot boxes, which complicated the voting process for illiterate citizens, also served the cause. Careful gerrymandering of electoral districts provided a final protection against black political action. Thus excluded from the polls, blacks no longer counted politically. In a state like Louisiana, for example, the number of black voters, still as high as 130,000 in 1896, had shrunk to a mere thousand in 1904.[210] Southern legislatures thus regained a free hand to pursue their program of "redemption," of which the policy of segregation formed the backbone.

Segregationist measures were put in place starting in the 1890s, a quarter of a century after the end of the Civil War.[211] These completely transformed daily life in the South. Whites and blacks were separated everywhere: in housing, schools, sporting events, theaters, restaurants, public transportation, prisons, orphanages, hospitals, cemeteries, and funeral homes. No place or institution escaped the process. The segregationist imagination knew no limits. The results were sometimes very odd. In Florida and North Carolina, for example, the law specified that textbooks for whites and blacks had to be stored in different places. These so-called Jim Crow laws were upheld by an 1896 Supreme Court decision in the case of *Plessy v. Ferguson,* which recognized the doctrine of "separate but equal."[212] A new South emerged, quite different from the old South of the slavery era. Back then, segregation was impossible: masters and slaves inevitably rubbed shoulders in the course of everyday life. Although vastly unequal in status, they were in constant direct contact. Social distance and physical proximity went hand in hand. Segregation changed the relationship between distance and inequality. Henceforth, blacks would be treated as a group, indistinguishable from one another, whereas in the slave era there had been a degree of individualization in relations between masters and slaves. Each slave was perceived as a specific individual and called by name on the plantation to which he or she belonged. Now, blacks became just "Negroes."

Two Histories of Segregation

There are two ways of talking about segregation, in terms of either social history or anthropology. Traditional (social) historiography focused on two major questions: the evolution of proximity/distance relations between whites and blacks and the comparison of forms of exploitation under slavery and free-labor systems. On the latter point, recent work has emphasized the reconstitution of certain types of "forced labor" in the post-slavery era, involving not only "ordinary" capitalist exploitation but also the development of novel forms of subjugation. For example, laws against vagabonds made it possible to force blacks to accept underpaid jobs and sign long-term employment contracts. Some judges sentenced defaulting debtors to make "reimbursements in kind," forcing them to work for their creditors. Collusion between judges and local officials and certain firms led to the establishment of actual "labor camps," where individuals convicted of minor offenses (such as boarding a bus without a ticket) were incarcerated. Major corporations such as U.S. Steel did not hesitate to participate in these shameful schemes.[213] The equivalent of the old indentured labor system was thus revived in the South under quasi-legal or even totally illegal auspices. In describing these various ways of reducing a portion of the black population to a situation of dependency, some historians speak of "re-enslavement," but this tends to minimize the differences between the new system and the old. For these historians, segregation was merely an adaptation of earlier forms of racial separation to new circumstances, just as new forms of dependency had emerged after slavery was abolished.

More recently, however, historians have emphasized the novelty of segregation. C. Vann Woodward was the first to do so.[214] He made two key points. First, the earliest segregation ordinances (pertaining to public transportation, schools, prisons, and cemeteries) were promulgated in early nineteenth century in the North, where there was no slavery. This observation led him to follow Tocqueville, who had described a sort of economy of separation, a zero-sum game involving two variables, legal barriers and cultural barriers. "Racial prejudice seems to me stronger in the states that have abolished slavery than in those where slavery still exists, and nowhere is intolerance greater than in states where servitude was unknown. . . . Thus in the United States, the prejudice against Negroes seems to increase in proportion to their emancipation, and inequality is enshrined in mores as it disappears from laws."[215] In the South, slavery had effectively created such a gulf between blacks and whites that the latter could not help seeing the proximity of the former as a threat. Hence there was no correlation between equality and proximity. The two types of relationships were totally distinct, and law and custom did not overlap. Hence duality was possible: ferocious laws could coexist with a certain comfort in everyday relations. In the North, things were very different. Social relations were singular rather than dual: "In the South, the master is not afraid to raise the slave to his own level, because he knows that whenever he wishes he can cast him back down into the dust. In the North, the White no longer clearly perceives the barrier that is supposed to separate him from this debased race, and he shuns the Negro all the more assiduously for fear that he might one day become indistinguishable from him."[216] Woodward interpreted segregation in similar terms, as a sort of restoration-displacement of an old mode of differentiation destroyed by emancipation. It was therefore important to emphasize the novel character of the new relation between the races established by segregation. Woodward extended this analysis into the economic sphere by showing how Jim Crow laws were related to the economic crisis of the 1880s and 1890s. Although the complaints of many whites against conservative southern leaders stemmed from the failure of the latter to restore the economic health of the region, those same leaders tried to shift the focus of discontent from fears of economic decline to a sense of racial superiority. Economics and race came together in a new arithmetic of distinction and similarity. The segregation of blacks enabled whites to experience a form of identity that distracted attention from the economic inequalities that separated them. Racial identity replaced social equality as the source of feelings of similarity among whites. Progressives campaigned in the South on that basis. The defense of white supremacy and opposition to the right to vote for blacks was coupled with left-wing social rhetoric. Whites joined in solidarity around the slogan "Send the blacks back where they came from." The call for a more democratic society was thus rooted in an openly racist worldview.[217]

An obsession with racial mixing plagued early twentieth-century American segregationists. European visitors in the 1830s and 1840s had already noticed the extreme reluctance of northern whites to mix with blacks. In the South, by contrast, the legal inferiority of slaves coexisted with a certain tolerance for sexual relations between the races, and the birth of a child of mixed blood was not considered a scandal. Emancipation radically changed things, however, as the sharp decrease in the number of mulatto births indicates.[218] Interracial relations became scandalous from that time forward. Most states in the new South passed laws prohibiting intermarriage. These were the capstones of the segregationist project.[219] The definition of "white" was simultaneously tightened, as an obsession with the "purity" of the white race became a key tenet of the segregationist system. This was reflected in the "one drop rule": a single drop of nonwhite blood sufficed to make a person "nonwhite" in the eyes of the law. The concern with strict criteria of racial differentiation even crept into the American census in this period. Despite challenges to the scientific soundness of biological and anthropometric racial distinctions, the government continued to classify people according to racial categories.[220]

The history of segregation, which these various innovations reveal, is quite complex and open to a number of interpretations. Some scholars deny that any qualitative change in black-white relations occurred. Even among those who accept the existence of a significant change, there has been controversy about when it occurred, with some arguing that the process began immediately after the Civil War. Still other historians insist on distinguishing between exclusion under slavery and the segregation that came later, warning against the idea that integration of some sort existed prior to emancipation. The same historians argue that, paradoxically, segregation may have been perceived as "relative progress" by the black population, because it gave access to property and services previously denied to blacks. Furthermore, segregation encouraged a certain positive identity among blacks as well as whites, and the idea of melting into the white population was not necessarily seen as desirable by all blacks.[221] Still, despite these controversies among historians about black attitudes, the advent of segregation marked a profound shift in white representations of equality. For the purposes of a social and philosophical history of democracy in America, this is the crucial point.

Equality and Racism

Gunnar Myrdal, in his masterwork *An American Dilemma: The Negro Problem and Modern Democracy*,[222] noted that racism in America was not just a perversion of democracy but also one of its structuring forms. Indeed, racism has played a crucial role in the construction of the egalitarian imaginary of whites. This was not always the case: at the time of the rebellion against England, the American revolutionaries' demand for equality and liberty was quite close to the French (although it is true that in America, the emancipation of whites from their previous condition of civil and political "slavery" was seen in relation to chattel slavery, which did not end). In both the United States and Europe, however, the combined effects of the Industrial Revolution and the market society quickly undermined the original promise. In this context, racism would impart a new meaning to the egalitarian ideal. The perception of social inequalities, including the most glaring, was completely transformed by the emergence of skin color as a defining feature of similarity. It was possible for whites to feel *solidarity* in shared contempt for a group deemed to be inferior, a group whose dimensions were immediately, physically apparent. The emergence of "whiteness" as a central category diminished the significance of other social representations.[223] In other words, American racism was distinctive. It was not based on simple hostility to something alien or different or threatening (in contrast to eighteenth-century European hostility to "savages"). It was rather a distinctively *democratic* racism. As

Colette Guillaumin perceptively observes, "the growth of racist ideology actually depended heavily on egalitarian values: it was a response to the demand for equality."[224] It was as if the emancipation of blacks and the ensuing demand for civil and political rights had undermined previous white ideas about identitarian equality. That is why so many whites insisted on a new, more corporeal notion of identity as the basis of equality in the post–Civil War era.

A racially based "equalization effect" gave rise to a concept of *collective equality*. Collective equality is different from democratic equality, which depends on *individual* norms of justice. It is closer in spirit to aristocratic equality. Beaumont, Tocqueville's traveling companion in the United States, saw this clearly: "Since the existence of a slave population establishes an inferior class, all southern whites consider themselves to be a privileged class. . . . White skin is seen in the South as a veritable token of nobility. Whites therefore treat one another with exaggerated respect and good will, even when they are thrown together with people they regard as beneath them. This imparts something of an aristocratic stamp to southern manners."[225] In early modern Europe, aristocratic sentiment was in fact similarly based on the idea of belonging to a distinct race, a separate branch of humanity sharing the same "blue blood." This was enough to establish a sense of parity between a great lord and a country squire, both set apart from the common run of humanity despite the enormous differences of wealth between them. "The aristocracy," Rousseau observed, "accepts only corporate rights, not individual rights."[226] Among southern whites, the lower down the social ladder one went, the greater the concern with keeping the blacks apart, as well as inferior. Segregation thus helped economically disadvantaged whites cope with fears of falling social status.[227]

As segregation took hold, older forms of sociability revived. The pure/impure dichotomy on which these were based suggested a society organized by castes. In such circumstances, equality could be conceived only as a group quality. It could exist only as homogeneity, not as a relation. Segregated America reverted to a society of this type, characterized by *segmented equality,* which was the antithesis of what a society of equals sought to create. At the inception of the American republic, the ideal was a society of semblables. Later, however, whites envisioned their equality in totally different terms dictated by racist objections to this sort of similarity.

Racism, Absence of Socialism, and Weakness of the Welfare State

The foregoing discussion has a bearing on the question of why there is no socialism in the United States. Leaving aside a few marginal groups, no true socialist party has ever existed there, nor have socialist ideas captured a significant portion of public opinion. America is exceptional in this regard: in no other industrialized country do we find such an absence of socialist influence. Many explanations have been proposed. Werner Sombart's explanation in 1906, the first formulated explicitly,[228] is related to Frederick Jackson Turner's frontier theory. Borrowing Turner's ideas about American exceptionalism, Sombart argued that the frontier operated as a "safety valve," defusing class antagonisms by giving tangible representation to the hope of a better world in which every individual could invest in the future—theoretically, at any rate. He logically concluded that the end of the frontier would lead to the emergence of socialism, which he saw as capitalism's "other." This hypothesis proved wrong, but many others have been proposed since Sombart's time.

Earlier, in the 1860s, Marx had emphasized the unusually heterogeneous nature of American workers, a group that comprised workers of many nationalities from successive waves of immigration. For Marx, this impeded the formation of a true working class. He naturally called attention to the most striking feature of this heterogeneity at the time, namely, the large number of Irish laborers, who often found themselves in open conflict with workers who had arrived earlier.[229] Many scholars have since explored the ethnic and social aspects of working-class heterogeneity and tried to expand on Marx's explanation.

The absence of an Old Regime or feudal past in the United States has also been discussed, in the first instance by historian Louis Hartz. Hartz believed that socialism was a response to feelings of oppression stemming from a society of orders and classes, so that it was unable to emerge in America, where society had initially been organized around independent labor and whose social representations remained closely associated with that original state. In the same vein, more general values of individualism and distrust of the state have often been invoked to explain why America is different. So has belief in equality of opportunity, which has remained strong and encouraged a preference for improving individual situations over changing structural conditions.

Political scientists have meanwhile focused on variables peculiar to the American political system.[230] The federal structure of the United States tended to disperse political demands and dilute social criticism. It was more difficult than in Europe to identify a center of decision making that could be taken over to change the political order. Hence the very notion of a conquest of power, an integral part of the very idea of revolution, never took shape there.

Seizing the White House as one seized the Bastille in France or the Winter Palace in Russia was unthinkable. The first-past-the-post electoral arrangement encouraged the emergence of a two-party system and discouraged the formation of minor parties (as in Britain, but there Labour had been able to push the Liberals out in the early twentieth century).

To be sure, the explanatory power of these facts of American history varies.[231] Taken together, however, they do shed considerable light on the absence of socialism in the United States. But to my mind, another, less frequently noted variable is the crucial one: the change in the perception of social antagonisms associated with racism directed against blacks. This racism was more important than so-called nativism: the feeling on the part of earlier settlers that they were superior to more recent immigrants. Marx and Engels were the first to point out the role of nativism in the formation of an "aristocracy" of skilled workers, a society of equals within the larger society, which kept other workers at arm's length, just as skilled workers themselves were kept at arm's length by the employer class.[232] The gulf created by racism was deeper and more fundamental, however, in part because it was permanent but also because it was more universal, lending itself to a clear and simplistic interpretation of social distinctions. As a result, whites developed a very particular perception of the condition of workers. Their feelings of exploitation were constantly counterbalanced by the racist staging of their supposed superiority to blacks in both the North and the South. As Chevalier lucidly explained, "White democracy stands on a pedestal, slavery. In order to stand out, it does not need constantly to pull down the bourgeoisie. It exercises its authority on those below rather than attack those above."[233] If one replaces the word "slavery" with "racism," it becomes clear that there was a very powerful impediment to presenting the proletariat as the generic figure of social suffering in the United States. And socialism is not possible unless misfortune can be universalized in such a way as to constitute the exploited as a class.

The historical weakness of the American welfare state and redistributive mechanisms compared to those of Europe can be understood in similar terms. There are many reasons for these differences.[234] First, any number of political and institutional factors hindered the development of highly organized national movements in favor of greater benefits (as we saw previously in the discussion of the absence of socialism). Cultural factors also played a role. For instance, Americans hold the poor responsible for their fate, whereas Europeans generally regard them as victims. And once again, racism appears to be a crucial factor. As Alberto Alesina and Edward L. Glaeser have shown, there is a strong correlation throughout the world between social homogeneity and redistributive policies: the more heterogeneous the country, the lower the expenditure on social programs.[235] This is no doubt related to what has been shown to be a relation between social homogeneity and a society's level of confidence.[236] In other words, the greater the solidarity among citizens, the greater the trust, whereas conversely, the greater the distrust among citizens, the lower the willingness to pay for redistributive policies. The cited authors note the racist aspect of this variable in the United States, where many whites implicitly suspect African Americans of being "welfare cheats" and "taking advantage of the system." Consequently, they are prepared to renounce redistributive programs from which they themselves might benefit solely because racial hostility leads them to want to exclude blacks.[237] Additional evidence in favor of this hypothesis can be seen in the fact that, across the United States, the states with the smallest percentage of African Americans in their population offer the most generous social benefits.[238] Once again we see the influence of American racism on the rules of social justice: racist stereotypes are part of the reason for rejecting the welfare state.

Racism and Worker Protection

Worker protectionism, which became part of the European and especially French political agenda in the 1890s, also met with considerable support in the United States. One immediate consequence was the restriction of immigration. In 1882 Congress passed the first laws imposing ethnic quotas on immigration, inaugurating a long series of quantitative as well as qualitative restrictions. For our purposes, it is especially important to note the violence against Chinese and Japanese workers that accompanied these laws.[239] Anti-Chinese racism developed very early in California. In 1879, a state referendum on the issue of Chinese immigration resulted in a stunning 161,405 votes against and only 638 in favor.[240] At the time, some members of the Workingmen's Party and Knights of Labor joined in physical attacks on Asian workers. Indeed, the 1876 charter of the Workingmen's Party stated that the party could not condemn impatient workers who failed to contain their hatred of the Chinese.[241] Owing to its overtly racist character, the violence against the Chinese was much more serious than Know-Nothing attacks on the Irish in the 1850s and 1860s.

As social distance increased in the West and many settlers from the East ceased to believe that they would soon strike it rich, racism served as a sort of "compensation" for downwardly mobile whites. White workers saw themselves being reduced to the status of "wage slaves," and both anti-Chinese and antiblack racism became substitutes for equality and ways of restoring wounded dignity.[242] Thus the question of equality in America became linked to racism in numerous ways. In the United States more than in other countries, equality was conceived in terms of exclusive homogeneity.

3

THE CENTURY OF REDISTRIBUTION

The Revolution of Redistribution

In the nineteenth century, the idea of equality was turned against itself by negation and perverse redefinition. A long crisis slowly came to an end as welfare states came into being in the early twentieth century. Thus began a century of redistribution, as universal suffrage spread throughout Europe. Within a few decades, inequalities had been spectacularly reduced. Three major reforms were responsible for this reversal: the institution of a progressive income tax, the advent of social insurance to protect individuals from life's risks, and improvements in working conditions stemming from the introduction of collective representation and regulation of labor.

The Institution of the Progressive Income Tax

It was not until the end of the nineteenth century that taxation was seen as a possible instrument of social reform. In order to reach that point, many old attitudes had to be jettisoned. The first of these obsolete attitudes was a visceral dislike of taxes, which had long been denounced as fundamentally illegitimate. Indeed, until the middle of the nineteenth century, even republicans and socialists viewed taxes with suspicion. The memory of illegitimate, coercive confiscation lingered from the Age of Absolutism. In France, rage against the tax collector accounted for 40 percent of seventeenth- and eighteenth-century rebellions, a far higher proportion than bread riots, which also survived in collective memory.[1] England was the only exception to this rule. Although the tax system there was also highly unjust, the existence of a parliamentary regime meant that the collection of taxes was more clearly linked to budgetary expenditures that everyone could judge. Britain was therefore able to have tax rates that were twice as high as France without spurring comparable opposition.[2] Even after the French Revolution gave new legitimacy to taxation by linking it to active citizenship, something of the old reflexive resistance remained deep in the collective unconscious. A feeling that the tax system was external to the social structure remained, even after the specter of the bureaucratic state supplanted the denunciation of privilege.

Until the end of the nineteenth century, moreover, even when taxation was viewed positively, it was seen only as the price paid for services rendered. This was the theory of *tax as exchange,* which was later supplemented by a theory of *tax as insurance premium.* For instance, Girardin defined tax as "the insurance premium paid by the owners of property to insure themselves against all risks apt to disturb their enjoyment of their possessions."[3] On this view, the appropriate tax was one that was proportional to the amount of property one owned or public services one used. "What is society," Thiers asked, "if not a company in which each person owns a larger or smaller number of shares, and in which it is just for each person to pay in proportion to the number of shares he owns."[4] In this framework the notion of *tax as solidarity* or *tax as redistribution* clearly had no place. Even a socialist such as Proudhon saw tax as "each citizen's share of the expenditure for public services."[5] This approach to the fiscal question seemed self-evident at the time. Hence there was nothing problematic about indirect taxes, which were considered just because they were proportional to individual consumption. The only controversy concerned the nature and necessity of the taxed goods. Indirect taxes were also easy to collect and therefore constituted the major source of state revenue.[6]

Within a few years of the turn of the twentieth century, everything changed, however, as most major countries adopted a progressive income tax. Two revolutions followed, one in the realm of taxation and the other in the realm of principles, where the idea of progressive taxation was linked to redistribution among social groups. The simultaneity of tax reform is striking, since the governments of these countries were politically quite different from one another. Germany started things off by establishing an *Einkommensteuer* (income tax) in 1891. The United States followed suit in 1894 (and while the law creating the income tax was overturned in 1895, a revised version was ultimately adopted in 1913, following ratification of the Sixteenth Amendment to the U.S. Constitution). The United Kingdom, which had already adopted a form of income tax in the nineteenth century, imposed a modern "supertax" on income in 1909. After bitter controversy, the French parliament joined the movement in 1914. At inception, all of these income taxes had very low rates. German rates varied from 0.5 to 4 percent. In the United States, rates ranged from 1 to 6 percent, while in France the initial top rate was 2 percent, compared with 3 percent in the United Kingdom. The tax applied only to the top income brackets and therefore affected only a small number of taxpayers. In Britain only 12,500 households paid the supertax established by Lloyd

George (inheritance taxes on large estates were also sharply increased at this juncture, and capital gains on real estate were taxed for the first time). The supertax fell only on households declaring an income of more than £5,000 per year, which in those days was 100 times the average annual wage of a skilled worker.[7] In the United States, one had to earn more than $500,000 per year to be taxed at the 6 percent rate, and scarcely more than a thousand people fell into this category.

Despite these low rates and the small number of households concerned, the imposition of new taxes aroused extraordinarily vehement debate everywhere. In fact, it was the very principle of progressive taxation that drew the wrath of conservatives from the moment the idea was first broached. They believed that the progressive income tax was discriminatory because it aimed solely at the rich. In their eyes, it was a Trojan horse that would inevitably lead to the destruction of liberal society. American critics loudly denounced the specter of communism.[8] In 1894, during the debate about the law that would eventually be struck down by the Supreme Court,[9] some newspapers attacked the income tax as a "socialist measure," "worthy of a Jacobin club," and "communist in spirit."[10] In Great Britain the tone was identical. William E. Gladstone himself had denounced the principle of the reform as "tending toward communism."[11] French conservatives were of the same opinion. In a campaign manifesto of 1877, a veritable political testament, Thiers thundered that "progressive taxation is socialism."[12] The leading liberal economists of the day, such as Léon Say and Paul Leroy-Beaulieu, made the fight against progressive taxation their primary focus, and the battle became the rallying point of the liberal bourgeoisie.[13]

Indeed, adversaries of progressive taxation were in no way reassured by the low rates envisioned. They objected to the principle of progressivity itself, but they were also alarmed by what they saw as the rampant "virus" of redistribution, which would spread until it ultimately undermined private property and the equality of all before the law, the very bedrock of society. In France, one deputy said this during the parliamentary debate: "Tomorrow [the income tax] will no longer be 2 percent. Once the tax rolls are established, it will be easy to tighten the screws. You won't stop. You'll go to 50 percent."[14] At the time this seemed excessive. Ten years later, in 1924, the top marginal rate reached 60 percent. Probably the most significant fact in the history of the progressive income tax was this rapid rise of the top marginal rates, even in the United States. By 1918, only five years after the United States ultimately adopted an income tax, the top rate stood at 77 percent. It was reduced in the 1920s (to 24 percent by 1929), climbed again to 79 percent in 1936, and reached as high as 94 percent in 1942.[15]

What took place was thus a true revolution, which altered the very essence of western capitalist societies. This revolution extended over two or three decades but is almost entirely forgotten today. The philosophy of taxation as exchange, which had prevailed throughout most of the nineteenth century, gave way to a new approach, whose guiding principle was redistribution. The transformation was as much intellectual as it was social and political. A few lonely voices had called for it long before it occurred. In 1848, for example, Charles Renouvier, then on the extreme left, had said that "the progressive tax is good because its effect is to level conditions."[16] Sixty years later, governments that were by no means controlled by socialists adopted the same social philosophy. In 1909, when Lloyd George presented the fiscal reform project that would become famous as "the People's Budget," he said that "it was for raising money to finance implacable warfare against poverty and squalidness."[17] The Labour view had won out. Philip Snowden, the Labour Party's specialist on fiscal issues, wrote that "socialists look to the budget not only as a means of raising revenue to meet unavoidable expenditure, but as an instrument for redressing inequalities in the distribution of wealth."[18] To be sure, Snowden looked ahead to further changes, indicating that the ultimate goal was to place a confiscatory tax on all "unearned income," to strictly limit inheritances, and to socialize the means of production.[19] In sociological terms, his analysis depended on the idea that landed wealth had been created by the equivalent of a tax unduly levied on the people, hence that great wealth was essentially parasitic. "The rich do not contribute in proportion to the benefits they receive or to their ability to pay," he argued.[20] In his mind, moreover, landed wealth was associated with unproductive and risk-averse capital. For all these reasons it was legitimate to seek its elimination. But one did not need to go that far to consider tax reform. The general idea that fiscal policy ought to be redistributive and that taxation could serve as an instrument to reduce social inequalities was more broadly accepted, not only in Great Britain but also on the Continent and in the United States, despite vigorous efforts to dramatize and radicalize the stakes.

The Insurance Society

A similar revolution took place in dealing with the social question. Throughout most of the nineteenth century, those in power had attributed the misfortunes of workers to their own mistakes. Lack of discipline and planning, debauchery, and drink: these were said to be the causes of misery, so that ultimately the poor were chiefly responsible for their own wretched conditions (except for those who were the victims of accidents or physical handicaps). No one denied the existence of pauperism, and studies of the condition of the poor filled libraries. But no one concluded that the social order had to be turned upside down to make things right. In England, for example, when Charles Booth published his celebrated series on the *Life and Labour of the People of London* in the 1880s and 1890s, describing *Outcast London* and the *People of the Abyss,* the powerful Charity Organization Society, which played a pioneering role in the professionalization of social work, continued to base its view of poverty on a distinction between the deserving and undeserving poor.

The reforms that Otto von Bismarck introduced in Germany in the 1880s marked the beginning of a process that would ultimately transform the social landscape. In 1883, a system of compulsory health insurance was established, financed by a levy on workers and firms, and this was followed in 1884 by insurance covering accidents in the workplace. Old-age insurance was introduced in 1889, establishing the first compulsory retirement program. A Code of Social Insurance in 1911 extended this tripartite system. The inception of the German welfare state set off a veritable reformist fever throughout the Continent and, indeed, the entire industrialized world. Workmen's compensation for accidents in the workplace was introduced everywhere, marking a major improvement in the condition of workers.[21] Workers injured in the workplace, numerous at the time, were thus entitled to compensation and pensions if permanently disabled, without having to prove that the employer was responsible. Later, the first health insurance programs were established by the National Insurance Bill of 1911 in Britain and the 1928 social insurance law in France. Retirement programs were also introduced. In England the Old-Age Pensions Act of 1908 took the next step, using tax revenues to fund small pensions for those whose resources were deemed insufficient. Unemployment compensation also made an appearance. In addition to these public insurance schemes, state expenditures with a direct redistributive impact, such as France's 1893 free medical-assistance program, also proliferated. Various forms of assistance that had previously been left to private charitable organizations were transferred to the state and constituted as rights. Hence the state's social budget grew substantially everywhere. From this point on, the traditional sovereign state was therefore supplemented by what I have called the "state as institutionalizer of the social."[22] The state began to think of itself as an agency of social solidarity working to correct inequalities and intervening in a growing number of realms of everyday life, ranging from traditional areas such as education to new ones such as housing and transportation.

The Collective Regulation of Labor

Everywhere, unions also gained recognition as legitimate and necessary economic actors. The institutionalization of labor unions marked a decisive break with the liberal notion of the labor contract. "To this day," a French parliamentarian remarked during debate over what would become the trade union law of 1884, "the commodity known as labor has been sold retail, piece by piece, by isolated individuals. Now, by means of association, the imperative is to establish wholesale, collective trade in the commodity known as human labor."[23] Facing the kind of large firm that was said at the time to "deindividualize" production,[24] wage earners came to be seen as a single collective worker. Novel forms of social regulation were therefore put in place. From the English Trade Dispute Act of 1906 to the French law of 1919 on collective contracts, the industrial world moved definitively away from its earlier commitment to freedom of contract. A new body of law governed relations between unions and employers, and workers were recognized as a corporate entity *(le corps ouvrier)*.

Specific features of these new institutions and laws have been studied extensively. The most important thing, however, was the convergence of so many different reforms. A definite idea of solidarity and equality underlay them all. Thus similar changes took place everywhere. Our next task is to explain the sources of the profound rupture reflected in these changes and to describe the new type of equality that they established.

The Redistributive Revolution

The Reformist Moment

Throughout the nineteenth century, people were obsessed with the possibility that a new period of revolutionary turmoil might be on the horizon. The idea that the rise of capitalism, coupled with the emergence of a pariah class, might lead to social chaos was widespread, although some saw it as a threat, others as a hope. In France in the 1830s and 1840s, the specter of a "social conflagration" akin to Saint Bartholomew's Day in the Wars of Religion was frequently raised. At the end of his famous inquiry into the condition of the English working class, Buret concluded that Britain had embarked on a course from which there was no exit and that the situation could only lead "to inevitable ruin or to the most radical and perhaps terrible of revolutions."[25] For Buret, the growing distance between capital and labor would inevitably end in "social war and anarchy" unless the manufacturing regime was somehow reformed.[26]

In England, the repeal of the Corn Laws in 1846 and the 1847 legislation limiting the working day to ten hours temporarily reduced the severity of the social fracture. But in France and nearly everywhere else in Europe, 1848 signaled a change. Many governments realized that reform was necessary in order to avoid revolution. Outright reactionary policy no longer seemed viable. Girardin summed up the situation this way: "France must choose between a fiscal revolution and a social revolution."[27]

Reform was therefore the course that Napoleon III would adopt in France and, later, Bismarck in Germany. The French emperor authorized the organization of trade unions and supported the development of workers' mutuals, while the German chancellor created the institutions of the modern welfare state. For Bismarck, the reformist option was clearly a political calculation: its immediate purpose was to counter the spread of socialist ideas by showing government concern for the working class. The Kaiser himself supported this strategy. "If the workers' wounds are to be healed, we must not only repress the excesses of social democracy but also, in a more positive sense, foster the well-being of workers," he argued in a message to the Reichstag.[28] In Germany, in other words, the plan to reduce social inequalities and compensate for the vicissitudes of working-class employment stemmed from what we might call the reformism of fear. Most other European countries followed the German lead. The trend received a boost from the growing power of socialist parties at the ballot box (which reform, though it clearly helped to limit social unrest, ultimately proved unable to reverse).[29] Liberals and conservatives thus "resigned themselves to reform" in response to alarmist warnings that capitalist society as it had developed by the mid-nineteenth century was untenable. "Too much inequality of wealth and income, too much class warfare, will eventually undermine every political system," was the view expressed by the German economists and sociologists who signed the Eisenach Manifesto of 1872, thus providing an intellectual and moral framework to justify the shift in Bismarck's domestic policies.[30]

"Revolution can always be avoided by opportune reform," observed Gustav Schmoller, one of the leading "socialists of the chair," the derisive name attached to German academics who supported reforms to improve the lot of workers.[31] Schmoller's position was that of a professor with advanced ideas, which the German Social Democratic Party (SDP) did not support in the 1880s, any more than French socialists did. In fact, a new idea of revolution had emerged in the late nineteenth century. Under the influence of Marxism, the idea of revolution had ceased to be associated with images of insurrection and barricades. Instead, it became linked to belief in the inevitable collapse of capitalism: the contradiction between the forces of production and the relations of production, it was argued, would ultimately lead to transformation of the latter. Hence the emancipation of the proletariat, according to Marx, no longer depended on man's imagination, morality, or courage: it was rather a logical consequence of the laws of historical development. The spread of Marxism was directly linked to this deterministic conception of the future of capitalism and the coming revolution. Engels set forth the terms of this new gospel in his widely read text, *Utopian Socialism and Scientific Socialism* (1880). The terms in which Paul Lafargue, Marx's son-in-law and theoretician of the French Workers Party, summed up this political vision give us a glimpse of the way in which this vulgate was socially appropriated:

The ideal of communism has been rekindled in our minds. But that ideal is not a memory. It emerges from the entrails of reality.

It is a reflection of the economy. We are not utopians. . . . We are men of science, who do not invent societies but who will rescue them from capitalism. If we are communists, it is because we are convinced that the economic forces of capitalist production will inevitably bring society to communism.[32]

This "fatalistic" conception of history would remain for quite some time a source of resistance to reform. Many socialists were convinced that there was an "iron law of wages" against which it was pointless to protest, because employers would always take back with one hand what they were forced to concede with another. Hence any action by unions to improve the condition of workers and in particular to increase wages was destined to lead nowhere. Real change would come only with the collapse of capitalism. In such a framework the idea of fighting to reduce inequalities had no place. Furthermore, the very notion of inequality made no sense, for it assumed the existence of a divided world in which the determination of norms of justice and principles of equivalence between individuals was subject to permanent questioning. For Marxists, there were only two worlds: one of class struggle, the other of reconciled community. The *grand soir*, the revolutionary uprising that would change everything overnight, was as much an intellectual notion as a political or historical one. The revolution, it was believed, would usher in a conflict-free world in which only one homogeneous social class remained. Between structural exploitation and harmonious community, no "intermediate" state was possible or even thinkable.

The (at least partial) turn away from this catastrophist vision after the turn of the twentieth century would lead to validation of reformist projects. The name of Eduard Bernstein is symbolic of this change. In 1899, this Social Democratic leader published *Evolutionary Socialism,* in which he invited his allies to take note of the fact that Marx's predictions about the future of capitalism had turned out to be wrong. The concentration of capital had not led to the predicted elimination of small firms. The immiseration of the working class had not proceeded as envisioned. For Bernstein, this meant that there would be no apocalypse in the near future, so waiting for revolution made no sense. "If economic collapse is neither likely nor imminent," he concluded, "any tactics based on this notion are wrong and dangerous. They distract the party from sound reformist politics."[33] Thus began the revisionist debate. One should be clear about the significance of the virulent attacks to which Bernstein was subjected. He was attacked not only for his moderation and for the bluntness of his critique but in a far deeper sense for his dismissal of the left's historical imaginary, a dismissal that many at the time found shocking. Rosa Luxemburg, on the extreme left, was dismayed: "The theory of the collapse of capitalism is the keystone of scientific socialism. By rejecting it, Bernstein inevitably undermines the very concept of socialism."[34] In the center, Karl Kautsky was also angry, because he believed that the defeat of capitalism was inevitable. The SDP strongman was nevertheless in his own way a reformist, in the sense that he did not believe in *making* the revolution. But this meant only that he believed the party's task was to prepare for the inevitable collapse, so as to be ready to play its historic role when the moment arrived.

Bernstein lost the ideological battle in SDP congresses, but in practical terms he triumphed: socialist parties everywhere turned to reformist objectives in the early twentieth century. This was true of Jean Jaurès's Socialist party in France,[35] and obviously of the Labour Party in Britain, which had been a reformist party from the beginning, owing to its union roots. To be sure, the Russian Revolution of 1917 changed the terms of debate. Nevertheless, socialist parties still faced the same problem: how to formulate a new idea of equality and a new critique of inequalities simultaneously. And invariably they turned, if only for tactical reasons, to a policy of gradual conquest and class compromise, with redistribution at the center of their programs. Thus conservative fear and socialist rationality converged to make the reduction of inequality and the institution of a system of social security the crucial issues of the day.

Resistance to National Protectionism

The possibility of a redistributive revolution also stemmed from the resistance of European socialists to protectionism. This was by no means a foregone conclusion. The French case is symptomatic. In the 1880s and 1890s, some workers had been drawn to the protectionist position. Boulangist activists even took control of some unions,[36] at a time when part of the revolutionary left was seduced by nationalist ideology. Popular demonstrations fed the xenophobic climate. It therefore comes as no surprise to learn that in the mid-1880s, as the economic crisis deepened, a socialist leader such as Jules Guesde was receptive to nationalist sentiment in his working-class base, even if he simultaneously affirmed his intellectual attachment to proletarian internationalism. Several articles in the *Cri du peuple* attest to this. One of them, entitled "National Labor,"[37] defended a proposal to set a limit of 10 percent foreign workers on public-works projects financed by the city of Paris. Foreigners were characterized as "exotic labor," and the phrase "national preference" was cited approvingly. Shortly thereafter, Guesde published a vehement piece entitled "French Workers Are Dying,"[38] in which he defended protectionist measures. Indeed, he even went so far as to condemn the "invasion" in no uncertain terms.[39] But these positions would evolve. Although it is true that in 1880 the French Workers Party rejected both free exchange and protectionism at its Congress in Marseille,[40] when the Méline tariff bill was passed later on, the party vigorously denounced the effects of higher tariffs on the standard of living of the working class.[41] Furthermore, the socialists went on to oppose any bill that would have imposed a tax on foreign labor. "We, the deputies of the workers, will vote against any attempt to prohibit the employment of foreign workers in France, because we believe that every man has the right to work in whatever country he happens to be," said the socialist spokesman in the Chamber of Deputies.[42] Henceforth, any "so-called patriotic Mélinite" was to be condemned.[43] Jaurès also spoke out on several occasions against antiforeign discrimination and protectionist ideology.

Socialists in other countries such as Germany and Belgium had been quicker to reject protectionism. In Britain, of course, the Labour Party had from its inception adhered to the popular idea that protectionism is synonymous with a high cost of living. It was therefore only logical for the Socialist International to call upon its members, repeatedly and unanimously, to reject laws prohibiting the hiring of foreign workers.[44] Protectionism was simultaneously denounced as a deceptive illusion. Witness this resolution, proposed to the Congress of Amsterdam: "Whereas it is the policy of the capitalist classes and imperialist governments to divide the workers of the world by erecting tariff walls, and to protect the economic interests of owners, the wealthy classes, and monopolists by imposing duties on the workers' food . . . the Congress declares that protection is not favorable to the wage earner."[45] This course would be maintained in the years to come.

European socialists did not content themselves with general condemnations of this sort, however. By criticizing the idea of "national labor," they learned to redefine the nation in a nonnationalist way, that is, to conceive of it as a social form to be constructed rather than as a self-evidently coherent entity. Thus they came to see the nation as necessarily a zone of redistribution, in which it was important to understand the actual mechanisms by which redistribution was managed. During parliamentary debate on the Méline tariff, Jaurès developed this idea at length. He was responding to Paul Deschanel, who had asserted that "the worker can readily agree to sacrifices for the sake of his rural brothers."[46] Deschanel thus acknowledged that protectionism could restructure society. The problem, Jaurès replied, was to understand precisely how redistribution from "working democracy" (that is, the cities) to the countryside worked. In other words, *who* was the urban worker's "brother": the capitalist, the landowner, the tenant farmer, or the agricultural worker? He estimated that only one-third of the increased revenue from protection went to those who worked the soil, while two-thirds went to the landowner as profit. He therefore concluded that the issue was not protectionism in general but rather what specific social reforms should be enacted in order to build a nation in which various parties could negotiate the terms of economic redistribution and thus work toward greater solidarity.

Labourites said much the same thing in Britain. This was their line in opposing the Liberal dissident Joseph Chamberlain in 1903. Chamberlain had become a champion of tariff reform as well as imperialism.[47] The context was favorable to him, as English trade had stagnated somewhat in the face of a newly dynamic Germany, whose exports of manufactured products were rising sharply. He also struck a resonant chord when he called for a restoration of national pride in the wake of the British loss in the Boer War. But the candidate who presented himself as the "missionary of imperialism" was severely beaten in the 1906 elections, which he had tried to turn into a referendum on his views. He lost for the simple reason that the public bought the arguments of Ramsay MacDonald's Labour Party and Lloyd George's Liberals. The old arguments from 1846 about cheap bread surely played a part, but there was something else as well: the emergence of a current of social reformist thinking that did not end with the old defense of free trade. In *Imperialism*, a virulent critique of Chamberlain, Hobson argued that England's real economic problem was underconsumption.[48] Anticipating John Maynard Keynes, he suggested a program of public works to reduce unemployment. The solution to England's problems, he concluded, lay neither in protectionism nor in imperialism but in a new distribution of purchasing power. "Social reform" was the remedy to British ills. The objective, Hobson wrote, was to "draw into the public exchequer for public expenditure the 'unearned elements' of income."[49] MacDonald came to the same conclusion in 1903 in *The Zollverein and British Industry*. He, too, argued that the key question was the efficient redistribution of income. For him, socialism was thus the true alternative to protectionism.

The socialist critique of protectionism therefore led to a rejection of the nation as identity, as Barrès and Paul Déroulède conceived of it, and a return to the revolutionary idea of a nation founded on internal bonds of solidarity and reciprocity. Socialists therefore moved away from internationalism as the only possible progressive position. Although the ideal of internationalism as global reconciliation remained, the nation again represented an alternative ideal of emancipation. Jaurès became its champion in France and Kautsky in Germany. Kautsky understood the nation as a space for experimentation with social cohesion through reduction of economic antagonisms.[50] In this way he easily integrated the socialist struggle for a classless society into a doctrine that recognized the relevance of national boundaries. The nation was both an essential moment in a larger struggle and a necessary element in the battle to reduce inequalities. Otto Bauer, an important Austrian social-democratic leader of the time, simultaneously developed a powerful theory of the nation as "common experience of a similar kind," thus rejecting the nationalist idea of simple passive identity decided by fate.[51] In other words, a nation, for Bauer, was a matter of permanent interaction, conflict, and compromise among its various constituent groups: "Hence the nation, in our eyes, is not a rigid thing but rather an unfolding process."[52] Understood in this way, the nation creates a social bond that is based not on an imposed external norm but rather on an emerging "internal force."[53] The development of redistributive institutions could easily be accommodated in this type of approach.

The Constitution of a Reformist Milieu

Further light can be shed on policies to reduce inequality by studying the sociology of the state and reformist milieus. The redistributive revolution was not limited to top-down interventions or national-level political decisions, though these were of course crucial in reshaping the fiscal order. When it came to social legislation and welfare institutions, however, change was piloted by a broad network of charitable organizations and citizens groups that infused government bureaus with new ideas. The French case is particularly noteworthy in this regard. Reform owed nothing to Jacobin centralization. It was conceived and driven by a *reformist milieu*, which brought together the ideas and policies of numerous politicians, progressive officials, committed intellectuals and academics, traditional philanthropists, and radical social experimenters. Diverse political and intellectual sensibilities combined and worked together toward practical goals.

In the early 1900s, the Musée Social was typical of the sort of crucible in which consensus was forged. Here, Social Catholics and liberal Protestants found common ground with republicans and pragmatic socialists.[54] A new institutional spirit was created by focusing different sensibilities on immediate objectives and encouraging reformers to take the concerns of the nascent trade unions into account. An undogmatic social-reformist culture gradually emerged in opposition to the doctrinaire character of conservative liberalism.[55]

War and the Nationalization of Life

The development of inequalities is closely related to the detachment of certain individuals from the common run of mankind and to the legitimation of their right to distinguish themselves and separate themselves from others. It is therefore linked by construction with placing a higher value on private norms than on public norms. The experience of World War I reversed this tendency. In a sense, the war nationalized people's lives. Private activities were largely shaped by collective constraints. Social relations therefore tended to become polarized between two extremes: either withdrawal into the family circle or absorption into the superior problems of the nation. Virtually no middle ground remained between family and country. Concern with one's immediate family and anguish over the fate of one's country absorbed everyone's energy. Civil society shrank accordingly and was relegated to a position of secondary importance relative to both family and nation. The forced simplification of social life and elevation of the nation to the status of a community undergoing an ordeal radically transformed the conditions of political life. The idea that every individual owes a *social debt* to the community gained currency. The fact that the war threatened everyone's existence revived the fundamental principles of the social state (the contract and the debt to society) at a time when the prospect of returning to a chaotic state of nature seemed quite real. When novel social forms were first proposed during the French Revolution, the justification was that society owed a "sacred debt"—the expression was ubiquitous at the time—to the defenders of the fatherland. Hence the first steps toward a welfare state took place in similar circumstances.[56] This objective radicalization of the notion of social debt, which simplified all the rules of justice and reduced uncertainty concerning their application, was amplified by a similar polarization of the category of risk. The state established itself as a source of security in the face of radical risk.[57] Thus the images of Leviathan and the social state merged in a natural way: the state as protector of life superimposed itself on the state as source of social security to form a single image: the state as general insurer.

The redistributive revolution thus stemmed from the context of World War I. Millions of deaths on the European Continent compelled people to think in new ways about what united them. "If the war didn't kill you, it made you think," George Orwell put it.[58] Of course, the soldiers' lot was the hardest. Each combatant learned in the mud of the trenches that his life was just as vulnerable as that of his comrade, as all were returned to something resembling a state of nature. No one expressed this feeling more vividly than Ernst Jünger. In *Storm of Steel* he extolled the thrill of power and will that he discovered in combat, but he also explored what he called the inner experience of the front. "I have been in this trench for an eternity," he wrote. "Such an eternity that my senses have gone dead one after another, and I have become part of nature, lost in the ocean of night."[59] Infantrymen experienced equality of conditions in the extreme form of a return to a state of nature, at the border between humanity and animality—naked existence. Living in terror of death, they knew the equality of being cannon fodder.[60] "The consciousness of a community of nature gave rise to a very vivid and comforting sentiment of equality," one of them wrote.[61] As a result of experiencing this kind of unity, they also constituted a nation in a novel, immediately physical way. As Robert Musil remarked, "Many German soldiers felt for the first time the exalting sense of having something in common with all other Germans. One suddenly became a simple, humble particle in an event that transcended the personal. Subsumed in the nation, one could almost feel it."[62] Death thus acquired meaning as a form of participation in the life of the community. It was the most radical expression of such participation and therefore did not feel like a useless waste. Soldiers thus felt that in combat they had both fully realized their individual freedom and experienced the ultimate human communion. The term "self-sacrifice" reflected the unprecedented strength of this mass feeling.[63]

The experience of World War I thus marked a decisive turning point in democratic modernity. It restored the idea of a society of semblables in a direct, palpable way. It revived the oldest meaning of the idea of equality, captured by the Greek word *omoioï*. The first sense of the epithet *omoiïos* applied to *polemos,* or combat: it characterized a battle "that is equal for all, that spares no one." The *omoioï* were therefore equals in the sense that they had fought together; they had experienced the common lot of the soldier in battle. World War I not only demonstrated this aspect of equality through the fraternal experience of combat but also publicly validated it in all combatant countries through the organization of national funerals to honor the "unknown soldier" fallen on the field of battle. The cult of the unknown soldier was carefully staged to heighten its symbolic significance, attesting to the importance bestowed on the humblest citizen as representative of the entire nation. The anonymity of the unknown soldier expressed in exemplary fashion the idea of radical equality, of strictly equivalent value: the most obscure individual embodied what was best in everyone and became the ultimate measure of the social order. In 1918, *every man* became the incarnation of the social individual.

Fraternity in combat and the commemoration of sacrifice are complex phenomena, but they helped to pave the way to greater social solidarity. The benefits awarded to veterans led to a general reconsideration of social benefits and other redistributive transfers. The very idea of "nation" was redefined in the ordeal of war. If the war strengthened the idea of the nation as identity, forged in negation of the other,[64] it also clearly imposed the idea of the nation as solidarity, which helped to legitimize the need for greater equality. Thus, in the French case, the first major social insurance legislation, the law of 1928, was presented by its sponsors as a law "born in the aftermath of war out of the solidarity demonstrated among the various classes of society; out of the determination to grant those who defended the fatherland in the trenches, members of the popular classes who were obliged to defend the common wealth, the necessary aid to see them through difficult days; and out of the great idea of national solidarity."[65] Identical arguments were used across Europe to justify social reforms in the postwar period.

America itself emerged from the war profoundly changed. The experience changed American attitudes toward taxation and redistribution. The Revenue Act of 1917, which increased the income tax to finance the war effort, was presented as a way of "equalizing the burden of public expenditures."[66] When the law was passed, there was talk of "conscription of income" and "conscription of wealth" at a time when young men were enlisting en masse. "Let their dollars die for their country too," one congressman said.[67] The call for fiscal patriotism helped to legitimate the progressive income tax in the United States. First conceived as an instrument for taxing only the highest incomes, the income tax gradually became a universal tax with a redistributive purpose. It was universal in the sense that, by 1944, two-thirds of American households paid income tax, compared with only 2 percent in 1913. But it was also highly redistributive because the marginal tax rate reached 94 percent in 1942. This high marginal rate was not considered confiscatory, however. It was well accepted by society: 90 percent of Americans considered it just in 1944.[68] The government's effort to link the income tax to wartime patriotism helped to create a "tax-paying culture" and to persuade the nation that taxation was central to an ethical society.[69] Hence it is fair to say that after World War I, all the capitalist democracies reconsidered their basic principles and institutions.

In Europe, an additional factor hastened change: reawakened fear of revolution. This played a major role in 1918. The October Revolution raised the specter of insurrection elsewhere. Leninism made political voluntarism respectable again, so that some

socialists—those who would eventually join communist parties—
were no longer content to await the inevitable disintegration of
advanced capitalism. In 1919, Europe witnessed a number of revolutionary uprisings spurred by the Soviet ideal. In Germany, it was
the Spartacists led by Karl Liebknecht and Luxemburg. In Hun-
gary, Béla Kun overthrew the government established by the bourgeois revolution and proclaimed the Hungarian Soviet Republic.
Large strikes erupted everywhere, shaking established governments.
"All of Europe is in a revolutionary state of mind," Lloyd George
warned at the Peace Conference on March 25, 1919. "The workers are
deeply dissatisfied with prewar conditions. They are full of anger
and outrage. The whole existing social, political, and economic order is being challenged by the masses from one end of Europe to
the other."[70] Workers had greatly increased their influence, moreover, and were organized on a wide scale. Trade union membership
skyrocketed in the immediate postwar years. British union membership rose to 8.3 million, compared with 4.1 million before the
war. German union membership tripled to 7.3 million, and French
membership quadrupled (from 400,000 to 1.6 million). The power
of workers therefore had to be dealt with. All these social and political factors converged to encourage governments to extend and
accelerate reforms initiated before the war.

The Deindividualization of the World

The redistributive revolution was made possible by the historical
and political conditions discussed in the previous chapter. But it
was also the fruit of an intellectual and moral revolution, which
made redistribution thinkable. In a word, redistribution became

possible because the economy and society were "deindividualized" by thinkers who rejected older views of individual responsibility and talent. What ultimately emerged was a new vision of enterprise itself.

A Moral and Sociological Revolution

A new understanding of the nature of society changed the way people thought about equality and solidarity in the late nineteenth century. As early as 1877, Alfred Espinas published *Des Sociétés animales,* which treated human societies as living organisms, complex collective realities, rather than as juxtapositions of individual sovereigns.[71] Émile Durkheim later said that this book was "the first chapter of sociology,"[72] and he built his own work on its organizing principles and institutions. "Our society must become aware of its organic unity," he stressed in his first lecture. "The individual must sense the social mass that encompasses and suffuses him. He must feel it as present and active, and this feeling must always regulate his behavior."[73] Durkheim spoke for his era. The founding fathers of European sociology—Albert Schaeffle in Germany, J. A. Hobson and L. T. Hobhouse in England, Alfred Fouillée in France—all agreed that society was an organic whole. If we delve into the vast sociological literature of the period, however, we find important differences of sensibility and areas of theoretical disagreement. For instance, there was a considerable gap between the use of the organic metaphor and its practical interpretation. Fouillée's "contractual organism" differed substantially from Schaeffle's "social bodies." The rejection of older liberal individualist understandings of social phenomena was clear in all cases, however. The new approach had a diffuse but significant impact on *political culture* and *social philosophy,* and for our purposes this was perhaps more important than its contribution to the nascent science of sociology.

Socialists of the chair in Germany, Fabians and New Liberals in Britain, Solidarist republicans in France: these various political and intellectual movements converged in the late nineteenth century. All three reformulated the question of how society is constituted in very similar terms. The idea of a society composed of sovereign, self-sufficient individuals gave way to an approach based on interdependence. "The isolated man does not exist," argued Léon Bourgeois, the author of *Solidarité,* a work that would guide a generation of republicans and radicals toward a refoundation of their political culture.[74] In *Liberalism,* which played a similar role in England, Hobhouse argued similarly that every individual is constituted by the "social atmosphere" around him.[75] The Pasteurian revolution underscored the idea that the individual is fundamentally social. "Thanks to Pasteur," Bourgeois wrote, "the idea of a new humanity entered people's minds. It was he who gave us a more accurate conception of the relations among men. It was he who definitively proved the profound interdependence that exists among all beings. It was he who, by formulating the microbial doctrine so persuasively, showed how much each of us depends on the intelligence and morality of everyone else."[76] With Pasteur, as with Espinas before him, science once again became "progressive," a substantial ally of social reformers.[77]

In this new context, the notions of right and duty, merit and responsibility, autonomy and solidarity were completely redefined. Equality as redistribution became not only thinkable but also possible. Thus the introduction of the progressive income tax and

changes in the estate tax were closely related to the growing popularity of Bourgeois's idea of the social debt, formulated in *Solidarité*. For him, everyone is born owing a debt to society. Every individual owes something to the accumulated labor of all mankind.
The individual comes into the world with all sorts of obligations to
society. This is true even of the humblest peasant: "The inventor of
the plow still works the field invisibly alongside the farmer," Bourgeois's friend Fouillée argued in a much-remarked phrase.[78] But it
was even truer of those with better jobs. Hence the need for what
Fouillée's *La Science sociale contemporaine* (his first work) called "reparative justice."[79] Arguing along similar lines, Bourgeois justified
a progressive income tax: "The use that men make of the whole
range of social tools, and the profit they derive from those tools, is
not proportional to their wealth," he wrote. "A man who sets to
work and tempts fortune without previously acquired savings or
instruction is in a far worse position, when it comes to profiting
from social tools, than a man who already possesses considerable
intellectual and physical capital. We profit progressively from social tools to the degree that we have more potent and varied means
of action. It is therefore fair to look for a tax system that takes that
progressiveness into account by making each person's contribution proportionate to his advantages."[80] Hobhouse made the same
argument. The progressive income tax thus came to be seen as a
strict measure of justice. Redistribution was a means of balancing
history's books by requiring everyone to pay his or her debt to the
community.[81]

In addition to "paying the social debt," there was also a structural reason for the redistributive principle underlying the progressive income tax. The tax made it possible to correct the income
distribution determined by the market and thus derived from the

principles of individual liberty and private party by taking into account the socialized nature of modern production. The system of production was an interdependent one, in which it was impossible to isolate each person's contribution. Hobhouse mocked the claim of the "self-made man" to be solely responsible for his success. "If he dug down to the foundations of his fortune," he wrote, "he would recognize that, as it is society that defends and guarantees his possessions, so also it is society which is an indispensable partner in its original creation."[82] Bourgeois summed up the point succinctly: "It is impossible to tally up each individual's account."[83] The two great American theorists of tax reform, Richard T. Ely and Edwin R. A. Seligman, used the same argument in their brief in favor of a progressive income tax: "No such thing as strictly individual production exists in any modern community," as Ely put it.[84] The idea that modern production is in essence social was also at the heart of Seligman's case.[85] Both men relied on this view of the organization of the economy as grounds for rejecting "tax as exchange for services," or "the benefits doctrine," as it is usually called in English, and for favoring a redistributive tax instead.[86] This new way of looking at economy and society lay behind the progressive tax everywhere. The new tax was seen as a necessary instrument of socialization, a corrective to the market bias in favor of privatization and individualization.

In other words, social justice was no longer based on a moral imperative of charity. It was instead necessitated by the social structure itself. The notion of solidarity in the socioeconomic order therefore tended to overlap with the notion of citizenship in the political order: these were two different ways of understanding society as a body, an organic whole. Accordingly, the idea of a *right to existence* and that of a *guaranteed minimum income* both emerged in this period.[87] The effect was to redefine the whole republican idea. "'Republic,'" Bourgeois concluded, "is not just the name of a political institution but an instrument of moral and social progress, a way of steadily diminishing inequality of conditions and increasing solidarity among human beings."[88]

Via the diverse mechanisms of taxation and the welfare state, the concern with greater equality was thus directly linked to the figure of the social individual. At the same time people began to look at the state in a new way. What had been seen as a more or less parasitic bureaucracy came to be viewed in a more positive light. It became possible to demand the expansion of the state as a necessary condition for achieving greater liberty and solidarity. Public expenditure and therefore taxes thus came to be linked to the progress of democracy. Adolph Wagner accordingly formulated a famous "law" linking the expansion of the state to the development of civilization and modernity to the process of socialization.[89] In Britain, the Liberals also championed this theory of the state as entrepreneur and redistributor.[90] In the United States, Seligman went so far as to say that taxation was justified by the fact that the state had become an "integral part of us."[91] New social representations thus played a key role in changing the perception of equality and paving the way for new institutions intended to reduce inequality.

The idea of a redistributive society also figured in the new conception of the nation that we discussed previously. Instead of looking at the nation solely in terms of an inherited identity, people began to think of it as a construct to be achieved democratically. Bourgeois typifies this view: the nation, he wrote, "should not be reduced to the resolve to defend the homeland against threats from abroad. It commands a larger duty, a duty within as well as without, a duty toward justice, peace, and fraternity, because domestic peace and fraternity are always in danger."[92] In other words, many people now looked to rules of justice and redistributive institutions as additional sources of national solidarity.

The Socialization of Responsibility

"To be in solidarity is to be responsible for one another": this formula, from a Forty-Eighter newspaper, would take on its full meaning at the end of the nineteenth century.[93] The fact that society was defined as a system of interaction and interdependence actually led to changes in the notion of individual responsibility. Instead of looking to subjective responsibility, as in the past, people began to take *objective* situations into account. The statistical idea of *risk* became crucial for understanding social issues. It became central to the construction of the welfare state after its initial application to policy concerning workplace accidents, as we saw earlier. The French case is enlightening in this regard, because the Civil Code had exhaustively defined individual responsibility. After twenty years of debate, a law passed in 1898 broke new ground: setting individual responsibility aside, workers were guaranteed compensation in case of an accident, regardless of the cause and circumstances and whether or not the employer was proven to be at fault. The system was financed by requiring firms to pay for compulsory workmen's compensation insurance.

This law marked the formal, official recognition of the fact that modern industrial society called for novel forms of regulation, owing to its complexity. According to a contemporary statistic regarding workplace accidents, the employer could be proven to be at fault in only 12 percent of cases and the worker in 20 percent. The other

68 percent involved were unavoidable accidents or cases of *force majeure*.[94] Thus 88 percent of all accidents were legally imputable to workers, even though they were by no means responsible that often. By awarding financial compensation independent of a determination of direct responsibility, the system *socialized* the very idea of responsibility. Taking the view that accidents were a consequence of industrial risk, workmen's compensation insurance made it possible to deal pragmatically with a social issue without having to delve into a complex set of interrelated mechanisms and procedures. "Modern life is more than ever a question of risk," commented the great jurist Raymond Saleilles. "The issue is not to inflict punishment but to determine who should suffer the damage. The penal view is not applicable; only the social view counts. It is no longer, strictly speaking, a question of responsibility but rather a question of risk."[95] Great Britain took the same course slightly earlier than France, passing a law to deal with these issues in 1897.[96] Interestingly, the law referred to "wounded soldiers of industry,"[97] thus linking the industrial regime to the battlefield, where everyone was indiscriminately at the mercy of fate.

Further elaboration of the new category of risk made it possible to treat a range of situations (including disease, disabling injury, unemployment, and old age) as objective social facts, which could be statistically measured and thus insured without reference to individual behavior. Thus the justification of redistribution via the tax code in the name of a social debt was soon complemented by the development of a system of insurance that equalized conditions by reducing the role of chance in determining individual outcomes. Social insurance was thus a horizontal system of redistribution complementary to the vertical system established by the progressive income tax.

A New View of Poverty and Inequality

The development of the welfare state and redistributive institutions was abetted by the fact that the social nature of inequality was increasingly recognized. People were more and more willing to see the organization of society rather than objective and justifiable individual differences as the structural cause of inequality. Socialist critiques of the social order thus gained currency in the first half of the twentieth century thanks to this new social representation. The shift was particularly marked in England, where class differences at the turn of the century were the starkest in Europe. The obvious importance of inherited wealth in Britain (where land ownership was concentrated to an almost incredible degree) fueled demands for a reduction of inequality. In *Equality*,[98] one of the great classics of English social thought, R. H. Tawney argued that the elimination of structural inequalities of the sort found in England was quite simply the mark of a "civilized society." Although he acknowledged that individual differences were a source of positive social energy, there was no reason to believe that these had to be associated with a high degree of inequality. Individual differences would be just as important if inequalities were reduced.

Views of poverty also changed. Here, too, Britain set the tone for Europe. After Tawney, postwar neo-Fabians such as Anthony Crosland, Richard Crossman, and Roy Jenkins theorized the need for greater equality and described poverty as a consequence of social dysfunction.[99] Richard Titmuss, a professor at the London School of Economics, shaped Labour thinking on the issue in the 1950s and 1960s.[100] He championed the right of the poor to social benefits without means testing, because in his view their situation was the result of a flawed economic system. To the question "Why are they poor?" he offered a striking answer: "*They* are poor because *we* no longer care: 'Because we are a very unequal society . . . because we are unwilling to tax ourselves . . . unwilling to reduce our demands for more and more consumption. Because we don't really want a more equal society.'"[101] It would be difficult to take a position more diametrically opposed to that of conservative liberals, who never tired of insisting that poverty was a consequence of failure or error.

The Consolidation of the Social Welfare State

By the late nineteenth century, reformism, in the guise of social redistribution, had emerged as an alternative to the national-protectionist response to the first globalization. In the period between the two world wars, however, reformism faced new competitors. Although the shock of World War I created an opening for new experiments in social solidarity, it also radicalized critiques of liberal-capitalist society. Totalitarian regimes emerged as the embodiment of these new critiques. The Bolshevik Revolution was the communist utopia made flesh. It proposed a far more audacious idea of egalitarianism than earlier reformers. Meanwhile, Germany and Italy also proposed their own reinterpretations of the socialist ambition. Fascism and, even more, National Socialism appealed to many minds and set Europe ablaze. Both revived and radicalized the idea of equality defined in terms of national identity and homogeneity.

The Temptation of Homogeneity Redux

The Nazi regime was responsible for the most monstrous forms of racist nationalism, of which state-sponsored anti-Semitism was the most appalling illustration. Germany's turn to irrationality and horror was no accident, however. The regime justified its action with a perverse but carefully elaborated theory of equality. The key concepts that unified its political philosophy and social theory were *identity* and *homogeneity*. In political terms, the idea of a homogeneous sovereign people represented a rejection of both the "arithmetic individualism" of majority rule and the deliberative ideals of liberal parliamentarism. Carl Schmitt, who proposed this theory, argued that democracy ought to be the expression and validation of a collective identity. "Democratic equality," he wrote, "is essentially homogeneity, the homogeneity of a people."[102] This was a central tenet of his work. He often spoke of a "democracy resting on a substantive equality and homogeneity."[103] His ideal was thus logically one of seeking unanimous agreement: the manifestation of the people as One. He therefore prized "acclamation" by the assembled people speaking in one voice above the mere counting up of individual opinions expressed in the privacy of the voting booth. "The political force of a democracy," he therefore reasoned, "manifests itself in its ability to eliminate or expel the foreign and alien, which threaten homogeneity."[104] By representing society as necessarily divided between friends and enemies, he defined equality in terms of the subsumption of individual men and women in an undifferentiated mass. The Nazis would follow this imperative to the letter, carrying it to the most radical extreme.

For Schmitt, equality as homogeneity was not the result of a consensus reached after negotiation over the principles of justice. It was exclusively substantive. "National Socialism," he wrote approvingly, "takes care to preserve each authentic substance of the people wherever it is found in nature, in race *(Stamm)* or condition

(Stand)."[105] It was urgent, he argued, "to consider the question of the substance of democratic equality."[106] In its extreme form, this insistence on substantive equality ended in the genocidal madness of anti-Semitism. The invocation of race led to the substitution of *natural homogeneity* for natural equality: some groups had to be banished from humanity in order to create the conditions of equality for others (in contrast to the democratic vision of equality, which broadened the definition of humanity to include those who had previously been excluded). The shift from the social to the racial had been brewing since the late nineteenth century. The first sign of change can be seen in certain representations of the enemy in World War I.[107] Only with the advent of Nazism was the danger fully realized, however.

This version of homogeneity was also diametrically opposed to democratic equality defined in terms of redistribution and the construction of solidarity. It was based on the assumption of work already accomplished and potentially destined to endure for a long time to come. It was fundamentally antipolitical, because it assumed that the question of the institution of society had already been resolved. Hence the fall of Nazism in 1945 was not simply the fall of a regime. It marked the historic disqualification of a radical perversion of equality—equality defined as exclusionary identity—while at the same time reinforcing the project of inclusive, redistributive equality as a central feature of the democratic spirit.

The Climactic Moment: 1945

The year 1945 marked a climactic moment in the consecration of equality as redistribution. The victory over Nazism had eliminated the prospect of a homogeneity of exclusion. The shared sacrifices of the war effort reinforced feelings of solidarity everywhere. The phrase "social security" rapidly took hold. Even earlier, on August 14, 1941, the Atlantic Charter had affirmed the goal of "securing, for all, improved labor standards, economic advancement, and social security," and before that, in an address to Congress on January 6, 1941, Franklin D. Roosevelt had listed "freedom from want" among the four basic freedoms. Three years later, in May 1944, the International Labor Conference in Philadelphia called for the establishment of social security, including a guaranteed minimum income, on the grounds that poverty represented a "danger to the prosperity of all" and that it was essential to guarantee "equal opportunity in education and occupations." At the same time, capitalism came in for severe criticism. For example, Henry Morgenthau, the American Secretary of the Treasury, warned at the Bretton Woods Conference that governments could no longer be content to protect people from the negative consequences of the capitalist economy.[108] In France, the National Council of the Resistance called for radical structural reform. This point garnered wide approval, extending well beyond left-wing groups. For instance, the Christian-Democratic Popular Republican Movement, influenced by social Catholic ideas, proposed in its 1944 manifesto that the state, "liberated from the power of the owners of wealth," should take control of the economy. Christian Democrats in Germany and Italy were also critical of capitalism. Significantly, between 1945 and 1950, no pro-market liberal party succeeded in joining a governing coalition in Europe.

The new spirit shaped the reforms of the immediate postwar period. William Beveridge's 1942 report on "Social Insurance and Allied Services" set the tone. By formulating "freedom from want" as a "practicable postwar aim," he had encouraged his country to prepare for peace while the battle was still raging.[109] "Citizens," he argued, "will be that much more likely to devote themselves to the war effort if they feel that their government is developing plans for a better world."[110] Beveridge's outline for a "New Britain" thus flowed naturally from the shared sacrifices and ordeals of wartime.[111] In substance, he saw protection against social risks and redistribution of income as complementary aspects of his program. He also made the reduction of inequalities a key tenet of desirable economic policy. All Englishmen, whether rich or poor, were equal in the face of German bombs, he argued, and he called on his fellow citizens to draw the consequences of this involuntary solidarity. The social revolution whose principles he laid down was thus really an extension of the "spirit of Dunkirk."[112]

The situation was perceived in quite similar terms in France. The rapporteur on the social security bill also favored rewarding the courage and sacrifice that had been demonstrated in the struggle against the occupier. In his view, the fraternal spirit of the Resistance called for a "redistribution of national income, which will take from the income of favored individuals the sums necessary to complement the resources of deprived workers and families."[113] Many writers picked up on the phrase "necessary revolution."[114] But the French did not feel that they were doing anything novel. "In the outpouring of fraternity and solidarity among the classes that has marked the end of the war," wrote Alexandre Parodi, who served as minister of labor just after the war, "all the countries of the world are working to implement a social security system for the benefit of workers or even, in some cases, for the entire population."[115] The new institutions created between 1950 and 1970 essentially perpetuated and fulfilled the "spirit of 1945."

In 1945, as in 1918, the fear of revolution once again reared its head.[116] Still, the essential force behind the redistributive revolution in democratic countries, especially in Europe, was the acute feeling that the social debt contracted in the ordeal of total war had to be honored. It was in Great Britain that the egalitarian ethos of wartime proved most durable. Labour, in power under Clement Attlee from 1945 to 1951, made this ambition its own. The very high tax rates set during the war in 1941 and 1942 were maintained,[117] and the reforms introduced by the Beveridge plan radically improved the condition of workers. The standard of living of the masses no longer depended solely on the workers' pay; the "social wage paid to all citizens" through the new machinery of the welfare state also counted.[118] Meanwhile, primary inequalities were substantially reduced within a decade. The after-tax purchasing power of wages increased by 25 percent between 1938 and 1948, while that of profits decreased by 37 percent.[119] Over the same period, the *average* tax on income above £10,000 (covering a total of 8,000 individuals) increased from 43 percent to 76 percent. As a result, there were no more than seventy people in Britain with an after-tax income greater than £6,000 in 1948, compared with £7,000 in 1938.[120]

Similar changes took place in Scandinavia and, to a lesser degree, in France and Germany. Everywhere, taxes became the crucial instrument of economic and social policy.[121] In addition to the spirit of 1945, the growing electoral power of left-wing parties naturally played a role in this evolution, whether these parties ruled directly (as in Britain, Sweden, and Norway) or in coalition with other partners. Together with the trade unions, the parties were at a minimum able to exert strong pressure on governments in the thirty years after World War II. Obviously, moreover, this social change by way of taxation and redistribution was greatly aided by the high rate of economic growth in postwar Europe, with growth playing the role of "social lubricant."[122]

A Rudimentary Communism?

This reduction of inequalities, which continued from the end of the war into the 1970s, was thus rooted in a widely shared vision of the economy and society, extending well beyond the intellectual and political left. It is therefore not surprising that, in the 1950s and 1960s, a number of theorists, including Raymond Aron and Peter Drucker, thought they saw a certain convergence of socialism and capitalism. They described this convergence in terms of a capitalist conversion to the virtues of planning rather than a socialist conversion to the market economy. Tawney went so far as to apply the phrase "rudimentary communism" to these developments.[123] The formula might seem incongruous or excessive, but it certainly could have been used by Disraeli or Thiers or even Marx in the middle of the nineteenth century if the world of 1945 had been described to them. In other words, the book had been closed on nineteenth-century capitalism and the type of society it created.

The work that best captured the tone of the post–World War II period, Karl Polanyi's *Great Transformation,* was a vast fresco depicting the rise and then the inexorable decline of the idea of the market. "The congenital weakness of nineteenth-century society," Polanyi concluded, "was not that it was industrial but that it was a market society. Industrial civilization will continue to exist when the utopian experiment of a self-regulating market will be no more than a memory."[124]

At the time, this vision was closely associated with the development of social security institutions and policies to reduce inequality.

The Enterprise as Organization

The history of the welfare state was closely related to the dominant place of Keynesian ideas in macroeconomics, with their concomitant emphasis on demand. To redistribute wealth was to contribute to growth. At the same time, a new "post-liberal" approach to the enterprise gained prominence. Writers such as Andrew Shonfield, John Kenneth Galbraith, and Drucker exemplified the new approach to the firm that became influential in the 1960s, as the social redistribution model reached its apogee. Let us use their work as a guide.

In *Modern Capitalism* (1965), Shonfield summed up a vast study of Europe and the United States by describing the modern private industrial firm as an organization that "sees itself as a permanent institution, entrusted with functions that transcend the search for maximum profits and are at times incompatible with it." Indeed, the corporation's style was "more and more reminiscent of certain public institutions."[125] Although competition had not disappeared, the large firm had emerged, he argued, owing to its ability to "tame the market" by virtue of its great size. In other words, big firms were no longer subject to disruptive short-term changes in the market. Indeed, all three authors agreed that the day of the market economy was over. "The modern industrial system," Galbraith wrote, "is no longer essentially a market system. It is planned in part by large firms and in part by the modern state. It must be planned, because modern technology and organization can flourish only in a stable environment, a condition that the market cannot satisfy."[126] In Galbraith's view, modern firms had become relatively autonomous organizations. Self-financed to a large degree, they had no need to rely on the stock exchange and had largely freed themselves from the power of shareholders, who were content to receive "reasonable dividends." As Shonfield wrote, "the situation of the shareholders, whom liberal theorists sometimes portray as a parliament dictating to ministers what they ought to do, is in fact far more comparable to a disciplined army, which the law allows to rise up against its generals if and only if is short on rations."[127] Not being obliged to borrow, corporations were also relatively free of the power of the banks. Galbraith reached the same conclusion, and a great deal of contemporary research confirmed the view that shareholder power had dramatically declined in the 1960s.[128] Finally, our three authors agreed that, thanks to their size and monopoly of certain production techniques, large firms exerted power over their own prices.

Paradoxically, the fact that these large firms were privately owned was seen as an additional guarantee of autonomy. Since they were theoretically and legally controlled by their shareholders, no outside entity could lawfully impose its power. Hence corporations were independent of the state, the market, and shareholders. Their complexity was a further guarantee of independence. No outsider could possibly possess sufficient information or expertise to contradict the decisions of the giant corporation. Corporations were run by what Galbraith called the "technostructure," a core group of managers and experts. "By taking decisions away from individuals and locating them deeply within the technostructure, technology and planning remove them from the influence of outsiders."[129] Safe from such interference, the firm was an anonymous organization in which power was essentially collective, independent of any individual will.

In the large modern firm, Galbraith concluded, "control passes smoothly from the entrepreneur to the technostructure," because only the group has the information necessary to make decisions.[130] This observation was crucial to his description of what might be called the "deindividualization" of power and the socialization of responsibility.[131] For the author of *The New Industrial State*, this transfer of power to the organization had a number of implications. First, it reflected the disappearance of the Schumpeterian entrepreneur: "The entrepreneur no longer exists as an individual person in the mature industrial enterprise."[132] The technostructure, a veritable collective mind, had replaced him. The advent of this impersonal power also reflected the fact that the success of the firm depended more on the quality of its organization and the pertinence of its management procedures than on the exceptional talents of this or that individual. It could therefore perform quite well even though staffed by perfectly ordinary people. The point is important enough to warrant another quote: "The real accomplishment of modern science and technology consists in taking quite ordinary men, informing them narrowly and deeply, and then, through appropriate organization, arranging to have their knowledge combined with that of other specialized but equally ordinary men. This dispenses with the need for genius. The resulting performance, though less inspiring, is far more predictable."[133] Talent was thus taken down from its pedestal. Drucker made exactly the same point.[134]

For Galbraith, these changes meant that the role of the firm's chief executive officer (CEO) was reduced to that of just another cog in the machinery of the organization. Evidence of this could be seen in interchangeability: the "retirement, death, and replacement" of a captain of industry, "however important for the individual involved, have no perceptible effect on the performance of General Motors or IBM."[135] The CEO of a large corporation is forgotten as soon as he leaves his job, and "there is only Stygian darkness." Executives, like other employees, had become "organization men." They were mere servants. Prestige belonged to the organization, not its members. "The mature corporation," Galbraith observed, "has the prestige which induces and encourages the individual to accept its goals in place of his own."[136]

The socialization of responsibility and productivity due to this type of organization changed the nature of the social question, in Galbraith's view. The productive efficiency of the system inevitably redistributed wealth and reduced inequality. The lot of the individual benefited from what were seen as collective achievements.[137] No one could claim these accomplishments as his own. Executives were better paid than workers, of course, but only within the framework of a functional hierarchy of skills (and recall, by way of illustration, that Drucker stated at the time that the pay ratio between the top executive and the humblest worker should be no greater than 20:1). Galbraith wrote at a time before executives were paid in stock options, so he could plausibly claim that their compensation "was not extraordinarily high."[138] He could even envision a time when the quest for profit would be reduced to a purely mechanical, almost technical exercise, independent of the self-interest of the firm's executives. In his view, the reign of the organization was linked to something like a psychological mutation of the individual, with the desire for profit "divorced from the egos" of company executives.[139]

Galbraith and Drucker were by no means original in describing the evolution of the firm. Although they were not always clear about which parts of their description were factual and which were speculative, the views they expressed were widely shared throughout the industrial world. The egalitarian ethos of the period was closely related to this image of a profoundly socialized world.

4

The Great Reversal

The Functional and Moral Crisis of Institutions of Solidarity

Back to the Nineteenth Century?

It is tempting to interpret the current state of developed societies in the Age of the Second Globalization as a spectacular reversal of fortune. Indeed, the case is easy to make. Once again, the market is king. Inequality of wealth and income has nearly returned to the colossal levels of a century ago. Equally symptomatic and troubling, reactions to the second globalization have reproduced some of the social and identitarian pathologies of the late nineteenth century. Today, national protectionism and xenophobia have returned in a variety of troubling political forms. The idea of the nation has also made a comeback. As in the time of Barrès, it is invoked not to give flesh to "the people," which the democracy of the ballot box had turned into an elusive abstraction, but rather as a way of conjuring away the pragmatic difficulties involved in constructing a society of equals. Once again, the nation has become a convenient if simplistic framework in which to think about common interests, a symbol of negative unity and assumed homogeneity. This return of the repressed leaves one with a certain bitter taste.

Yet the change we are witnessing should not be seen as a simple return to the past. Periods of change are always times of ideological clashes and intensification of social conflict, as disruption of the established order provokes blunt expressions of reaction and resistance. At the dawn of the twenty-first century, for example, a prominent official of the leading French business association urged his fellow business leaders to methodically undo everything that the spirit of the Liberation had achieved.[1] Such a massive change in attitude cannot be explained in simple terms, however. There must be deeper causes. And the change did not take place overnight. Early symptoms of the crisis of the welfare state had begun to appear by the 1970s. The idea of the European Union had supplanted the social question in many people's minds. "Europe" symbolized the ideals of social protection and justice that individual member states found it increasingly difficult to articulate. Then, however, disenchantment with Europe began to grow, marking a new turn in the debate.

Historical factors played a part. With the collapse of communism and the evaporation of revolutionary hopes, the fears that had once driven reform dissipated. Memory of the shared ordeals of the past faded, and with it went the sense of heightened solidarity. Structural factors also played an important role. Three of these deserve to be singled out: the functional and moral crisis of institutions of solidarity; the advent of a new type of capitalism; and the metamorphoses of individualism. Delving into these three aspects of the new "great transformation" will show that history was not simply repeating itself. New representations of the just and the unjust emerged, posing novel threats to the very fabric of democratic society.

The Hollowing Out of Institutions of Solidarity

The changing attitudes of the 1990s were accompanied by a considerable internal erosion of the institutions of solidarity. This was particularly clear in France. With the persistence of mass unemployment and the emergence of new forms of social insecurity, a gap began to develop between traditional social insurance programs and a new "regime of social assistance," which directed aid solely to the most excluded and deprived members of society. The universalist character of the social security system was therefore seriously impaired, and this undermined the system's legitimacy, particularly among the middle classes. The *social insurance paradigm*, the technical and philosophical underpinning of the welfare state, also suffered. The concept of risk, central to the very idea of social insurance, was refined and particularized to the point where it ceased to serve as the unifying idea of the whole system. Basic distinctions—between the sick and the healthy, workers and unemployed, active workers and retirees—were predicated on the assumption that everyone faces similar risks. The implicit principle of justice and solidarity inherent in the welfare state rested on the idea that risks are equally shared and essentially random. It gradually became clear that this was no longer the way in which risk was perceived. Outcomes were no longer seen as randomly distributed individual *situations*. The phenomena of exclusion and long-term unemployment reconstituted poverty as a veritable *condition* with a strong social determinant, which consistently and durably affected certain subgroups of the population.

Furthermore, the spread of knowledge about the state of society and individual behavior rent the "veil of ignorance" on which the operation of the welfare state depended.[2] The social insurance principle assumes that individuals face equal social risks; the sense of fairness therefore depends on a certain opacity of the social, in the sense that there is no a priori method for determining the probability that a given individual will face a particular misfortune (such as accident or illness). If the nation is perceived as homogeneous with respect to risk, then a sense of solidarity can develop. Increasingly, however, this assumption of homogeneity was called into question. People became more aware of their life expectancies and learned how individual behavior and situations affect health and job prospects. This increased knowledge of individual and group differences posed a challenge to the basis of the social contract. Human beings may feel natural solidarity in the face of an unknown common fate, but they are less likely to feel solidarity if they perceive a link between individual choices and outcomes. In an opaque universe, justice is essentially *procedural*: it can be defined in terms of a universal rule. Growing knowledge of inequalities and differences called this definition of justice into question, however.

The American political philosopher John Rawls propounded what he called "the difference principle," according to which inequalities are acceptable only if they benefit the most disadvantaged members of the population. This is a stringent condition, which can entail a substantial redistribution of wealth, but in Rawls's argument it is formulated behind a "veil of ignorance." The parties to the agreement must believe that they themselves may be among the most disadvantaged. If it is possible to anticipate the probability of one's future position in society, then it no longer follows logically that the difference principle will be accepted as the principle of justice.[3] Under such conditions, procedural fairness, indifferent to the variety of individual situations, may be preferred to fairness of outcomes according to a principle that takes such variety into account. Knowledge of such differences did not simply drive a wedge between insurance and solidarity. Risk classes shrank in size, undermining the very basis of social insurance. Insuring these smaller groups still makes sense, but the result is no longer *social* insurance, strictly speaking. It is rather something closer to classic *private* insurance. As long as the veil of ignorance remains in place, insurance serves an aggregative social function, but growing knowledge of relative risk erodes solidarity. Information promotes differentiation. Ultimately, if everyone is different, then there is nothing left to insure: no "insurable" population can be constituted.

The relationship between justice and solidarity changed as a result. Indeed, the rending of the veil of ignorance revived the traditional opposition between distributive justice and commutative justice—an opposition that the classical welfare state had partly transcended, because the social insurance system combined rules of fairness with mechanisms of redistribution. In fact, solidarity can in a sense be defined as a way of compensating for differences. It is characterized by positive acts of sharing. Justice is defined in terms of the norm that governs this sharing. With insurance behind the veil of ignorance, justice and solidarity coincided: the sharing of risk was both a *norm of fairness* and a *procedure of solidarity*. Fairness and redistribution coincided. The tearing of the veil of ignorance changed this. Justice again became problematic: no a priori definition was possible once differences ceased to be random. Rawls's *Theory of Justice,* based on the idea of a principle of justice formulated behind the veil of ignorance, was a theory of the old welfare state, which collapsed in the 1990s.[4] The post-Rawlsian age of social theory therefore began in the 1990s.

Strong Institutions and Weak Theory

The institutions of solidarity established after 1945, and the policies that accompanied them, were also left vulnerable by the absence of a coherent theory of equality. The plain fact of intolerable suffering, coupled with the impact of great events such as the war, had initially sufficed to establish a consensus in favor of reform. But no theory of justice emerged to justify subsequent changes to the system, especially in regard to financing. When it came to managing the welfare state, pragmatism prevailed. For instance, most European countries adopted a system of "fair pay," under which remuneration for specific types of jobs was codified in schedules negotiated with unions, but no philosophical justification for this wage hierarchy was ever articulated. Pay scales were supposed to reflect a "just order," but on the whole they simply ratified socially accepted differences based on levels of education and training. Similarly, tax schedules were determined more by immediate budgetary needs and considerations of political feasibility than by explicit agreement about maximal acceptable differences.

A case in point is the evolution of social contributions to health insurance in France. When the system was first created in 1945, individual contributions were proportional to pay, up to a certain ceiling (originally set at twice the minimum wage). Thus, the principle of horizontal redistribution by way of insurance (from the healthy to the ill) was linked to a limited form of vertical redistribution between income categories. The assumption was that the consumption of medical services was not a function of income (or was to only a limited degree). But as the amounts required to finance the medical insurance part of social security increased, the ceiling was gradually raised before being completely eliminated in

1984. Small adjustments passed in response to budgetary emergencies slowly changed the nature of health insurance. And hardly anyone noticed at the time, because each time the ceiling was raised, it was said to be a "temporary" response to the social security deficit. To be sure, a 1983 white paper on social protection noted that the ceiling increases "might be seen as both a way of tapping new resources and an initial step toward a more just apportionment of social effort." Yet the report failed to describe any specific relation between the two goals. Throughout the 1980s, additional technical measures concerning unemployment insurance, workmen's compensation, and welfare assistance to families further contributed to the vertical redistribution effects of the system.[5] The relation between insurance and solidarity as conceived by the founding fathers of the 1945 regime was thus completely redefined without any explicit statement of principle.

It was not until the early 1970s, following the upheaval of May 1968, that the principles of justice on which the social security system rested were for a brief period directly challenged. This occurred in France and Italy, for example, where a demand for "equal wage increases for all" was heard in a number of labor conflicts. This posed a challenge not just to extreme inequalities but also to the whole pay hierarchy for white- as well as blue-collar workers. Differences in the remuneration of manual and intellectual labor were also questioned, along with the relative status of different professions.[6] Labor unions such as the Democratic Confederation of Labour in France and the General Confederation of Labour and Confederation of Trade Unions in Italy contributed to the theoretical debate.[7] But the moment did not last, and rising unemployment after the first oil shock of 1973, which marked the end of the period known in France as *Les Trente Glorieuses* (The Thirty Glorious Years,

1945–1975), imposed new priorities. As a result, the question of appropriate rules of justice and norms of solidarity was never properly addressed, while the cost of the social security system continued to grow.

The Delegitimation of Solidarity and Its Consequences

Tax policy was the first place where the silent delegitimation of the redistributive welfare state was felt. Suspicion of taxation has a long history in democratic societies. Broadly speaking, the general trend was to justify taxes on the grounds that the state provides services to its citizens. Only small businessmen and merchants continued to look upon the state as a predator standing outside society.[8] Things begin to change around 1980. Indeed, it was even earlier, in the mid-1970s, that California's famous "Proposition 13" marked an abrupt shift in attitudes toward taxation. Growing numbers of Americans began to link the fight against taxes, associated with bureaucratic growth, perverse forms of solidarity, and "legal expropriation," to the original spirit of democracy.[9] In Europe, the shift in opinion was less dramatic, but the results were similar. To be sure, the movement had direct political consequences, symbolized by the names Ronald Reagan and Margaret Thatcher, and later, George W. Bush.[10] The change was also reflected in ideology: the efficiency of the market was contrasted with the alleged inefficiency of the state. In fact, however, the progressivity of the income tax decreased everywhere, regardless of the ideological complexion of the government in power. In Sweden, the top marginal rate decreased from 87 percent in 1979 to 51 percent in 1983. In Britain, it went from 83 percent in 1977, the year of Crosland's death, to 40 percent in 1999 (while the standard rate declined from

35 percent to 23 percent). By the early twenty-first century, there was no developed country with a marginal rate above 50 percent. The change was dizzying.

The feeling that there was a social debt to be honored was also severely eroded. We have already mentioned some of the historical reasons for this. But there were also other reasons. For one thing, the focus of the social debt sentiment shifted. Empathy for the plight of others took novel forms. For instance, ecological concerns led some people to believe that man's relation to nature had become an essential feature of the social bond. Concern for future generations thus became a moral imperative, which for some took precedence over traditional forms of social justice. It is largely in this new mode that a *reobjectification* of the imperative of solidarity has taken place in recent years. Symbolically, future generations have replaced the proletariat in the collective imaginary as the focal point of public concern.

Meanwhile, the older, narrower sense of social solidarity faded, owing to a certain *deobjectification* of misfortune. The idea that poverty is a consequence of laziness, which historically had been limited to the United States, began to spread insidiously in Europe, where social injustice or the overall economic situation had previously been the dominant explanation of poverty.[11] There is no better example of this change than the views of a writer like Peter Sloterdijk. The rector of the University of Karlsruhe in Germany, Sloterdijk came to prominence as the critical sociology of the Frankfurt School began to decline. Sloterdijk's summary of his social philosophy is striking.[12] The state, he alleges, is a "kleptocratic monster," "intoxicated with Keynesianism," and the introduction of the progressive income tax was nothing less than a "functional equivalent of socialist expropriation." The only function of the welfare state is to perpetuate a society in which "unproductive citizens live indirectly at the expense of productive citizens." This new form of exploitation, Sloterdijk argues, "trumped the far less plausible socialist thesis of the exploitation of labor by capital." It would be hard to find a starker expression of the growing suspicion of institutions of solidarity, but what is even more surprising is that Sloterdijk's article drew no response, as if it merely stated in a particularly extreme form ideas that were widely shared in Germany.

These intellectual and cultural shifts were crucial, because they made impending changes thinkable and acceptable. And yet the redistributive social welfare state remains resilient. Even if it is tottering on its foundations, its basic institutions are still functioning. But if the gap between existing institutions of solidarity and recognized ideas of social justice continues to widen, further changes are not out of the question.

The Economy and Society of Singularity

The Capitalism of Singularity: The Meaning of a Mutation

Organized capitalism, as described by writers such as Galbraith and Shonfield in the 1960s, differed from earlier forms of capitalism with respect to its mode of management, the role of stockholders, and its relation to the market. When it came to the organization of labor, however, continuity prevailed. From workshop to factory, the work force was treated as it always had been. The worker was still reduced to his labor power, that is, to his fungible generality. He remained a perfectly interchangeable part in the system of capitalist production, whose true subject, according to Marx's *Capital,* was the "collective worker." The Fordist factory rationalized this reality by perfecting the assembly line. In assembly-line production, differences of age, sex, origin, and training ceased to matter. Manual labor became a pure commodity, abstract labor power. In this sense, the exploitation of the worker was inextricably intertwined with a veritable deindividualization of the laborer. Capital also reified intellectual work by incorporating social knowledge into machines, thus transforming it into fixed capital and expropriating the worker in yet another way. Indeed, this is why Marx defined emancipation as a *return to particularity*. In the most radical version of this doctrine, he identified free labor with the work of the artist, that is, the expression of an irreducible singularity. For Marx, social liberation therefore required making it possible for every worker to become a full-fledged creator. Throughout the long nineteenth century, the workers' movement would continue to praise independent labor while advocating the abolition of wage labor.

The capitalism that began to emerge in the 1980s differed from earlier forms of organized capitalism in two ways. First, its relation to the market changed, as did the role assigned to stockholders. Second, labor was organized in a new way. Fordist organization, based on the mobilization of large masses of workers, gave way to a new emphasis on the creative abilities of individuals. What now counted most was the ability to respond to rapidly changing conditions; the old emphasis on workplace discipline receded. Labor thus became more singular, for two reasons. First, the nature of production changed. New technologies of information and communication were themselves products of knowledge, and new technologies incorporated scientific knowledge in essential ways. Creativity thus became the principal factor of production. Phrases such as "cognitive capitalism" and "productive subjectivity" were coined to describe this change.[13] Second, the growth of the service economy meant that the quality of customer relations took on increasing importance. In the service sector, customer relations are central, and here, too, we can speak of a singularization of the labor process. The change is obvious in fields such as health care, consulting, teaching, and skilled crafts such as cooking. But it is also true of work in delivery services and home repairs, industries that now count among the largest employers of those classed as "workers." *Quality* has thus become a central feature of the new economy, marking a sharp break with the previous economy of quantity. Work routines have consequently become more diverse and product offerings more varied.[14]

These broad changes in the organization of production have given rise to more particularized forms of work. We see greater flexibility in the labor process. The era of planning has given way to a new era of permanent adaptation. It is no longer enough for workers to carry out assigned tasks by rote. They must be able to take the initiative, respond to unforeseen problems, and exercise responsibility. Although rules are still imposed from above, workers must often take the lead in applying those rules effectively. Organizations cannot function effectively unless workers enjoy some measure of autonomy, even in tasks that seem repetitive. Many practical consequences flow from this. Some job categories are perceived differently. The relatively broad notion of *skill*, referring to a general aptitude or specific level of knowledge or know-how that can be precisely measured and standardized, has given way to the notion of competence. As one sociologist has written, "the competent subject is one who is capable of making the right decisions in the face of unforeseen contingencies."[15]

The word "employability" came to express the idea that there is an interaction between the personal qualities of an individual and features of the labor market or industrial organization. Again, the old paradigm of strictly prescribed work routines was rejected, along with such negative consequences of factory discipline as psychological pressure and stress. Thus the Marxian antithesis between the artist and the wage worker ceased to hold.[16] Individual workers no longer saw themselves as members of the working class, as they did when coercive organization reduced them to abstract labor power. The use value of the worker—in other words, his singularity—became the key factor of production. The worker's productivity depended on his ability to mobilize his own resources and invest himself autonomously in his task. Older modes of collective regulation of labor therefore had to be modified. Pay could no longer be determined automatically by skill level. What was considered just and unjust in the workplace also changed, as did the sense of exploitation.

The mode of production in the new capitalism of singularity was shaped by the economics of permanent innovation. Evidence of this can be seen in the fact that the list of leading firms in the major industrial countries remained relatively constant from 1950 to 1980. Some firms on this list were decades old. During the 1990s, however, the hierarchy underwent considerable change. In the United States alone, the leading firms in terms of stock-market capitalization were relative newcomers such as Microsoft, Apple, and Oracle, while many once-giant firms had disappeared. The industrial and financial landscape was transformed everywhere, and this further accelerated the shift to new modes of organization and labor mobilization.

The Metamorphoses of Individualism

These changes, which precipitated a crisis in societies ruled by the spirit of equality as redistribution, also had a sociological dimension. This is not easy to see, because unbridled individualism came in for a great deal of criticism. Critics charged that the pursuit of wealth had undermined social solidarity and encouraged privatization. Although the critics clearly have a point, their criticisms do not help us to understand the origins of the phenomenon. In particular, they overlook a striking paradox: the new age of inequality and diminished solidarity has also been a time of heightened awareness of social discrimination and tolerance of many kinds of difference. The picture is contradictory, to say the least, and while some ground has been lost, there have been undeniable advances in regard to the status of women, acceptance of differences of sexual orientation, and individual rights generally. If we want to understand recent changes in our societies, we must take note of all of these divergent tendencies. One way to do this is to look at the *internal* transformation in the "society of individuals." This did not suddenly appear at the end of the twentieth century. For more than two centuries it has formed the framework within which modern institutions have developed. Succinctly put, what we need to understand is the transition from an individualism of universality to an individualism of singularity.

The Individualism of Universality

Revolutionary individualism does not refer to a social state or moral fact. As we saw earlier, the term did not appear in the revolutionary period. It describes the constitution of man as both legal subject—the bearer of rights guaranteeing freedom of thought and action, property, and autonomy—and political subject, sharing in sovereignty through exercise of the right to vote. The term therefore defined a way of making society, a novel approach to creating a social and political order in place of the old corporatist and absolutist order. Revolutionary individualism was therefore intimately related to the idea of equality and recognition of human similarity. It characterized a relational form, a type of social bond, rather than the condition of a single social atom taken in isolation.[17] Simmel used the phrase *individualism of similarity* to describe in general terms the tendency of European societies in the eighteenth century.[18] His point was that the aspiration to autonomy and liberty was intimately related to a universalist egalitarian ethos. The individualist perspective, he argued, "rested on the assumption that individuals freed of social and historical fetters would turn out to be essentially similar to one another."[19] In this context, liberty and equality were overlapping values.[20] Once imposed orders, disciplines, and structures were removed, individuals would be able to assert themselves fully as human beings. Everyone would become "a man *tout court.*" Everyone possessed a share of generality, a fact denied by societies in which individuals were confined to the condition in which they were born and thus condemned to a truncated existence. Under such circumstances, to be oneself was the same as being like others. As Simmel summed up this line of thought, "the individualism that then came into being was based on *natural equality* among individuals, the idea that all impediments to similarity were artificially created inequalities, and that if these were set aside, along with their historical contingency, their injustice, and their oppressiveness, the ideal man [meaning the universal individual, the pure semblable] would emerge."[21]

Such an individualism of universality was fundamental to the constitution of a society of equals. In no way did it fuel a process of differentiation leading to an atomization, division, or segmentation of society, nor was it a vector of particularization. On the contrary, it contributed to the generalization of the social by directly attacking the society of orders and corporations that rested on the institutionalization of particularity. The universal individual was in essence a juridical and political principle. It also had a psychological aspect, in that the affirmation of the universal individual was linked to the experience of humiliation and inequality in aristocratic society. But this psychological effect depended on the fact that a great distance separated individuals of different stations. Interpersonal relations were a very different matter, as we know from the work of seventeenth-century moralists such as François de La Rochefoucauld, Blaise Pascal, and Jean de La Bruyère, who were minute observers of interpersonal relations in this broader sense. These revolved around a logic of imitation and distinction and mechanisms of envy and jealousy as much as sympathy and sharing. The court of Louis XIV constituted a sort of laboratory for such relations because court life was totally taken up with games of power and appearance.[22] We turn next to an exploration of this terrain and what might be called the individualism of distinction.

The Individualism of Distinction

With the decline of the Ancien Régime, the psychological dimension of individualism was most fully and recognizably achieved in the artistic realm. It was the artistic milieu that gave existential depth to what had previously manifested itself mainly in caricatural form in the royal court. Artists defined their identity in terms of dissidence from the common run of mankind.[23] They turned away from a bourgeois society defined by conformism, that is, by the bourgeois class's inability to exist other than as a prisoner of its own narrow objectives and lack of imagination. Artists also stood apart from the supposedly gregarious masses, which they took to be slaves of immediate self-interest and unreflective passions. Nineteenth-century artistic individualism combined Romantic bohemianism with lingering elements of aristocratic pride. The aristocratic aspect of artistic individualism at times resulted in ambiguous attitudes toward democracy. Hatred of the bourgeoisie led to outright dismissal of limited-suffrage regimes, but doubts about the masses gave rise in some cases to skepticism about universal suffrage or to a fastidious refusal to mingle with the vulgar horde. Stendhal gave memorable expression to the contradictions inherent in the attitude of the republican artist: "I abhor the rabble (when it comes to communicating with it), while at the same time, if I call it *'the people,'* I passionately desire its happiness."[24]

This individualism of distinction was the precursor of today's individualism of singularity. Although it pointed the way to the future, it long remained the exclusive property of the artistic world in which it originated. Artists lived under material constraints but could aspire to a more ample existence by producing a body of original work.[25] The masses, reduced to a mere workforce, could not dream of deriving nourishment from what artists produced. Their emancipation depended entirely on transforming their condition in general.

The individualism of distinction would find its first social expression in a phenomenon midway between the old aristocratic distinction and the new ambition of artists, namely, in the phenomenon of fashion. Fashion provided a restrained form of expression, caught between the traditional principle of similarity and the new affirmation of particularity (in one form or another). Fashion did not exclude the idea of similarity but did limit its scope to particular subgroups of society. Sociologists at the turn of the century took note of the phenomenon. For instance, Tarde discussed "the reign of fashion," which he contrasted with the old "reign of custom." For Tarde, the reign of fashion described a modern process of singularization of the individual, who began to measure himself against others in new ways.[26] In this perspective, which we might call the interactive view of the social bond, individualization went together with hopes for unprecedented intimacy based on selective similarity. In assessing the new individualism of singularity, we will want to compare it with this first stage in the socialization of the individualism of distinction, which remained limited in its objectives and influence.

The Individualism of Singularity

The individualism of singularity can be seen as a generalization of the individualism of distinction. Distinction became commonplace and lost its elitist connotations: in short, it was "democratized." This process inaugurated a new phase in human emancipation, defined by the desire to achieve a fully personalized existence. Its advent was closely related to the growth in the complexity and heterogeneity of social life and therefore to changes in the nature of capitalism. At a deeper level, it was also linked to the fact that the life of each individual is now shaped more by personal history than by personal condition. Today, most lives are determined by the confrontation with events, by the trials one endures and the opportunities one encounters. Two people with similar backgrounds and similar educations may, for example, lead quite different lives because one has to endure a period of unemployment or divorce while the other does not. Psychological research has shown that people are less influenced by what they have at a given point in time than by what they are afraid they might lose or hope to gain.[27] People tend more and more to look at their lives in dynamic terms. The individual as history—necessarily singular—has therefore eclipsed the individual as condition, more closely identified with a group.

Another sign of this evolution is the fact that the nature of inequality has changed. Although inequalities between different social groups remain (rich and poor, management and workers, etc.), they have to a certain extent become individualized, and this changes the way in which they are perceived. Inequalities are now as much the result of individual situations, which are becoming more diverse, as of social conditions, which reproduce themselves. Economists describe these new inequalities as "intracategorial."[28] They are ambiguous in nature. At times, they are more bitterly resented than other inequalities because they are attributed to personal failure or lack of ability. They lack the clearly objective and therefore psychologically "reassuring" character of traditional inequalities of condition. Even if they can also be blamed on injustice or misfortune, they are still associated with an idea of responsibility. Indeed, responsibility automatically comes to the fore in a society that values singularity, as both constraint and positive value.

The individualism of singularity also reflects new democratic expectations. In democratic regimes associated with the individualism of universality, universal suffrage meant that each individual had a claim to the same share of sovereignty as every other individual. In democracy as the social form of the individualism of singularity, the individual aspires to be important and unique in the eyes of others. Everyone implicitly claims the right to be considered a star, an expert, or an artist, that is, to see his or her ideas and judgments taken into account and recognized as valuable.[29] We see this in the media, which exploit games and advertising as ways of mobilizing the individualism of singularity for their own ends.

Equality has lost none of its importance in this new context. The most intolerable form of inequality is still not to be treated as a human being, to be rejected as worthless. Hence the idea of equality still implies a desire to be regarded as *somebody,* as a person similar to others rather than excluded in virtue of some specific difference. To be recognized as being "like" others therefore means to be recognized for the *human generality* one contains (harking back to the original sense of "humanity" as a quality of unity without distinction). But this human generality has taken on a broader, more complex meaning. It has come to include the desire to have one's distinctiveness—one's history and personal characteristics—recognized by others. No one wants to be "reduced to a number." Everyone wants to "be *someone.*"

The advent of the age of singularity has given rise to new types of social conflict. For instance, the growing aspiration to achieve individual autonomy often comes into conflict with the narrowly utilitarian response of firms. But at the same time the individual's relation to society has changed in ways that have profoundly influenced judgments as to the most viable forms of equality, as well as the most tolerable forms of inequality.

The Era of Distributive Justice

The welfare state introduced ideas of corrective and compensatory justice. Its redistributive approach focused on achieving an objective *final state* of equality with respect to individual resources and standards of living, which became the basis of its legitimacy. The notion of need was central. By contrast, in a society of singularity, a distributive (as opposed to redistributive) concept of justice prevails. The relation between an individual's actions and his condition is central. Legitimacy is defined primarily in individual terms, in relation to the subject and his behavior, and only secondarily in relation to the general state of society.

Luck and Merit

In the age of singularity and responsibility, luck and merit are two different ways of reconciling actual differences with the principle of equality. Both are considered to be socially and psychologically justifiable. Take luck, for example. It is a structural equalizer, in the sense that no one can control an outcome based on luck, as in the drawing of lots. The positions of winner and loser take on objective reality, exempt from social or moral judgment. Losers can attribute their failure to bad luck. Psychologically, this is useful, because it attenuates the responsibility of the individual, which is such a fundamental feature of the society of singularity. The idea that outcomes are determined by luck may thus help to salvage self-esteem.

By contrast, merit is not so easy to characterize. David Hume spoke of its "uncertainty" and "natural obscurity."[30] It is a product of both nature (talent) and behavior (virtue) in varying degrees. In

Meritocracy, Michael Young proposed the lapidary formula *merit =
IQ + effort.*[31] This is misleadingly simple, because the meaning of
the terms of the equation is unclear, as is the distinction between
them. What we make of them depends as much on our idea of a good
society as on the implicit science of anthropological measurement.
The only useful definition of merit is negative: it is that part of a
given outcome that cannot be ascribed to luck. Significantly, it was
in theological debate over the respective roles of divine grace and
individual piety in salvation that merit became a value in Western
Catholicism, *in opposition to* the Protestant understanding of the relation between faith and works.[32] Despite the fundamental ambiguity
of the term, the concept of merit took hold because of the essential
role it plays in the democratic imagination. Modern societies must
believe in merit in order to function properly.[33] Merit fulfills a psychological function: knowing his merits, the individual develops
the self-esteem necessary to confront society and master it. It is
therefore a "necessary fiction,"[34] which enables individuals to make
sense of their experiences and reconcile the philosophical principle
of equality for all with the social fact of unequal outcomes.

Luck and merit thus support two distinct views of equal opportunity: one *probabilist,* the other *possibilist.* In French, equality of
opportunity is *égalité des chances,* and the word "chance" suggests
not only luck but also the possession of sufficient resources to seize
opportunity and succeed. In other languages we do not find the
same semantic range. The English "equality of opportunity" has a
more instrumental connotation and lacks a probabilistic dimension. The polysemy of the French term has helped to give particular centrality to the idea of *égalité des chances* in France.

The proximity to "games of chance" is also important, as Roger
Caillois has shown in *Les Jeux et les Hommes.* Caillois points out that

there are two ways to ensure strict equality between participants in a game: *agon* and *alea,* that is, a contest governed by rules or a contest governed by pure chance.[35] In the first case, the player alone decides his fate. Whether he wins or loses depends on his commitment and skill. He is fully responsible. The contest is supposed to be organized so as to ensure that the winner demonstrates incontestable superiority. By contrast, *alea* (Latin for the game of dice) indicates that fate decides the winner. The player's abilities do not count; his role is purely passive. Both types of game are quite popular today: sports on the one hand, lotteries and other forms of gambling on the other. Their social functions and psychological roots are opposed but complementary: opposed, because the purpose of competition is to reveal natural abilities and mental qualities, whereas games of chance are intended to "negate natural or acquired superiorities so as to make each player absolutely equal before the blind verdict of chance."[36] But *alea* and *agon* are also complementary, Caillois argues, because *alea* represents a "trial of substitution": since it depends on pure chance, it "helps to bear the injustice of a fixed or oppressive competition." The degree to which *alea* corrects *agon* can be gauged in prosaic terms by looking at the amounts that can be won in lotteries, where payoffs are exceptionally high compared to the typical prize in a sporting competition.[37]

The Metaphor of Athletic Competition

Athletic competition can be seen in this perspective as an illustration of both *agon* and *alea.* There are many ways to understand why sports have become so important in modern society. Some sociologists, working in the tradition of Norbert Elias, emphasize the contribution of sports to the "civilization of morals." Thus games in the twentieth century might be compared to "gentle commerce" in the eighteenth: they are an instrument for calming political and social conflict and diverting it to the circumscribed arena of sports. Other social theorists, following in the footsteps of Michel Foucault, call attention to the role of sports in training and disciplining the body, which emerged in the final decades of the nineteenth century. If we want to understand the symbolic function of sports, we must turn our attention to what we might call the politics of athletic competition. In fact, sports serve as a *theater for the equality of opportunity*, whose spirit and values they sustain and propagate.

The essence of the athletic contest is one of minutely regulated competition. Participants, whether individuals or teams, are carefully selected to ensure that the outcome remains uncertain. That is why it is common to create a number of divisions or categories of competition, taking account of varying athletic abilities and physical characteristics such as weight, age, and sex. Each contest is calibrated to isolate the variable one wants to measure in the various competitors. In a foot race, for example, one might emphasize endurance rather than acceleration. Each type of trial demands different talents and physical builds. In this way, veritable "similarity classes" are constructed, and competitors are sorted into various groups. Athletic leagues and event organizers try to ensure that contestants are equally matched. In many sports, handicaps are assigned to the same end.[38] Although handicapping is rarer today than it once was, in part because competition is more diverse and setting records is emphasized, it persists in sports such as golf, Nordic skiing, and horse racing. In the latter, handicappers calculate the additional weight that each horse in a race must carry based on past performance and presumed ability. The goal is to allow for more equal competition with other horses believed to be less capable. Athletic authorities enforce respect for the rules and try to eliminate any unfair advantage, such as might be gained through the use of drugs. The use of drugs is not only subject to athletic sanctions but is also against the law in many countries.[39]

In sports, then, the ideal is to eliminate structural inequalities and even to compensate for natural inequalities through training: when competitors are chosen for their relative homogeneity, superior training is supposed to make the difference. The objective of selection is to make the contest as unpredictable as possible, on the borderline between *agon* and *alea* (although bettors will try to anticipate the outcome). Ideally, the finish should be as close as possible, so close that only a camera or precision chronometer can decide—a "photo finish" in the parlance of horse racing. Under such conditions, a certain equilibrium subsists between winners and losers. The winner can savor his victory because the loser has demonstrated his talent. "To win without risk is to triumph without glory." To say this does not merely pay conventional homage to the value of participation. It means that winner and loser are in a sense united: one cannot exist except in relation to the other. Each needs to recognize and respect the other. Although the outcome of the contest divides them, sometimes cruelly, the difference between them derives its meaning from this act of reciprocal recognition.[40]

The internalization of this athletic notion of equal opportunity helps to explain the influence of the competitive model of society based on radical equality of opportunity, along with its mode of construction and ideology.

The Society of Generalized Competition

The idea of generalized competition as a perverse radicalization of equal opportunity is not just a reflection of the all-encompassing triumph of the market economy. It is at once an ideology and a social form. As an ideology, it is often associated with the term "neoliberalism," whose meaning, as we shall see, is ambiguous because the word refers to a number of heterogeneous theories. As a social form, it describes a general way of constituting the social bond. To form an accurate image of what generalized competition means, we must distinguish it from both market society and market order.

Market Society and Market Order

Contrary to what some writers have claimed, the idea of market society is not a twentieth-century invention marking a qualitative break with the earlier idea of "Manchester liberalism," that is, with the theory and practice of laissez-faire capitalism in a strictly economic sense. Indeed, the concept of the market acquired a sociological and political dimension as early as the eighteenth century. It did not refer simply to the regulation of economic activity by way of competitively determined prices. Indeed, "market" was understood at the time to refer to a general form of social organization. As conceived by the founding fathers of political economy, Adam Smith foremost among them, the market was closely linked to civil society. For Smith, the market represented the self-organization of a nascent civil society, which sought to emancipate itself from traditional authorities. It thus stood in opposition to the idea of contract and to political concepts of the social bond. Smith was therefore the first theorist of the withering away of politics, just as he was the founder of modern economics. He was, strictly speaking, the anti-Rousseau.[41] In contrast to formal hierarchies of authority and command, the market represented the possibility a new type of organization and decision making freed from any form of institutionalized authority. It made automatic adjustments and effected transfers and distributions without the intervention of human will in general or governing elites in particular. It eliminated the drama of face-to-face encounters, drained the passion from human relations, and blunted the potential for violence inherent in relations of power. The market thus empowered an "invisible hand," whose action was neutral because it was impersonal. It instituted an abstract mode of social regulation, in which "objective" laws regulated individual relationships without any need for subordination or command. For Smith, the idea of the market therefore incorporated a moral and social dimension.

Was this a utopian vision of the economy? We are of course inclined to think so today, because the opposition between the virtues of gentle commerce and the vices of wicked politics seems so naïve. But we forget that people in the eighteenth century lived in a precapitalist society under despotic governments. The market was still a novel idea, with which they had little or no experience. The nineteenth century took a more prosaic view: economic liberalism no longer proposed the market as a substitute for politics. None of the great conservative European statesmen of the period, such as Guizot, Thiers, Disraeli, or Gladstone, subscribed to the market religion. Indeed, all sought to make the economy subservient to the political order. They were in no sense "Manchester liberals."

Friedrich Hayek's theory of the market order took a different tack from Smith. Whereas Smith thought in terms of natural order and harmony of interests, Hayek stressed the need for permanent intervention to allow market mechanisms to operate as intended. In other words, the market must be continually reinstituted. Furthermore, Hayek understood the market in terms of a theory of information, which "complicated" the traditional notion of market equilibrium. The market, he observed, is the only known procedure for "the utilization of factual knowledge widely dispersed among millions of individuals."[42] On the same grounds he criticized state intervention, because of the "impossibility of knowing all the particular facts on which the overall order of activities in a Great Society is based."[43] Hayek coupled his cognitivist approach to the market system with a genetic discussion of its origins. In his view, the market was not an "invention" that emerged full-blown from the brain of some economist. It was rather the result of a cumulative, adaptive process based on human experience. For him, competition was a process of "tentative exploration."[44] (With this approach, moreover, Hayek borrowed far more from Burke and his evolutionary understanding of the production of rules and tradition than from Smith.)

Only through the market order can a true "government" of generality be established. Political authority is doomed by its limited and incomplete knowledge of the variables governing social interaction. It is structurally mired in the narrow world of particularity. Its interventions are inevitably distortionary, and despite its good intentions it cannot avoid creating rents or privileges for some at the expense of others. By contrast, the market, Hayek argued, creates an *invisible order* (the metaphor of the invisible hand too strongly implied the existence of a subject and a will for Hayek's taste), which delegitimates the claim of any human power to take command of society.[45]

Generalized Competition

The society of generalized competition can be defined as a radicalized form of the market society and market order. It magnifies the key features of market society in three ways:

- By basing itself on a philosophy and anthropology of risk and autonomy.
- By establishing the consumer as the symbol and measure of the general interest.
- By making competition the social form that "establishes the proper relations among members of society."

To understand the place of risk in the society of generalized competition, there are no better guides than François Ewald and Denis Kessler, France's leading ideologists of risk.[46] "Risk," they write, "describes man's ontological condition.... Having to take risks is inherent in man's status on this earth." They then invoke Pascal in support of their view ("One must wager. It is not optional. You are on board from birth."). They also invoke existentialist ethics, which Simone de Beauvoir summed up with the observation that "the essence of any ethical system is to regard human life as a game that one can win or lose and to teach man how to win."[47] Our authors hammer their point home: it is by confronting risk that man becomes who he is; the dignity of the individual depends on facing up to risk; risk is the root of the human condition, the source of all values; it constitutes the *episteme* of the modern world. Their style is by turns lyrical and sententious in describing risk as the source of all morality, all political philosophy, and all economics. But the true purpose of their celebration of risk becomes clear when they turn to practical recommendations. They blast the wage regime for valuing the externalization of risk and accuse the welfare state of fostering a culture of overprotection and diluting individual responsibility. Income inequality is regarded as a minor issue. They sum up their argument by noting that their "goal is to enable each individual not to shift as much risk as possible to others but to shoulder as much risk as possible himself." They present risk in a new light. Rather than something one assumes by choice or an adventure that one willingly undertakes, risk becomes a constraint that one endures. The same is true of autonomy. In principle, autonomy is a value that one seeks to achieve, an ideal synonymous with independence and emancipation. But in the society of generalized competition, it becomes a norm to which one must submit, an injunction that one must obey. The individual's aspiration to find his own way is thus turned against him in a sort of internal perversion of liberty and singularity.

In the society of generalized competition, the image of the consumer becomes sacred. The consumer becomes the symbol and touchstone of the general interest. In the consumer the egalitarian project merges with the elimination of rents and monopolies and with the right to increase one's purchasing power and expand one's range of choice. In contemporary ideology, the destruction of privileges has taken on a new face with the exaltation of competition. A new culture of choice flourishes under competition's banner: instead of an enlarged existence, the individual now seeks an ever-wider range of choice among competing products. The palpable benefits allow the consumer to forget his or her disillusionments as a citizen and to compensate for his or her powerlessness. The undeniable expansion of market choice makes up for the loss of social equality. The elimination of monopoly takes the place of the reduction of inequalities. Protection of the consumer becomes the ideal of the good. Defense of the consumer passes for the ultimate in political activism and public spirit.

The introduction of competition as the generic form of the social bond is the third distinguishing characteristic of the society of generalized competition. This idea is by no means original. The best-known nineteenth-century reference work on political economy tells us that commercial competition is but one of many forms of a "general competition that occurs in all aspects of human activity." General competition is the law of the new society of individuals.[48] In this context, to be equal means simply to be in the game, to participate in the competition. To borrow a phrase from Montesquieu, it is as if competition is what now determines the "true relation among men." What remained a formal possibility in the nineteenth century has become central in the twenty-first: the individual's aspiration to gain recognition of his singularity has radically altered his relation to others. Meanwhile, the mode of production increasingly recognizes the distinct contributions of different individuals, thus intensifying competition among them. The open society has consequently become the society of generalized competition.

Meanwhile, various institutions have restricted their purview to the protection of competition (in Europe, this has become the explicit doctrine of the European Commission, the central institution of the European Union). But the ideology of generalized competition was not imposed by force, nor was it foisted on people by some "neoliberal" pressure group. It is important to understand that it took hold as disenchantment with democracy spread throughout the developed world. It progressed slowly at first, as a sort of substitute for the failure of political will, or, more precisely, because the idealized expression of political will seemed to have become inoperative or ceased to be socially acceptable.[49] The ideology of generalized competition flourished in this political vacuum but did not create it (though it obviously helps to sustain it). It came to the fore as the more problematic or controversial definition of the general interest receded, because it reflected the modest but palpable reality of greater freedom of individual choice, whether in the mundane realm of consumer products or in the more consequential area of school choice. Individuals were able to express their discomfort with the deflation of the political, but they were not yet ready to renounce their limited powers, no matter how insignificant. The society of generalized competition was therefore openly and universally criticized even as it was silently validated.

Ideology and Reality

Although the ideology of generalized competition has become widely influential, it has proved to be incapable of establishing an acceptable new world order. Not only are this ideology's underpinnings open to moral, social, and anthropological criticism, but the fact is that actual capitalism bears little resemblance to the enchanted image propagated by its advocates. Actual capitalism suffers from any number of functional failures and depends on a variety of unspoken "arrangements." Capitalist economy and society are not at all like a minutely regulated athletic competition. Above all, the principles of capitalist economics cannot justify existing disparities of income and wealth. Labor economists can explain the differences in pay between a worker and an engineer or a manager in terms of differences in education and in respective contributions to the production process in a given sector of the economy.[50] But economic theory has nothing to say about the very top of the income distribution, which is precisely where the problem lies. If the "ordinary" compensation ratio (covering 99 percent of all employed persons) is 6:1 and has been more or less stable for many years, the compensation of CEOs has diverged sharply from that of other employees since about 1990. In the United States, the CEOs of the two hundred largest firms earned 150 times the average production worker's salary in 1990, compared with only 35 times that amount in 1974.[51] The ratio in other countries has evolved similarly.

There is a moral and cultural aspect to this spectacular change (the acquisition of great wealth has become more socially acceptable), but sociological rather than economic factors have been crucial. There has been collusion, for example, between CEOs and members of the compensation committees of the boards of directors of large firms. These people form a socially homogeneous milieu, yet economic theories of the firm assume that these are arm's-length relationships. In other cases, CEOs are complicit with stockholders, who receive higher dividends in return for approving generous pay packages. Some CEOs have become identified with their firms in the eyes of market actors.[52] Thus high pay is explained more by power relations than by market-related factors.

Dramatic increases in the income of the best-paid artists and athletes are also a long way from reflecting market realities. The "economics of superstars" turns on the globalization of celebrity via the media.[53] In a world of mass culture, small differences of talent can result in dizzying increases in remuneration. The concentration of income at the top in sports and show business is a consequence not of economics but of the existence of a quasi-religious consecration of planetary idols and rationing of supply. Under such circumstances, the winners take all.[54]

The even more spectacular pay packages in the financial sector are not the market's reward for contributions to the productive process either. Why, for instance, have hedge funds been able to claim a lion's share of financial market rewards in recent years? The answer is that their managers were able to capitalize on global trading in stock options and other derivatives.[55] George Soros's Quantum Fund, which employs three hundred people, made more money over the past thirty years than such prosperous firms as Alcoa or Apple, which employ tens of thousands of workers.[56] And a substantial share of hedge fund profits go to the fund managers, whose gains can be astronomical. One fund manager, John Paulson, made $3.7 billion in 2007, and a handful of traders earned more than many CEOs.[57] One can imagine a mathematician of genius or a supremely lucky gambler achieving mastery of time and capturing nearly all the profits generated by the economy. Such an ultimate winner would become a veritable god, vanquishing uncertainty and thereby controlling the world.

From these examples, which illustrate the central mechanisms at work in the explosive increase of incomes at the very top of the distribution, we see that neither virtue nor merit nor individual talent is responsible for the extraordinary increase in compensation. What is more, the big winners have suffered little from recent economic failures. Their increased compensation has mainly been the result of cunning, manipulation, power, complicity, and even corruption. This is the Achilles heel of the society of generalized competition, which stands in the way of its achieving full legitimacy: it is totally disconnected from any theory of justice.[58]

Radical Equality of Opportunity

The idea of equality of opportunity is closely related to the merito-cratic ethos in which democratic individualism has bathed from the beginning. But the connection is misleading for a number of reasons. The first is its polemical content. Many authorities have used the idea in an essentially rhetorical way to discredit, in the name of equality, proposals to redistribute wealth. Equality of op-portunity has thus long played a role in social conflicts and ideo-logical controversies around the idea of equality. It was introduced as an antidote to the demonized term "egalitarianism." Yet the idea of equality of opportunity has always resisted simple defini-tion. In its broadest, most consensual meaning—that everyone should begin life on the same starting line—everything depends on how the obstacles to achieving this goal are perceived and what conditions must be met to ensure that it is realized. As a result, equality of opportunity has assumed a number of different guises.

Five Definitions

During the revolutionary period, equality of opportunity was un-derstood in negative terms: it was identified with the elimination of privileges and legal or corporate barriers to social mobility. By incorporating this program, the Declaration of the Rights of Man and the Citizen gave a minimalist definition of equal opportunity by establishing a legal framework of equal rights. All careers were formally opened to talent and virtue, but the social and cultural inequalities that determine each individual's actual starting point (and which are essentially inherited through the family) were ignored.

With this in mind, the notion of equality of opportunity was expanded to eliminate such distortions. We might then speak of *social* (as opposed to legal) *equality of opportunity*.[59] There are essentially two ways of implementing this. The first is institutional, with the goal being to create an artificial environment from which existing sociocultural differences have been eliminated and in which the ordinary rules of society do not apply.

From the beginning this was the project of the republican schools. These were meant to be open to all and to create the equivalent of an ideal countersociety, a "classless microsociety." The rules under which the schools functioned were intended to arrive at an objective classification of individual students based solely on their personal attributes. The hope was to achieve an *institutional equality of opportunity*.

A second way of neutralizing sociocultural differences was also envisaged. The intention was to compensate for initial handicaps afflicting certain individuals and groups. We can describe this as *corrective equality of opportunity*—an instrumental approach. There are many ways to design correctives for inherited social and cultural inequalities. All involve selective or adaptive distribution: of human capital endowments (Gösta Esping-Andersen), of cash (asset-based welfare), of primary goods (for Rawls, rights and material goods), of resources (Ronald Dworkin), of capabilities (Amartya Sen), of means of access (to institutions, networks, or help, for Gerald Cohen). Recent theories of justice have placed particular emphasis on this point, seeking the best ways to achieve the ideal of equalizing the conditions under which individuals compete in a fair contest for meritocratic rewards.

Equality of opportunity is most commonly related to conditions early in an individual's life. But discrimination also occurs later in life, reducing the likelihood that members of certain groups will arrive at certain desirable positions. "Glass ceilings" of one sort or another exist, owing to a variety of handicaps that distort social relations. The result is not institutional discrimination but discrimination as a social fact, reflected in statistical measurements, such as career disparities between men and women, denial of certain posts to women, or ethnic discrimination in hiring. The law and the courts can help to remedy such discrimination when the facts are clear, but there is also a need for more general social remedies. Efforts in this direction fall under the head of *statistical equality of opportunity.*

A Formula for Radical Equality of Opportunity

Although these different ways of conceptualizing equality of opportunity figure in the background of various debates, no new theory of justice has yet emerged from them. Sen counsels us not to worry about this because the fight for equality has never been a question of absolutes. It has always been anchored, rather, in some specific situation and aimed at some concrete improvement or specific reform.[60] There are good reasons for such militant pragmatism, which is not without nobility. But in a time of bitter controversy over redistributive social policies, there is also a need for a new theoretical justification of their legitimacy. What we require is a theory of equality that can be mobilized against equality's detractors.

Dworkin was the first to propose such a theory in two fundamental articles published in the early 1980s.[61] In today's world, he argued, a useful theory of equality could only be a theory of equal opportunity. In order to be socially acceptable and to withstand criticism in the age of singularity, it would have to recognize the principle of individual responsibility. All human beings are equal in dignity and value and entitled to live under the same conditions,

Dworkin granted, but justice must nevertheless take different levels of individual ambition and commitment into account. A fair distribution of income must therefore recognize the importance of this variable while rejecting inequalities due to inherited factors.[62] In other words, income inequalities that are the result of personal *preferences* and choices are acceptable, while those that stem from disparities in individual *resources* are not. Dworkin's conceptualization of the problem has been popularized as a distinction between *choices* and *circumstances:* equal opportunity is achieved when the influence of circumstances is completely eliminated by adequate compensatory policies.

Dworkin's approach marked a turn away from Rawls's theory of justice. Rawls refused to limit himself to a narrowly meritocratic view, no matter how radical. He favored a principled equality according to which individual talents should be regarded as collective goods for the benefit of all.[63] For this Rawls proposed the term "democratic equality." His thinking thus continued to be shaped by the vision of the 1950s and 1960s according to which society was a collective order of which individuals were merely component parts. Indeed, his *Theory of Justice,* published in 1971 but written over the two previous decades, provided a retrospective philosophical justification for the classic redistributive welfare state gradually established over the course of the twentieth century. In no sense was it conceived as an alternative to the "neoliberal" concept of a society of generalized competition. Rawls's work provided a solid intellectual foundation for the idea of "reparative justice" that had barely been sketched out by Fouillée and Bourgeois. Dworkin saw himself as the theorist of the next stage, that is, of a society in which the idea of society makes sense socially only if it somehow incorporates the notion of individual responsibility.

Dworkin pushed the idea of compensated meritocracy quite a long way. He even argued that because "natural" talents are individual resources, those who do not have them should be adequately compensated for their lack. His work was praised by many who believed that both an intellectual and political response had to be found in critiques that accused the redistributive welfare state of encouraging passivity and reliance on welfare assistance. Even the Marxist philosopher Gerald Cohen praised Dworkin's work for that reason.[64] Cohen took the argument a step further, however, by treating the distinction between choice and chance as a criterion for distinguishing between acceptable inequalities and differences calling for corrective policy interventions.[65] Following Cohen, a number of authors laid the foundations of what has been called "luck egalitarianism."[66] This radical version of equality of opportunity insists on neutralizing all consequences that can be ascribed to chance in the broadest sense of the term. Rather than emphasize the positive consequences of individual choices, which are always difficult to establish, they accentuate the negative, arguing that anything that is not clearly attributable to individual effort should be subject to compensatory redistribution. What they propose is thus a strictly limited form of meritocracy.

A Paradoxical Theory

This radical version of equality of opportunity is intellectually appealing but unsustainable in practice, because its conceptual underpinnings are paradoxical. If all consequences of chance and circumstance must be compensated, the range of policies to correct potential handicaps is subject to unlimited expansion. Virtually nothing is the result of a pure choice. Each of our actions and decisions is informed by social factors and therefore subject to a variety of deterministic mechanisms. Luck egalitarianism also relies, paradoxically, on an idealized view of the individual and individual responsibility. On the one hand it advocates extreme "generosity" on the part of the redistributive state, but on the other hand it is strictly unmoved by the consequences of choices deemed to be authentically personal, no matter how devastating. For a luck egalitarian, it can be just for an individual to ruin his life because he makes a tiny error of judgment. One sees this asymmetry clearly in some of the examples proposed by John Roemer, one of the principal proponents of this view. If a person is run over by a truck in a marked crosswalk, he argues, it is just for him to be indemnified, but if the same person is run over after "choosing" to cross the street elsewhere, he must bear the consequences of his decision.[67] Here, then, the choice/chance distinction has resulted in a step backward with respect to the historical trend toward greater socialization of responsibility. What we have here is a combination of "progressive sociology" with "conservative ontology."

Another interesting example has to do with the treatment of smokers. According to Roemer, the issue is complicated.[68] If it is just to hold the smoker responsible for his addiction, he argues, it must also be granted that smoking appears to be a socially determined behavior. In the United States, for example, workers and African Americans smoke more than other groups. What, then, is the responsibility of an individual afflicted with lung cancer? There is no simple way to know. How can this difficulty be resolved? Roemer suggests that we construct "risk classes" based on observed behavioral differences for people of different family, social, or ethnic backgrounds, sex, etc. The individual smoker's responsibility can then be gauged by controlling for the median behavior of the groups to which he belongs. Merely stating this point is enough to show how impractical it would be to act on it: not only would it be difficult to devise an appropriate insurance policy, but there would also always be room for controversy about the relevance of this or that reference group or the definition of risk classes.

To base a theory of equality of opportunity solely on the distinction between voluntary and involuntary behavior is also likely to generate social distrust. The effect would be to cause people to pay closer attention to the behavior of others, who would then become objects of resentment, stigmatization, or suspicion. Distributive justice would enter into fatal conflict with social ethics.[69] So conceived, radical equality of opportunity thus ends in an impasse. It can inspire corrective action but is incapable of establishing a *political theory* of justice.

The Absolute Individual

Radical equality of opportunity leads, moreover, to treating individuals in abstract, absolute terms. This point bears emphasizing as we conclude our review of this approach. If we adopt the radical approach, *individuals have to be desocialized* in order to treat them as true equals. A case in point: the French revolutionary Michel Le Peletier proposed to create schools based on meritocratic ideals. In his 1793 report, he referred to these schools as "houses of equality."[70] The idea was to take young children between the ages of five and twelve away from their families. This was believed to be the crucial period for shaping young minds. At school, "in accordance with the sacred law of equality," all would be given "the same clothes, the same food, the same instruction, and the same care," so that "only talent and virtue" would set them apart, as meritocracy required.

The family, which otherwise would shape the destinies of these children, was thus designated as the enemy of equal opportunity.[71] This idea justified the republican goal of creating "schools of opportunity," but the practice fell far short of this ambitious ideal.

The problem of inheritance in a democratic system was understood in similar terms. Here, too, the initial concern was to enhance equality of opportunity by reducing the material basis for the reproduction of inequality. In France, the decree of April 8, 1791, stipulated that the property of a person who died intestate should be divided equally among his or her heirs. This provision passed, but not without difficulty. Other provisions covering gifts between living individuals and the freedom to make a will were also questioned. The section of the law covering wills was entitled "Effects and Limitations of Individual Dispositions." The issue was whether individual wills should be allowed to prevail over social compacts in regard to equality. A few days before his death, Mirabeau delivered one of his most interesting speeches, in which he urged his colleagues to impose equality by nullifying any will that favored one heir over others.[72] No individual should be allowed by an act of will to establish legal distinctions not permitted under public law, he argued. In his view, the freedom to dispose of one's property after death "artificially" made one member of a family rich while leaving the rest poor. It had the potential to transform a father's relationship with his children into a relation of power between "a haughty protector and obscure subordinates." Furthermore, wills that were used to create posthumous distinctions were mere "instruments of vanity" in the hands of men "with proud imaginations of . . . a long line of descendants praying to their ashes." Empowering the "individual will" in this way was tantamount to perpetuating feudal inequalities by way of the laws of inheritance.

By contrast, equal legacies were fully in accord with the new spirit of postrevolutionary institutions. Mirabeau's words were not heeded, however, and it was not until 17 Nivôse, Year II, that the principle of equal shares was adopted. The new law placed great emphasis on the fragmentation of large estates that would result from it. This was seen as a way of limiting the reproduction of inequality. The lawmakers had briefly considered an even stronger measure, which would have placed a ceiling on the maximum amount of property that could be inherited. Jacques Nicolas Billaud-Varenne made an even more radical proposal: a system of *national inheritance,* which would have endowed Frenchmen of modest means with a nest egg to give them a start in life.[73] Although these proposals did not pass, the issue did not go away.

What to do about inherited wealth was also a central issue in revolutionary America.[74] Thomas Jefferson favored heavy taxation of bequests in order to prevent the reproduction of inequality and the emergence of a caste of rentiers. In his work, the word "inheritance" was often linked to "feudalism" and "aristocracy," and he believed that landed property had to be subdivided constantly in order to preserve a government of liberty and equality. In 1778, he sponsored a Virginia law that granted seventy-five acres of land to all residents of the state. In his eyes, a democratic society belonged to the living; the dead played no role. Inheritance empowered the past, transforming once-legitimate differences into unacceptable inequalities.[75] To combat this and establish a material basis for the idea of equal opportunity, Paine proposed establishing a social fund financed by a tax on inherited wealth. This would have made it possible to give each citizen a sum of money at age twenty-five, enough to provide a start in life, and would also have offered a small pension starting at age fifty.[76]

Liberal thinkers would continue to consider similar ideas throughout the nineteenth century. For instance, John Stuart Mill suggested limiting the amount that one person could obtain through the kindness of another. "I see nothing objectionable in fixing a limit to what any one may acquire by the mere favor of others, without any exercise of his faculties, and in requiring that if he desires any further accession of fortune, he shall work for it."[77] He also favored limiting the amount that could be inherited. Socialist platforms frequently broached the idea, and many technical schemes were proposed to equalize opportunity by restricting inherited wealth.[78]

The only way that an individual could be made fully responsible for his own achievement was thus to eliminate the influence of his family through education and limitation of inheritance. Ultimately he would then become a child of society alone. Ideally, however, he would also have to be divorced from his history, or be allowed to start his history over at any time. This problem stemmed from the idea that initial positions also had to be equalized. Life is such that there is no true initial position, because each individual situation is constrained in various ways by what came before.[79] To envision *permanent equality of opportunity* was therefore a contradiction in terms: there would be no opportunity to seize or effort to make if outcomes were equalized at every turn. Equality of opportunity would then be reduced to simple economic equality. Here is yet another way that equality of opportunity fails to establish a theory of justice. The idea wavers constantly between two extremes: pure social equality and simple equality of rights. It may serve as a guide for specific reforms but cannot point the way to a true social philosophy.

The Apotheosis of Ability and the Advent of a Hierarchical Society

Furthermore, a society subject to the meritocratic principle alone would be rigidly hierarchical. This was the society envisioned by the Saint-Simonians. They went farther than others in making the elimination of inheritance and destruction of the family central tenets of their doctrine. They never tired of repeating the slogan "Shame on hereditary idleness! Honor merit and work!"[80] Unlike the socialists who came after them, the Saint-Simonians never advocated the socialization of property. For them, the essential thing was simply to prevent wealth from being passed on to the next generation. They therefore drew a contrast between "property by birthright" (that is, inherited property), which they proposed to abolish, and property "by right of ability," which they recognized as legitimate (though they did not propose to allow it to be passed on).[81] They also planned to establish "houses of education" in which children would be raised "in accordance with their natural abilities" rather than their birth.[82] *Le Globe,* the movement's newspaper, summed in its masthead, which highlighted three tenets of Saint-Simonian doctrine: 1) "The purpose of all social institutions should be to improve the moral, physical, and intellectual lot of the poorest and most numerous class"; 2) "All privileges of birth shall be abolished, without exception"; and 3) "To each according to his ability, to each ability according to its works." The third of these three tenets was fundamental. It shows that Saint-Simonians were committed to a society strictly organized around abilities, which they believed to be objectively and hierarchically ranked. Enfantin went so far as to say that Saint-Simon's followers "believe in *natural inequality* among men and regard such inequality as the very basis of association, the indispensable condition of social order."[83]

A hundred years later, Tawney criticized the Saint-Simonian position for offering "equal opportunities to become unequal."[84] Young painted a very dark portrait of meritocracy in which the old aristocracy of birth was supplanted by a new aristocracy of talent that was even more oppressive because it believed its ascendancy to be justified on the most impeccable grounds.[85] Indeed, the more fully the program of radical equality of opportunity is achieved, the more strictly hierarchical the result: this is the second impasse to which the doctrine leads. Hence it is no more capable than the society of generalized competition of serving as a new foundation for the idea of equality.

5

The Society of Equals

A Preliminary Outline

From Equality as Distribution to Equality as Relation

The Limits of Distributive Justice

Equality of opportunity is the dominant idea of equality today. As we have seen, however, it has the paradoxical consequence of ending in the consecration of inequality. The more its proponents advocate its "real," "strong," or "radical" versions, the more powerfully the justifications they offer for unequal outcomes. In other words, equality of opportunity underwrites a theory of justice that legitimates certain kinds of inequality. There is nothing inherently unacceptable about the equal opportunity approach, but if we are to gauge its applicability and limitations correctly, we must be aware of three blind spots.

First, equality of opportunity tends to separate distributive from redistributive justice. By attempting to define a fair distribution of resources, it tends to minimize the importance of redistribution and undermine its legitimacy. This should not come as a surprise, because, historically, equal opportunity regained its centrality in the 1990s by taking on board some of the more telling criticisms of the redistributive welfare state (for instance, the allegation that it fosters irresponsibility and passive dependency). The distinction between distribution and redistribution was crucial to the thinking of the leading British theorists of the "third way."[1]

Second, the theory of equal opportunity says nothing about acceptable differences of outcome. It can even justify the most extreme instances of personal enrichment, as long as the acquisition of immense wealth can be explained in terms of merit. "We are intensely relaxed about people getting filthy rich, as long as they pay their taxes," said Peter Mandelson, a minister in Tony Blair's cabinet.[2]

Third, the theory says nothing about what minimum level of resources society ought to provide. Equality of opportunity is often linked to compassion but not to social rights. Most theorists in the equal opportunity school conceive of the ultimate social safety net in terms of humanity rather than citizenship.

Each of these three blind spots touches on a key feature of the social bond. Taken together, they force us to think about what determines the structure and quality of a society. The problem is that theories that rely on equality of opportunity see the question of inequality in terms of the justice of individual situations alone, but inequality also has a societal dimension. The nature and degree of inequality in its various forms determine the cohesiveness of a society, as the authors of *The Spirit Level* have clearly shown. They point out that well-being depends on the quality of personal relationships, individual recognition, and feelings of usefulness.[3] In addition, they show that in more egalitarian societies, people are healthier and delinquency rates are lower than in less egalitarian ones.

The key point is that inequalities not only affect the disadvantaged but are in fact deleterious for everyone. Rousseau already pointed this out in his *Discourse on the Origins of Inequality* and *Confessions*. Inequality, he showed, is always experienced jointly. It defines a social state and affects the entire society. His vivid term for this was *égale gueuserie* (roughly, equality in misery), which ultimately engulfed rich as well as poor in cities where extremes of wealth and poverty coexisted cheek by jowl.[4]

Equality is thus as much a political idea as an economic one. It deals with the common as well as the just. By the 1980s this distinction had already been developed in the earliest critiques of modern theories of justice. But these critiques emphasized the opposition between individual values and the communitarian ideal. They called attention primarily to factors of collective identity and cultural homogeneity.[5] In this work, which would today be characterized as "neo-republican,"[6] individual and collective values were pitted against each other in a zero-sum game. At the same time, early treatments of the "politics of difference," which were also critical of theories of distributive justice, suggested that the concepts of domination and oppression be used instead of exploitation in discussions of equality.[7] There was consequently a tendency to oppose principles of recognition and redistribution. In reaction to these early theories of diversity, some authors reverted to a basic social-democratic position as the best response to the contemporary crisis of equality.[8]

The time has come for a new, more open approach. The idea of equality must be reformulated in a way suited to an acknowledged age of singularity. The goal is to develop an "expanded political economy" of the social bond as a step toward a general theory of equality in all its dimensions. Only such a theory can provide a firm basis for reform.

The Spirit of Equality and Classless Society

To that end, a revival of the revolutionary spirit of equality—the desire to create a society of equals—is urgently needed. During the nineteenth century, in the age of triumphant capitalism, this imperative was encapsulated in the idea of a "classless society." In *The Communist Manifesto* (1848), Marx offered the following definition: "In place of the old bourgeois society, with its classes and class antagonisms, we shall have an association, in which the free development of each is the condition for the free development of all."[9] Socialists of various stripes shared this vision of equality as freedom. They never understood equality in simple arithmetic terms as equality of income or wealth. The term "equality" was originally identified with ideals of emancipation and autonomy and thus with the creation of a society of proud individuals, living as equals not set apart by humiliating differences. The critique of economic inequalities was always linked to the goal of a society without barriers in which individual differences did not lead to exploitation, domination, or exclusion. In this connection, a classless society is one in which work is not subject to predatory powers and the dignity of all is guaranteed. Social virtues are primary.

The phrase "classless society" proved to be particularly pregnant in Britain, where rentier wealth had the greatest influence on the social structure, and economic, social, and cultural barriers made a veritable caste of certain elites. The concept was central to Tawney's manifesto *Equality*. "What is repulsive," Tawney wrote, is not that one man should earn more than others, for where community of environment, and a common education and habit of life, have bred a common tradition of respect and consideration, these details of the counting-house are forgotten or ignored. It is that some classes should be excluded from the heritage of civilization which others enjoy, and that the fact of human fellowship, which is ultimate and profound, should be obscured by economic contrasts, which are trivial and superficial.[10]

The idea of a classless society was also developed in the 1950s by Crosland, the leader of the neo-Fabians, in his book *The Future of Socialism.* Orwell struck a similar note with his idea of "common decency," which he discussed in a number of essays. In *Homage to Catalonia,* the terms in which he describes the emancipated, fraternal atmosphere of republican Barcelona in the winter of 1936 are particular eloquent.[11] There he breathed "the air of equality," by which he meant the simplicity of social relations in a society in which everyone was on the same footing, money was not a central topic of conversation, and there was "no boot-licking." "To the vast majority of people, socialism means a classless society, or it means nothing at all."[12] Our task now is to conceptualize this idea in more precise terms using the notion of a society of equals.

The revolutionary spirit of equality revolved around the principles of similarity, independence, and citizenship—three ways of conceiving of equality between individuals. The notions of similarity and citizenship remain as important today as they were two centuries ago, but they need to be expanded. The new expectation of an equality of singularities has to be superimposed on the original project of constituting a society of semblables. Although universal suffrage has been achieved in many places, the idea of citizenship also needs to be extended. The problem today is not just to share political sovereignty but also to participate together in the making of society, hence the imperative of communality. By contrast, the ideal of a society of autonomous individuals has lost much of its relevance in the modern world, where interdependence in all areas is inescapable. This old ideal is to some extent expressed in a different way in the form of singularity. As far as the rules of individual interaction are concerned, however, the generic principle of reciprocity has supplanted the narrower and economically irrelevant view of market equality. Accordingly, we will approach the society of equals in terms of singularity, reciprocity, and communality. In the following pages I sketch a preliminary outline of the reconceptualization I have in mind.

Singularity

The Society of Singularities

The aspiration to singularity can take shape only in the individual's relation to others. If the meaning of a person's life lies in his difference from others, then he must coexist with them. It is important, however, to distinguish between singularity and autonomy or identity. Autonomy is defined by a *positional* variable and essentially static. Identity is defined by *constitutional* variables: a composite quality, it is basically given, although it may evolve over time. By contrast, singularity is defined by a *relational* variable; it is not a state. The difference that defines singularity binds a person to others; it does not set him apart. It arouses in others curiosity, interest, and a desire to understand. Equality of singularities does not imply "sameness." Rather, each individual seeks to stand out by virtue of the unique qualities that he or she alone possesses. The existence of diversity then becomes the standard of equality. Each individual seeks his or her own path and control over his or her history. Everyone is similar by dint of being incomparable.

This form of equality defines a type of society whose mode of composition is neither abstract universalism nor identity-based communitarianism but rather the dynamic construction and recognition of particularity. This shift has significant implications. First, it suggests that individuals now seek to participate in society on the basis of their distinctive rather than common characteristics. The value of singularity is thus directly social. Singularity is not a sign of withdrawal from society (individualism as retreat or separation). Rather, it signals an expectation of reciprocity, of mutual recognition. This marks the advent of a fully democratic age: the basis of society lies not in nature but solely in a shared philosophy of equality. It follows, moreover, that democracy as a type of political regime is no longer distinct from democracy as a form of society.

The Sign of Discrimination

Every singularity establishes itself in relation to the singularities that surround it. Hence singularity becomes a vital force only in a democracy of recognition, and lack of recognition prevents singularity from taking shape. Discrimination—defined as unequal treatment of individuals on the basis of origin, faith, beliefs, sexual orientation, gender, or handicaps—is among the more obvious manifestations of the absence of recognition.[13] The cause of unequal treatment, and the reason why it is illegitimate, is the negative identification of the individual with one of his or her characteristics. The subject of discrimination is not the individual but the category: women, people of color, homosexuals. Discrimination can therefore be defined as a joint denial of similarity (or generality) and singularity; it combines both dimensions. That is why discrimination is the key form that denial of equality takes in the contemporary world. It is essentially a pathology of singularity in the sense that it assigns an individual to a denigrated or maligned "singularity class." For instance, an individual may be reduced to his or her ethnic background or gender, to the neglect of all other characteristics. The person's true singularity goes unrecognized. He or she is not regarded as *someone,* but at the same time his or her true individuality is denied by confinement within a social category. The person discriminated against is thus doubly excluded, from both the society of semblables and the society of singularities.

Discrimination is a strictly modern way of producing inequality. Indeed, it is an "internal" perversion, intrinsic to democratic society, of the principles of similarity-generality and singularity. But it also revives old forms of inequality and exclusion in the form of specific practices and rules. The chiasmus that constitutes these practices and rules suggests two distinct ways of combating them. One possible corrective is to rehabilitate ordinariness. The person who is discriminated against aspires simply to be a human being like any other. In France, for example, experiments have been conducted in which job applications are submitted anonymously. In this way, prospective employers are forced to consider only those characteristics relevant to performance of the desired job, excluding irrelevant characteristics likely to be grounds for discrimination, such as gender or ethnic background. The rehabilitation of ordinariness can also occur through the generalization of a norm. For instance, to declare that a ban on homosexual marriage is discriminatory means that the definition of "marriage" as a union between one man and one woman has been deemed to be insufficiently general and replaced by another, namely, the union of two individuals.

By contrast, discrimination can also be challenged by attributing rights to a specific category of individuals or, more generally, by ascribing value of one sort or another to a group. To continue with the previous example, one might insist that homosexuals have the right to marry.[14] Or one might envision various actions to compensate for the discriminatory characteristic. The term "affirmative action" has been applied to corrective action aimed at a particular group. The goal is to fight discrimination with discrimination. The person subject to discrimination may then transform the denigrated characteristic into the basis of a proudly proclaimed identity or a claim of certain rights. In the first case, the person may turn to the courts, whose function is to consider the "individual in general." In the second, he or she might turn to lawmakers, who have the power to create norms applicable to specific groups.[15] Thus we have two distinct ways of conceiving equality in a society confronted with inequalities due to discrimination.

Finally, the struggle against discrimination can lead to two diametrically opposed ends: *separatism* (the extreme case of imposing specific norms) or *indistinctness* (ending discrimination by imposing indifference). In the first case, you get *identity politics*, to borrow the American term. Identity politics is a response to the fact that the experience of discrimination creates groups of people who have been excluded or disrespected. In the United States in the late 1960s, some black leaders turned away from the integrationist goals of the early civil rights movement in favor of a new separatist identity politics. Radical feminists later followed a similar course. Subsequently, other "identitarian communities" demanded special rights of their own. Universalism, based on abolition of distinctions and shared humanity, ceased to be the fundamental principle of this new egalitarianism of identity. Society was instead understood as comprising a number of different groups, all of which were to be treated equally. Diametrically opposed to this view was what the French call the "republican" approach, which views society in radically abstract terms. But no less than the identitarian approach, the republican approach also denies the individualism of singularity.

The Question of Equality of the Sexes

The question of gender equality is the key to a history of equality because it is situated at two crucial intersections. The first of these is the intersection between singularity and similarity, and the second is the relation between singularity and difference. For a long time the condition and rights of women were determined by essentialization and naturalization of their singularity, which became the grounds for denying their similarity to men. "The two sexes are not equal; *to treat them as equal is to denature them*," was the way Rétif de la Bretonne summed up the issue in the eighteenth century.[16] Sex was seen as the equivalent of a species in a physical if not moral sense. Woman was not man's equal because she was not like him. There were qualitative differences between the sexes. During the French Revolution, women were therefore denied the right to vote because they were not authentic individuals.[17] They were seen as mere constituent parts of the "family body," whereas man was not only an authentic individual but the head of that body.[18] At the turn of the nineteenth century, the political exclusion of women was therefore a sign that revolutionary individualism had failed to complete its task in two senses: anthropologically, in defining the status of women, and sociologically, in shaping the perception of the family. Women thus floated between the old and the new, between corporate society and individualistic society. Madame Germaine de Staël captured the situation perfectly: "The social existence of women remains in many respects uncertain. . . . As things stand, women for the most part belong neither to the natural order nor to the social order."[19] At the same time, the difference between men and women was not seen as the generic expression of a form of singularity.

Although the similarity of men and women is today fully recognized, the basis of their equality remains surprisingly vague. Nearly everyone agrees that they enjoy equal rights, but the discrimination to which women are subjected in many areas suggests that the issue is far from resolved in either cultural or intellectual terms. This judgment is partly corroborated by the very variety of the arguments proposed to defend their cause. In France, for example, the debate on parity for women (in political representation) mobilized both universalist and differentialist arguments.[20] To resolve this dilemma, Mill was the first to suggest treating gender equality in terms of the *relation* between men and women. For him, the issue was the "fitness to live together as equals."[21] In other words, the question of women's rights was first of all a question of their *relation* to men and not simply of their possession of certain attributes.

Men and women do not exist separately at first only to enter into communication later on. Relation is the very condition of their existence.[22] They are "individuals in relation," whether as cooperators or competitors. Indeed, they constitute the best possible example of an equality of singularities. "In gender difference," Étienne Balibar suggestively argues, "we are dealing with a supplementary singularity. . . . Equality here is not neutralization of differences (equalization) but a necessary and sufficient condition of the diversification of freedom."[23] Precisely so. Gender relations are thus the most powerful expression of the individualism of singularity. The gender distinction is fundamental to a deeper understanding of the egalitarian ideal and a laboratory for exploring ways to intertwine similarity and singularity ever more closely. Republican abstractions must therefore be viewed with a skeptical eye, as must the idea that gender distinctions will ultimately disappear.[24]

Ethics and Politics of Singularity

If we are to establish a society of singularities, individuals must first be given the means that achieving singularity requires. Social policies must be redirected toward that end. In addition to passive monetary transfers (such as unemployment insurance, income support, negative taxes, etc.), which can compensate for the loss, inadequacy, or absence of income, individuals must be equipped with the tools they need to achieve autonomy. There is nothing original about this proposition. It has been extensively explored since the mid-1990s by proponents of the "capabilities approach" such as Martha Nussbaum and Amartya Sen, and it has also been embraced by writers like Esping-Andersen and others who have incorporated the theory of human capital into their work on reforming social institutions such as schools and health care systems.

There is no need to enter into the details of this work here. The important point is that in one way or another it views social policy as an instrument in the construction of the individual subject. The goal is to remove obstacles that limit the individual's view, confine him to his condition, and prevent him from hoping for a different future. These goals lead to policies that partake in one way or another of an expansive interpretation of equality of opportunity. In this respect, the way forward is clear in principle, although proponents of a more legalistic view of equal opportunity continue to resist. The problem now lies with the resources devoted to making these policies work. They are expensive, because they require that public action be tailored to individual cases rather than entire groups.[25] If taxpayers are to pay for such programs, the expense must be seen as socially legitimate. Therefore, the implementation of an active singularity policy cannot be separated from the development of policies of reciprocity and communality, which we will examine more closely in a moment.

This individualization of public policy marks a new departure with an important consequence: it blurs the line between the work of private associations and charitable organizations on the one hand and government action on the other. The new "service state" or "enabling state" is not simply a distributor of benefits and administrator of universal rules. In one way or another it enters into the lives of individuals and evaluates their behaviors. The very notion of *rights* has been redefined as a result, in the course of developing criteria of freedom and autonomy.

If social rights are modeled on civil and political rights, they are seen as attributes of the universal individual. Access to allocations and services is considered to be automatic and unconditional. Individualization is inconceivable in such a framework. There is only one way out of this dilemma: social rights must be defined as *procedural*.[26] The norm then becomes *fairness of treatment* (where "fair" means that everyone has an equal right to equivalent treatment), so that the needs of the singular individual can be taken into account. The development of procedural rights of this sort marks a new stage in the evolution of the individual's relation to society. As formulated by natural right theorists in the seventeenth century, the classic subjective right aimed to protect the individual from the prerogatives of government. Promoting individual autonomy meant keeping the powers-that-be at arm's length. Classical rights drew an inviolable boundary around the individual, creating a protected space.

Social rights were originally modeled on this kind of subjective right. This approach ceases to be adequate, however, when the content of a right involves the social relation itself. The constitution of a society of singularities therefore requires rights of a new kind. Little work has been done on this, however. Some have invoked the notion of "care," but this has been used mainly to avoid the issue by shifting attention to situations outside the realm of law. To be sure, the idea of care rightly calls attention to the fact that principles of justice are not enough to found a humane politics and that it is important to distinguish two dimensions of ethics: the elaboration of just *rules* (the pole of generality) and the definition of forms of *attentive behavior* (the pole of particularity). But we also need new notions of social rights and public policy.[27] Instead of attempting to manage the general and the particular separately, attention must be focused on singularity in public policy.

This new approach to social rights and public policy may entail new risks and injustices, and these have to be dealt with as well. Within the classical social rights framework, benefits are automatic and can be managed administratively in such a way as to guarantee equality for all. A more individualized approach, involving a form of *judicialization of the social,* is acceptable only if there is a possibility of appeal in order to reduce the likelihood of arbitrary treatment by social workers. Individuals must be able to challenge decisions easily. What is needed is something other than the equivalent of courts with complicated procedures that would be difficult for individuals to deal with. Rather, there should be some form of representation for clients of the social support system. The principles on which various agencies operate should be widely published, and mediators should be available to hear client complaints. Only then can the individualization of the social hope to avoid an insidious return to outmoded forms of social paternalism.

This question forces us to consider the possible ambiguities of singularity. Singularity is a consequence of individual fulfillment, but it can also be turned against the individual. We see this in modern firms. Firms call upon each of their employees to invest their special talents in the success of the firm. In return, the distinctive gifts of the individual employee are recognized. But this reward is often coupled with a coercive imperative to commit body and soul to the firm. "Be independent! Be responsible! Take the initiative!" Such appeals to the individual employee to demonstrate his or her mettle can easily become orders, with the result that individuals are caught in what psychologists call a "double bind," which can be a source of mental pressure and stress. Individualization as emancipation may therefore end in fragilization of the individual.[28]

Reciprocity

Interest, Altruism, and Reciprocity

"Rational choice theory" is still the dominant paradigm for explaining human behavior in the social sciences. According to the theory, individuals, before taking any decision, will compare the costs and benefits of different courses of action in order to maximize their self-interest. In other words, the theory is based on the paradigm of *homo oeconomicus,* which is useful in that it lends itself to ready modeling. This explains its appeal, especially to those who aspire to give social analysis the appearance of mathematical rigor. Yet there is no shortage of examples of the theory's fragility. For instance, it is difficult to explain on rational-choice grounds why anyone votes, since the influence of any one vote is negligible, while the act of voting imposes costs in terms of traveling to the polls and gathering information. Or again, why deny oneself the comfort of using water freely when consumption is restricted during a summer drought? If individuals were rational, self-interested decision makers, as the theory posits, they would not vote and would not see any reason to curtail their selfish use of water. Other explanatory factors must therefore be considered.

Many authors have looked into alternatives to rational choice such as limited rationality and disinterestedness.[29] There is also a vast literature on gifts and altruism, in which these subjects are studied from the standpoints of anthropology, economics, sociology, ethics, and even biology.[30] A century ago, the anarchist Peter Kropotkin, a trained zoologist, was one of the first to call attention to the importance of cooperative behavior in certain animal species, refuting Darwin's "liberal" interpretations.[31] Evolutionary biologists have since explored the issue in great depth,[32] while a number of authors have studied empathy in animals.[33] Meanwhile, social scientists have become increasingly interested in the idea of *reciprocity.*

What we find, in fact, is that man is neither completely selfish nor truly altruistic. He is always a composite of both in proportions that vary with the individual and the circumstances. By contrast, reciprocity is an essential part of his makeup. Some go so far as to speak of *homo reciprocus* or *homo reciprocans*.[34] Reciprocity can be defined as equality of interaction. It is similar in character to procedural equality, which Tocqueville regarded as the only rule that everyone could accept in a society in which everyone was seeking to rise at the same time.[35] Furthermore, there is consensus about the reciprocity rule because it stems from a principle of equilibrium in social relations. Some argue that it therefore constitutes an essential social and cultural norm as universal as, say, the incest taboo.[36] The equilibrium on which it depends takes two forms: equilibrium of exchange or involvement.

Reciprocity in exchange has been studied ever since Aristotle wrote *The Nicomachean Ethics*. The idea of a reversible relationship (which is the meaning of *reciprocus* in Latin) can be limited to material transactions (market equality is one form of this) or expanded to include symbolic goods, the gift of which entails the obligation to return the favor. To be sure, we must distinguish between market exchange as understood in classical economics and the kinds of "total gift" described by Mauss in his *Essai sur le don*. In both cases, however, reciprocity implies a fair division in exchanges between individuals.

Reciprocity of involvement refers to another type of parity. Its object is the social relation itself, which is simultaneously produced and consumed. It may take various forms, including coproduction of relational goods and parity of social engagement.

The Production and Consumption of Relational Goods

In one of his essays, Simmel writes that "the eye performs a unique sociological function: linking, and establishing reciprocity between, two individuals who are within sight of each other."[37] When two gazes meet, he explains, there is an effect of direct and absolutely pure reciprocity. The social bond created in that moment dissolves immediately afterward. It has no objective basis, unlike speech that is uttered or heard, which has an independent existence. The bond established by the gaze is fragile: it can be destroyed by a slight shift of focus, leaving no trace of its fleeting existence. The exchange of glances is perfectly reciprocal in the sense that "one cannot take in another person at a glance without giving something of oneself." The glance is thus a simple but exemplary form of what we may call a "relational good."

The notion of relational goods is a recent development. It was first proposed in the 1980s by Martha Nussbaum and Carole Uhlaner.[38] The term "relational good" applies to goods that can be possessed only if shared and that are produced and consumed simultaneously. They cannot be consumed by any one individual. Furthermore, they are elective goods and not universalizable: one cannot be everyone's friend or lover. By contrast, respect and recognition are relational goods, even though they can be expressed in a variety of ways. They are in fact *social* goods, founded on a relation of reciprocity. These two social goods are especially valued in a society of singularity. With them, a multitude of singular individuals can form a society while remaining fully themselves. More than that, their attention to singularity becomes the basis of a relation of equality. It is therefore essential to promote and protect these relational goods and to look upon their destruction or erosion as a major threat to social life and individual rights. Hence the law must severely punish forms of contempt, humiliation, and harassment that threaten human dignity and equality.

Reciprocity as Equality of Involvement

Reciprocity can also take the form of equilibrium of social engagement. *Homo reciprocans* does not aspire to strict quantitative economic equality (egalitarianism), which is difficult even to conceive of in a society of singularity. Nor does he seek equality as independence, which is unattainable in a complex economy. By contrast, he is especially sensitive to equality of involvement in civic life. This means that rights and duties should be the same for all, and anything that disrupts equality with respect to institutions and rules is unacceptable. Equality of involvement can be expressed in negative terms as hostility toward free riding, favoritism, and other ways of "taking advantage of the system" that are not available to everyone. These things are the modern form of what used to be called "privilege." Privilege is no longer a matter of legal exceptions or distinctions of birth but rather a form of asymmetry in the relation of individuals to rules and institutions.

This redefinition of privilege can be related to a broadened representation of rights and duties. Rights are no longer seen solely as abstract norms imposed on everyone, nor are they taken to be individual prerogatives, as if they constituted a sort of capital on which everyone may draw at will. An expectation of reciprocity exists, so that rights function as a social institution. Formal equality before the law is no longer enough; actual equality in using the rules that define civic space also matters. In a society of equals, rights therefore function as a constitutive principle. They are always *relational,* whether construed as claims to liberty or to certain assets. Rights are faculties and capabilities that individuals confer on one another in order to *create a society* based on the freedom and responsibility of each and every individual. The state is merely the guarantor and organizer of these relations, which stand on their own. Duties and obligations should be understood in a similar light. They cannot be understood solely as constraints and limits that the authorities impose on individual freedom, or as mere moral injunctions intended to bring individual behavior into line with collective values. They too have a relational character and play a part in the institution of the social. Furthermore, rights and duties can no longer be seen as contrary forces subject to the competing demands of individual autonomy and social constraint. They are convergent and complementary instruments for producing a society of reciprocity, in which each person's commitment and individuality can be simultaneously consolidated.

Tocqueville placed great stress on the idea that selfishness is "to societies what rust is to metal."[39] Today, one might say that the absence of reciprocity is the most important source of corrosion. Many studies have shown that political commitment is conditional, depending on how individuals perceive the commitment of others. More specifically, people are more likely to contribute to collective projects or expenditures if they believe that other citizens feel the same way.[40] Conversely, any perceived disruption of reciprocity can lead to withdrawal in one form or another. Inequality is most acutely felt when citizens believe that rules apply differently to different people or when they see intolerable differences in the way different individuals are treated by certain institutions. They resent the double standard and the sense that they alone are "playing by the rules" while others find a way to circumvent those same rules for their own advantage. Richard Sennett has noted "modern society's hatred of parasitism."[41] Sentiments such as these are a crucial source of social distrust, which in turn undermines the legitimacy of the welfare state and fosters aversion to taxes.

Other consequences include the increasing prevalence of insurance fraud[42] and tolerance of petty corruption,[43] as if these transgressions were justifiable compensation for perceived imbalances. Distrust thus leads to generalized resentment and erosion of the public spirit.

Today, the feeling that reciprocity has broken down is directed primarily at the two extremes of the social ladder. Some point to the fact that the wealthiest members of society contribute proportionally less than others to the collective effort and often find ways to exempt themselves from common rules, most notably in regard to taxation, either by way of specific legal deductions or because they can afford to hire lawyers and accountants to turn complex regulations to their advantage. But those at the bottom of the scale are also viewed with suspicion. The belief that they somehow receive benefits to which they are not entitled has spread insidiously. The welfare regime is deemed to be too generous or too indulgent, and its clients are accused of cheating to obtain benefits. Reality and fantasy have combined to create both a sociological problem and a political problem.

In sociological terms, the crisis of reciprocity is reflected in the malaise of the middle and working classes. Members of these groups who are employed see themselves as doubly penalized: their situations are not bad enough to receive the benefits of the welfare state, yet they are not wealthy enough to enjoy the fiscal and other advantages available to the rich. Politically, their resentment has fueled the rise of the extreme right in Europe. Extreme right-wing parties have capitalized on frustrations due to the diffuse feeling that reciprocity has broken down, directing their fire at both the privileged elite and immigrants said to be taking advantage of the taxpayers' generosity.

Toward a Politics of Reciprocity

If the breakdown of reciprocity is the driving force behind the rise of social distrust and therefore of resistance to greater solidarity,[44] no task is more urgent than to restore reciprocity as a first step toward a society of equals. Two things are needed: a redesign of the mechanisms of solidarity and a return to universalistic policies. In order to separate fantasy from reality when it comes to unequal treatment of individuals and groups, we first need to gain a better understanding of the facts. Equality as reciprocity means above all equality of treatment and involvement. Unless situational inequalities are clearly established, the fantasy machine is free to wreak havoc. Fiscal and social statistics must therefore be made transparent if democratic debate is to be fair and productive. Abuse of the welfare and tax systems must be vigorously opposed in order to maintain confidence in these institutions. No one should be considered a suspect a priori, but the principles of reciprocal involvement and equal treatment must remain intact in the eyes of all. In a society of equals, social rights should be constitutionally guaranteed.

The welfare state has also been undermined by a gradual loss of universalism. The change began imperceptibly in the 1980s. The growing difficulty of financing the welfare state led to a more selective allocation of benefits. The "underclass" of people "excluded" from the labor market became the primary beneficiaries. The redistributive state was transformed into an "assistance state." The concern with reducing inequality gave way to a new concern with alleviating poverty. The latter task is essential, to be sure, but a society of equals must envision its goal in a more democratic, universal way—one that includes the middle class in its mission.

Commonality

There are two ways of looking at citizenship: as a bundle of rights or a social form. The juridical definition is the more familiar of the two. A citizen is clearly an individual member of a community who is protected by the laws governing that community. If he has reached the age of majority, he is also a member of the sovereign body of the people, endowed with the right to vote. Because universal suffrage had to be fought for everywhere, this legal face of citizenship has been fundamentally important. Although the right to vote remains a crucial feature of any democratic regime, citizens in many countries take it so much for granted that they have begun to express disillusionment with what it represents.

Civil citizenship and the notion of human rights that goes along with it have reshaped the very idea of the individual. But citizenship is also a social form. The citizen is not merely an individual endowed with certain rights; he is also defined by his relation to others, his *fellow citizens*. What Émile Benveniste tells us about the etymology of the word *civis* is especially enlightening in this regard.[43] The Latin *civis*, he argues, was originally a term applied to people who shared the same habitat. Implicit in the meaning of the word was a certain idea of reciprocity. It was thus a term of relative order, as can be seen by comparison with the root of the Sanskrit and Germanic words for friend, relative, and ally. The *civis* was a person who joined with his peers in the construction of a *civitas*, a common society. I propose the term "commonality" as a name for this dimension of citizenship, citizenship as a social form, as distinct from its legal dimension.

The Denationalization of Democracies (I):
The Age of Secessions and Separatisms

Commonality was intimately associated with the rights of man and the citizen in the age of the American and French Revolutions. It was also at the heart of the idea of equality as relation. There is no denying that this association is considerably attenuated today. Does the fault lie with an excess of individualism, to the detriment of the general interest? Or is it the outsized importance attached to human rights, to the detriment of the political? It is tempting, perhaps, to pose the question in these terms. The writer Michel Houellebecq gave striking expression to this shift when he won the Prix Goncourt in the fall of 2010: "I am not a citizen," he said, "and I have no desire to become one. We have no duties to our country. No such thing exists. We are individuals, not citizens or subjects. France is a hotel, nothing more."[46] These words reflect a time in which there is apparently no vital need to defend one's community, and in which the idea that the citizens of a country face a common set of ordeals can no longer be taken for granted.

Nevertheless, if we focus exclusively on the tension between the individual and the political, between self-interest and the general interest, we risk missing the essence of the present moment. This tension has been present since the inception of democratic society, although its expression has varied over the years. If, at the beginning of the twenty-first century, collective values command relatively weak assent of citizens of Europe and North America, this calls for historical explanation, but the really important issue of the moment is somewhat different. It has to do with what I propose to call the *denationalization of democracy*.

We see a sign of this denationalization in the collapse of the sociological, not to say anthropological, basis of the shared social order. Take, for example, the *secession of the wealthy:* that is, the fact that the richest sliver of the population now lives in a world unto itself. Tax exiles are the most striking illustration of this. These are individuals who flee their country in order to avoid taxes, overtly seceding from the nation. Legally they remain citizens, but in practice they have ceased to partake of commonality. In Antiquity, the Theodosian Code already denounced *fiscal anchorites,* meaning those who evaded their social obligations by leaving the cities to which they were attached. Doing so put them outside of society, like monks. Today's tax exiles are not numerous, perhaps a few thousand or tens of thousands per country. But many of them are well-known as industrial leaders or athletes or artists, so they have become the most glaring symbol of the separatism of the wealthy. What is more, the gap between the wealthiest 1 percent of the population and the rest has grown so large that it has become explosive. We seem to have reverted to the days when there existed "two separate and hostile nations." When this happened before, in the middle of the nineteenth century, it signaled the beginning of a new revolutionary cycle.

Social change has not been limited to the secession of the wealthy, however. Other forms of separatism have also been at work at all levels of society, as Éric Maurin has shown.[47] There has been a tremendous reorganization of collective identities in recent years, as our sense of social proximity has fragmented. Economists speak of "assortative matching" to explain the tendency of people with similar characteristics to form groups.[48] The notion of similarity has been redefined in light of this phenomenon. It no longer refers to general equality of conditions throughout a given territory. Only a narrow set of sociocultural characteristics count in determining who is similar to whom. The concept of "similarity" has therefore lost its anthropological and democratic dimension. It has become a signifier of class. Contemporary societies are characterized not, as has been alleged, by diffuse "individualism" but rather by generalized social separatism.

What once was common has been dismembered into a set of segregated similarity groups. Rules of avoidance govern contacts between group members. This is especially apparent in the organization of urban space, where the new inequalities manifest themselves most directly. In many countries we find growing numbers of gated communities.[49] Social diversity increasingly expresses itself through the juxtaposition of homogeneous spaces, each isolated from the others. In the United States, neighborhoods and even entire cities are populated by individuals who not only exhibit common social and cultural characteristics but also share the same religious beliefs and even political ideas.[50] At the same time, the least favored groups are forced to live in neighborhoods from which others have fled. Urban space has thus become more and more homogenized. We are living in the age of *homo munitus*,[51] barricaded man, who gathers behind fortress walls in the company of his own kind.[52]

The Denationalization of Democracies (II): Depoliticization and the Return of the Citizen-Owner

The delegitimation of redistributive taxation and the trend toward generalized social separatism are both consequences of depoliticization. The type of depoliticization I have in mind should not be understood in ideological terms, as reflecting, for instance, diminished difference between the right and left, nor as a reflection of decreased citizen interest in the outcome of elections. The problem is deeper, involving a loss of vitality of what has defined the democratic order itself ever since the Greeks, namely, a deliberate effort by people of different sorts to organize life in common. This was Cleisthenes's crucial innovation at the dawn of democracy in ancient Greece. Attica was in the throes of major change at the time, with trade on the increase and populations on the move, and Cleisthenes recognized that society could no longer be understood in terms of fixed groups of families governed by ancestral traditions. In place of this "natural" social organization, he created a more abstract social form capable of accommodating a more complex and composite world.[53] To govern the *demos* that had supplanted the ancient *genos,* he overhauled the political framework in order to "melt" (to use Aristotle's term) the inhabitants of Athens down into a unified civic body.

The creation of Athenian democracy thus involved the establishment of a certain distance between the political order and the newly homogeneous social order. Athenian society had become a composite of people born elsewhere who had to be reconstituted as a political community. It was in this context that the principle of *isonomy* was invoked to create a common space. Laws were adopted to create solidarity among the members of this civic body.[54] In addition to new laws and institutions, the nascent democratic regime promoted new forms of sociability to bring people closer together. For instance, both Aristotle and Plato mention the *syssitia,* or common meals, organized by certain cities.[55] Aristotle remarks on their democratic character and says that the convivial atmosphere of these dinners fostered a sense of equality: "As to common meals, there is a general agreement that a well-ordered city should have them."[56]

This brief historical detour brings us to a key point: a human group that thinks of itself only in terms of a fixed and foreordained homogeneity of any sort is not only nondemocratic, it is also nonpolitical. Yet the secession and separatism that we are witnessing today is taking us back to this type of social organization. Democratic citizenship is being eclipsed by the old figure of the citizen-owner.

In the eighteenth century, the citizen-owner was the positive model and natural referent of political rights. For Enlightenment thinkers, the citizen was a stockholder in the social enterprise. Writing in the *Encyclopedia*, Baron d'Holbach observed that "it is property that makes the citizen; any man who owns property in the state is interested in the good of the state, and regardless of the rank to which he is assigned by particular conventions, it is always as an owner of property, and on account of his possessions, that he must speak, or that he acquires the right to be represented."[57] Here, d'Holbach was merely pointing out something that his contemporaries would have regarded as historically self-evident: the fiscal origin of systems of political representation. The movement for the reform of provincial assemblies in the late 1770s created an intellectual climate in which tax reform went hand in hand with recognition of citizenship. The representation of citizens (as opposed to orders) marked a new departure in politics, reflecting what was already a modern conception of equality, but the idea of the citizen as individual was still a long way off. The three principles of equality, individuality, and universality of political rights had yet to be accepted. The political order was still seen in predominantly "administrative" terms and not yet as a society-defining institution. The new vision would not take hold in France until 1789, but in America it drove the revolutionaries who rose against England in the name of "no taxation without representation." At the time, the theory of the citizen-owner was perfectly consistent with the idea that taxes were a form of quid pro quo for public services. The modern idea of democratic citizenship rejected this model, ultimately culminating in the idea of redistributive taxation, yet some of the old notion of the citizen-owner remained. A striking illustration of this can be seen in the difference between taxation at the national level and taxation at the local level.

In the United States, France, and many other countries, local taxation remains nonredistributive. Local taxes are generally proportional to the value of land and buildings owned by the taxpayer. The assumption is that towns are responsible solely for communal services and bear no responsibility for the corporate social existence of their inhabitants, whereas the national government defines the nation as a social body. This distinction is especially pronounced in France, where the desire to avoid divided sovereignty of any sort has always been strong. Hence towns have always played a purely administrative rather than political role.[58] Interestingly, it was not until the late nineteenth century that a measure adopted during the Restoration, which allowed the largest local taxpayers to participate in municipal council deliberations on borrowing and major public works, was rescinded.[59] This procedure was known as "inclusion of the largest taxpayers," and it had the effect of treating the town as a sort of "syndicate of interests" rather than a political community: the people with the largest interests at stake consequently deserved and received special representation whenever extraordinary expenditures needed to be made. Thus the figure of the citizen-owner continued to be a real presence at the local level. Even after the measure was rescinded, its underlying philosophy remained influential. The 1884 law on the organization of municipal governments, which still defines the system of local government in France, incorporated the idea that municipal councilors are merely administrators who should not assume a political role. In short, local government was conceived on the model of a partnership or condominium association.[60]

The case law established by the Conseil d'État (or Council of State, the highest administrative law body in France) has confirmed the republican vision of local government as "administrative" in nature. With a series of important decisions in the early years of the twentieth century, the council reaffirmed the notion that there was a community of taxpayers distinct from the community as a whole. The point of these decisions was to distinguish between the social existence of the town (as a community of people sharing the same living space) and its economic function as manager of collective expenditures. The great jurist Maurice Hauriou invoked this idea in justification of taxpayer petitions, protesting excessive expenditures by local governments. If voters could punish elected officials politically by voting them out of office, he reasoned, then taxpayers ought to be allowed to petition administrative courts for relief if they believed that their material interests had been harmed. In his remarks, Hauriou distinguished between the *public* (which falls within the purview of politics) and the *collective* (which has to do with the management of town business), stressing the importance of the latter.[61]

The French system repeatedly reinforced this distinction. In recent years, the structure of local governance has been altered by the development of interurban or regional agencies dealing with transportation, waste management, and economic development. These new institutions are explicitly charged with the management of issues affecting a number of towns jointly. Such a reform was needed to reduce the wasteful fragmentation of governance in a country with some 36,700 separate municipal governments (or slightly less than 40 percent of all the local governments in all twenty-seven member states of the European Union combined). Increasingly, these new agencies deal with big-budget projects and other controversial matters. The problem is that they are strictly functional institutions created for some specific purpose, and democratic representation is nonexistent at this level, except via local government representation on agency boards. Hence all the old problems of indirect democracy have reappeared, as decisions are made without input from citizens. The state has begun to transfer more and more functions to these regional agencies, resulting in massive depoliticization. What we see, then, is a quiet extension of government by co-owners, while political democracy, already damaged by secession and separatism, is further weakened.

I chose the French system as an example only because it is the most extreme, but the same general trend can be seen across Europe, where it is often linked to the affirmation of regional identities, thus contributing to another form of separatism. In America one sees a cultural shift in which the taxpayer eclipses the citizen, and "fiscal federalism" is proposed as a way of reducing the redistributive function of the federal government. One also sees a proliferation of private construction in unincorporated areas not under the jurisdiction of any municipality. These places are managed like giant condominiums in which there are no public services; any services provided are paid for privately. Schools, shopping centers, megachurches, theaters, stadiums, and security—all are private services. There are no public parks, no sidewalks, and of course no political activity. These developments are almost always inhabited by whites, who live in a world of their own, where the only law is homogeneity.

The Temptation of Homogeneity

Housing developments in unincorporated areas are one sign of a temptation to replace democracy with homogeneity, which also implies shared identity. This conception of civic space stands at the opposite extreme from Aristotle's original idea of the polis as a place of plurality and mixing.[62] A number of sociologists have recently tried to portray homogeneity in a positive light, as a key ingredient of trust. In an article that attracted a good deal of attention, Robert Putnam argued that the Scandinavian countries have been able to maintain a robust welfare state because they are socially and ethnically homogeneous, thus allowing them to avoid the distrust that has eroded solidarity elsewhere.[63]

The idea that there might be a connection between homogeneity and acceptance of egalitarian principles has a long history in sociology.[64] It is often formulated as part of a culturalist paradigm, but this approach has come in for extensive criticism. As the theory is usually formulated today, the chief methodological problem concerns the meaning of the observed correlation.[65] Two interpretations are possible. It may be that ethnic or cultural diversity is an impediment to solidarity. Or it may be that reduced heterogeneity makes it easier to express egalitarian feelings. At bottom, we need to distinguish between two rival notions of homogeneity. One sees homogeneity as a determinate quality, equivalent to a fixed identity. The other understands it in terms of a *process of homogeneization*, related to an effort to reduce inequalities and engage in a highly deliberative democratic exercise. It may be possible to move in this direction, however, without having to deal with this level of ambiguity.

The Production of the Common

Understood as identity, "the common" is often little more than a catalog of nostalgias and clichés. It can only be conceived of in the singular, moreover, as an unanalyzable brute fact. It is therefore structurally inert and conservative, useless for illuminating the future interpreting ongoing change. What democracy needs in the age of denationalization is a more active, creative concept, a more complex understanding of the common, encompassing three primary dimensions: participation, mutual comprehension, and circulation.

The *common as participation* is the simplest to describe. Events are experienced together, as in a pop concert or sporting event. In the past, carnivals, street dancing, republican banquets, processions, and other public gatherings filled a similar function. The phenomenon may be even more important today than it was in the past, owing, for example, to the construction of ever-larger stadiums and concert halls and to the vigor of the protest ethos. Apart from the *common as celebration and demonstration,* there is also the *reflexive common,* which is a consequence of the fact that everyone is bombarded with the same information about the day's most urgent and pressing social issues. The vitality of a community depends crucially on this, which in turn depends on the curiosity and involvement of citizens as well as on the quality of the media and the free flow of ideas.

This brings us to the *common as mutual understanding.* Mutual understanding depends on meetings, pictures, surveys, narratives, statistics, social analyses, incisive journalism that combines knowledge and observation, interviews, and sociological research. Understanding can help to overcome prejudice and undermine simplistic slogans and conventional wisdom. It depends on the work of intellectuals and journalists, on political activists and government investigators, on the authors of blogs, and on artists who express the life of society in image and song.

The *common as circulation* can be defined in terms of shared space. It usually manifests itself in unspoken forms of civility that nevertheless generate a diffuse kind of knowledge. Fleeting exchanges complement the sense that one has of living alongside others, which helps to develop an egalitarian ethos. Exchanges occur in public transportation, public buildings, and even on the street. People share the constantly shifting scene, which is a product of the quality of the urban environment. This type of exchange is inhibited, however, by barriers of various kinds: by the existence of isolated neighborhoods and enclaves, by social intimidation, and by unwarranted privatization of urban space. The common as circulation is a fragile public good. It decays if public services are allowed to dwindle. Urban policy is therefore at its core and must be a crucial element of any program to revitalize the egalitarian spirit.

These various dimensions of commonality all work together to enhance communal feeling. Many obstacles must be overcome to achieve a democratic outcome, and there is no single way to reach the goal. Many initiatives must be taken, and many experiments tried along the three axes described above. It is essential to bear in mind that the common is by its very nature intertwined with the idea of interaction, of *communication,* as the etymology suggests. *Munus* in Latin implies an exchange, a form of reciprocity, suggesting a gift that is given and that calls for something in return, a complementary gift. It cannot be stressed strongly enough that the common is not a form of property but a kind of relation. A community is a group of people united by a bond of reciprocity, a sentiment of joint exploration, and a shared set of hurdles to be overcome and hopes to be realized.[66]

Toward a General Economy of Equality

How can we be similar and singular, equal and different, equal in some respects and unequal in others? These are important questions today. The future of democracy will depend on how we answer them. In the precapitalist world of the American and French Revolutions, in the age of universalist individualism, they did not arise in these terms. The ideals of similarity, autonomy, and citizenship seemed readily compatible. This was the golden age of equality. The struggle to achieve it had drawn a clear line between its friends and its enemies. The legal principles and institutions that fleshed out the ideal—the rights of man, universal suffrage, the market—were taken as self-evident. Justifications of economic inequality were easily conceived and implemented. The economy of equality was simpler when the society of equals was first conceived. In an age of singularity, we need something more complex. Equality is multidimensional, and the tensions among the various dimensions are greater now than they used to be. There is also more doubt about what kinds of institutions are necessary if equality is to be achieved.

Equality in Difference: A Historical Overview

Although the issues raised in the preceding paragraph are controversial, and the terms in which we discuss them now are new, philosophers dealt with similar questions in the past. Rousseau in particular foresaw that the tension between equality and difference would become the great issue of modern times. At stake was more than just the contrast between the individual and the citizen. An implacable double bind runs through all his discussions of equality. If equality is not the same as leveling, if difference must be tolerated, a problem exists, because difference ramifies throughout the structure of society itself and thus tends to harden into destructive inequality. For Rousseau, the problem could not be solved simply by returning to the state of nature, where the absence of distinction is so complete that the very notion of equality loses all meaning (because equality assumes the ability to compare distinct individuals). Hoping to avoid the twin abysses of undiscriminating absence of differentiation and differentiation so obdurate as to pose a threat, Rousseau found himself drawn to the liberty of solitude. Many commentators have remarked on his frequent use of the adjective *seul* (alone, single, lonely). "A truly happy being is a solitary being," he wrote in *Émile,* while elsewhere he observed that "when one lives alone, men seem more likeable."[67] The idea of an equality forged and mastered by the power of the imagination makes complete sense in this perspective. It is linked, in fact, to a radical incommensurability (equality is unthinkable without some common measure).

Rousseau was not the only writer to explore the "imaginary equality" of isolation. In nineteenth-century America, Ralph Waldo Emerson and Henry David Thoreau built their work on similar themes. In *Der Einzige und sein Eigentum* (The Ego and Its Own), Max Stirner also called for a world of pure particularity, in which an "omnipotent ego" was the symbol of true freedom. For him, a "society of equals" meant a society of freely cooperating "egoists" (a term to which he gave a positive connotation), a collection of radically autonomous individualities. "We must no longer aspire to community," he argued. "Let us look to *particularity* instead. Stop searching for the largest collectivity, for 'human society.' . . . No one is *mon semblable,* but man for me is similar to all other beings, a property."[68] More recently, Roland Barthes described "a socialist utopia of distances," with *idiorhythmia* as the sign of a potential society of equal but radically autonomous individuals.[69]

A more venerable tradition views friendship as a distinctive combination of the similar and the singular. Many classical authors touched on this theme. Plato's *Lysis* as well as books VII and IX of Aristotle's *Nicomachean Ethics,* which are devoted to *philia,* are closely related to these philosophers' more general views of the political constitution of the polis and the rules of social justice.[70] Doing political philosophy means thinking about the ways in which the ideas of commonality, similarity, and equality relate to one another. Friendship is in fact a paradigmatic way of experimenting with this relationship. The essence of friendship is to enjoy spending time together and to share interests, tastes, and judgments. "And the proverb 'What friends have is shared in common' expresses the truth," Aristotle notes.[71] This production of a common environment is inextricably intertwined with a feeling of identity, proximity, and belonging to the same world. Friendship therefore relies on a judgment of close similarity. There is a saying that "Birds of a feather flock together."[72] In this respect we may speak of an *elective* similarity, which establishes total harmony between friends, putting them on the same footing. Friendship is a form of practical sociability, marked by generosity and confidence. It is sustained by overt reciprocity, defined not by an arithmetic equality of exchange but by an insistence that the emotional and moral commitments of both parties are symmetrical. "Friendship," Aristotle observed, "asks a man to do what he can, not what is proportional to the merits of the case."[73] In other words, the principle of justice in friendship is "from each according to his abilities, to each according to his needs." Attention to the singularity of the other is therefore a constituent part of what makes the friendship. Friendship thus embodies the principles of similarity, reciprocity, and commonality. That is one reason why it has a place in political philosophy, if only as a sort of magical metaphor. What makes friendship even more interesting in this context, however, is its relation to difference.

The bond of friendship is exemplary in that it relies on a completely nonquantitative notion of equality. What exists between friends is not a distributive norm but a *relationship* of equality. "When people are friends, they have no need of justice," Aristotle wrote in *Politics*. Friendship can tolerate a degree of economic inequality. But how much? The Stagirite does not say, noting simply that friendship between a man and a god is impossible because the distance between them is incommensurable.[74] To clarify this point, one might suggest a rule: the relationship of equality remains intact as long as the gap in resources between the two friends is not such as to undermine the relationship of commonality, similarity, and reciprocity that unites them. Or, to put it another way, friendship should be understood in terms of a *general economy of equality*, which in each particular friendship assigns the equivalent of "coefficients" of intensity or importance to the various components of the friendship: the feeling of elective similarity, the existence of commonality, and the various expressions of reciprocity. Socrates proposes the following definition of friendship to Menexenes: "It is the tendency of opposites to compensate each other."[75] The stronger these three elements, the less likely the friendship is to be affected by economic inequalities. People who have been through terrible ordeals together sometimes develop indestructible bonds that are unaffected by the subsequent appearance of economic inequalities between them. The closer the friendship, the greater the disproportion it can tolerate. Its capacity for "compensation" is directly proportional to the strength of the structural bond. Conversely, a weak bond is much more vulnerable to inequality.

With the foregoing in mind, it is easy to understand why the temptation to develop a "politics of friendship" adapted to our time was hard to resist. In formulating this aim, Jacques Derrida stressed the need to "conceive of an alterity without hierarchical difference" in order to reconstitute democracy.[76] Unfortunately, he demonstrated the difficulty of the problem without finding a solution. The model of friendship, like the prospect of an equality of solitary individuals, may be useful as a tool of thought, but neither can serve as the basis of a political philosophy. The reason is simple: friendship is not universalizable, because it is based on an elective bond, and a society of equal but isolated individuals is simply impossible in a developed economy. Hence today, the relation between equality and difference must be conceived in political, juridical, and institutional terms.

We can imagine doing this in three ways: in a positive mode, based on an articulation of the three principles of singularity, reciprocity, and commonality; in terms of a hierarchical ordering of equality as relation and equality as redistribution; and finally, on the basis of an identification of the turning points in the egalitarian ideal. In the pages that follow, I will not explain in detail how this might be accomplished. As a conclusion to this book, however, I would like at least to outline a broad conceptual approach.[77]

Plural Equality

It is never possible to speak of equality in general and only in the singular. Equality is always associated with some property that individuals have in common, whether it be physical (beauty, intelligence, height, or genetic endowment), psychological (desires, needs, or passions), economic (income or wealth), political (citizenship), cultural (level of education), or what have you. Individuals are therefore always both equal and unequal, since any number of properties may distinguish them to one degree or another. Given the multiplicity of distinguishing factors, total equality would imply an absence of all distinctions, leaving us with the aporias that Deschamps and Rousseau discovered long ago.

Therefore, setting aside the unrealizable and nightmarish form of equality that would result from an utter absence of distinction,[78] we must think in terms of selective equality. This implies a hierarchy of properties, some of which we will declare to be more socially important than others, and therefore not one but several distinct projects of equalization. For instance, one might grant the highest priority to reducing inequalities of income and wealth, or, alternatively, inequalities of access to medical care or education, on the grounds that these properties shape the social structure. Or one might think of a range of different types of equality and inequality. Each individual would enjoy certain advantages while suffering in other respects from certain disadvantages. The criteria of equality and inequality are not entirely objective, however; equality also has a subjective dimension. Economic, social, and cultural variables must be combined with other factors such as self-esteem and individual values. For example, a person may have a low income and still not feel unequal to others with much higher incomes if he or she believes that he or she is culturally "superior" (as is often the case among artists). The categories of inferiority and superiority thus combine with those of equality and inequality (a person might, for instance, be contemptuous of the ostentatious consumption of the nouveaux riches). In this case, we might speak of an *equilibrium inequality* as a social ideal, equilibrium being achieved when no individual considers himself to be in an irreversible or psychologically destructive situation of inequality in a multiplicity of dimensions.

The crucial point in the transition from equilibrium to disequilibrium is the point at which inequalities combine to form a counternature, an insuperable obstacle to greater equality. If we wish to liberate individuals from confinement to the unsatisfactory conditions in which they find themselves, we must design our policies carefully and implement them strategically. The outcome will be determined individual by individual. The politics of singularity becomes important, because each individual must be allowed to develop his or her specific qualities. Increasing individual differences enhances the likelihood of finding equilibrium. This is what Michael Walzer means by complex equality.[79] The goal is to reconcile different categories of inequality by taking a negative approach to equality. Ultimately, it comes down to *reducing* different types of inequality.

Conversely, thinking in terms of relations allows us to take a more positive approach and set realistic goals for achieving a democratic society of equals. In effect, we simplify the idea of equality by relating it to the three ways of being with others: in a relative position, in interaction, and through a bond of participation. Our approach is to bring these three things together and explore their interactions. It is not a question of reconciling "values" such as recognition and justice.[80] It is rather a question of simultaneously developing and optimizing categories of relationships. The affirmation of singularities, the attention to reciprocity, and the development of commonality are not all on the same level. Each type of relation can be developed independently, without competing with the others—a characteristic feature of this form of equality, which is both plural and absolute: absolute in the sense that its concept can be fully realized (indeed, we can envision the advent of a society of equals as a perfectly realistic utopia), and plural, because it conceives of the social bond in terms of its three constitutive figures.

The Lexical Order of Equality

A general theory of equality requires an ordering of its various dimensions. Equality as relation must come first, not only because it defines the spirit of equality but also because it has a universalizing dimension. Everyone can agree that it is preferable to live in a society of equals. Equality as relation is to everyone's advantage: it makes the world a calmer, less dangerous, more convivial place. It also makes it possible to include liberty in a theory of equality, because liberty can also be defined as a relation. It can be seen in terms of relative autonomy and necessary reciprocity. Indeed, equality and liberty are in contradiction only if equality is structurally associated with the state as its agent of realization, while liberty is merely a capacity attributed to individuals. When equality and liberty are understood jointly as social qualities, as relations, they tend rather to coincide.

Equality as distribution and equality as redistribution are secondary concerns. What this means is, first, that a method for redistributing income and resources is acceptable if it does not undermine equality as relation in any of its three dimensions: singularity, reciprocity, and commonality. Conversely, we can justify the direct or indirect limitation (through taxation) of high incomes and inherited wealth on the grounds that these things may impair participation in the common society. In addition, redistribution becomes mandatory when needed to restore degraded commonality, though it must be constrained by the requirement of reciprocity. Thus we have simple criteria that we can use to determine the degree to which economic and social inequalities must be reduced in various areas. To be sure, exact amounts will always be subject to debate and controversy, but at least the terms of the discussion are clearly specified.

Furthermore, to say that equality as redistribution is secondary also means that its legitimation depends on and is subordinate to equality as relation. Redistribution cannot be maintained or expanded unless the vitality of equality as relation is assured. This is an important caveat at a time when the legitimacy of redistribution is being questioned directly or indirectly in many places. If the meaning of taxation is to be restored in order to enable ambitious programs of redistribution, we must first build up equality as relation and make it the centerpiece of political action.

The Poisons of Equality

In order to grasp fully the nature of equality, we must also consider the structural factors that threaten to destroy it. Three in particular stand out: social reproduction, extravagance, and separatism. These define the limits beyond which economic inequalities become destructive poisons. Since the eighteenth century, these dangers have been denounced in both the United States and France by way of attacks on privileges, luxury, and corruption of the civic bond. Lately, however, they have taken on increased importance, and ways of dealing with them have also changed.

Start with social reproduction, defined as the transmission of structural factors of inequality, such transmission being the modern equivalent of hereditary privilege. Existing social differences are at some point transformed into inexorable fates imposed on subsequent generations. In a world in which the distribution of wealth shows signs of reverting to nineteenth-century patterns, this has become a crucial issue. Hence the laws of inheritance and inheritance taxes have become important determinants of social justice. On this point, we would do well to review some of the bold proposals made by nineteenth-century liberals and socialists who also pondered the issue.[81]

Extravagance is another destructive feature of contemporary society. It cannot, however, be regulated as in the past by moral and social dicta alone (as in the eighteenth century, with its praise of frugality). Today's imperatives stem from ecological limits to economic growth. The mania for ever-greater accumulation—an important source of the growth of inequality—can only be controlled by moving to a new developmental model. Sobriety has become a condition for the survival of the human race. In any case, economists point out that a new developmental model is needed because growth will inevitably stabilize at around 1 or 2 percent. In addition, the reduction of economic inequality must be linked to "decommodification," which will require the development and sharing of public goods.[82] In a world in which income and wealth inequalities persist, public goods and public spaces are important as means of correcting the harmful effects of these forms of inequality. In this context, commodification is not simply a sign of problems with market mechanisms but also a factor in the shrinkage of egalitarian public space.

The third and final poison threatening equality is separatism of one kind or another. Separatism undermines the very basis of equality by demolishing the principle of commonality. It is more damaging to the spirit of equality than the simple fact of quantitative difference. Separatism affects the very way in which space is organized, the structure of the national territory; hence action to curb its destructive potential is essential. All pro-egalitarian politics must therefore begin with a dynamic urban policy designed to increase the number of public spaces and ensure greater social mixing.

A World of Equality?

What is the proper extent of the egalitarian imperative? Is it not morally essential to envision equality as extending to the entire world? Why should a society of equals not be a world of equals? The bond of humanity stands at the opposite extreme from the bond of friendship, to take our paradigmatic figure for equality within difference. Although both may stem from the same source (as the etymology of the word "philanthropy" suggests[83]), the philanthropic spirit is quite different in its application from the egalitarian spirit. Philanthropy depends on a maximal differentiation of individual situations and a minimal definition of equality. For the philanthropist, similarity is limited to mere recognition that the object of his gift is, like himself, also a member of the human race. Philanthropy is therefore directed against threats to this common humanity: the risk of starvation or disease, the threat of civil war and genocide, subjection to humiliation or slavery, or discrimination on the basis of background or lifestyle.

International organizations seek to combat such affronts to the human condition as well as to formulate laws that might be used to punish them. There has been an undeniable globalization of this aspect of the egalitarian spirit. People everywhere belong to the same human race—the point has been driven home repeatedly. But in this context the reduction of economic inequalities is but a minor consideration. Just a little over 1 percent of global output goes into sustaining "human solidarity," whereas democratic welfare states devote up to 50 percent of their output to either direct redistribution of wealth or provision of public services. In short, the tie of humanity, along with the recognition of singularity, revolves around a fairly limited conception of equality and coexists with a certain indifference to social inequalities.

Poverty does not really elicit solidarity unless it is extreme enough to pose an existential threat (as in the case of famine or epidemic), and even then it is limited by the fact that it involves different peoples living in alien worlds. Commonality is not a goal of humanitarianism conceived in such terms. Boundaries—between states, subcontinents, and development zones—physically delineate the different types of solidarity.

Will the globalization of inequality[84]—by which I mean the fact that inequalities nowadays do not divide nations in general (except in Africa) but rather exhibit similar characteristics everywhere— change the way we see the phenomenon? The question is important. At the end of the eighteenth century, the difference in *average* income between the most developed and the poorest countries was 3:1, but within each country there were enormous variations.[85] By the end of the twentieth century, the wealth gap between nations had increased considerably (74:1). Conversely, inequalities within the developed countries diminished considerably until 1990. Hence the problem of justice at the international level became central. In structural terms, we are headed back toward the pattern of the eighteenth century. What will be the consequences of this change? Paradoxically, it seems likely that the result will be greater indifference to inequality within countries. Globalization has led, as we have just seen, to a limited definition of equality in humanitarian terms rather than to a demand for greater commonality. Nations are growing closer together, while the class divide is growing wider in both the material and psychological senses. Classes are thus once again becoming the equivalent of separate nations within the nation, as they were in the nineteenth century. Global inequality is becoming mixed up with social inequality. That is why the *renationalization* of democracy (through greater social cohesion and reappropriation of the political by citizens) is one way of combating both simultaneously. This struggle must therefore be a top priority for our time.

NOTES

1. Major works on the subject include Thomas Piketty, *Les Hauts revenus en France au xxe siècle: Inégalités et redistributions* (1901–1998) (Paris: Hachette, "Pluriel," 2006); Thomas Piketty and Emmanuel Saez, "Income Inequality in the United States, 1913–1998," *Quarterly Journal of Economics* 118, no. 1 (2003): 1–39; Anthony Atkinson and Thomas Piketty, eds., *Top Incomes over the Twentieth Century: A Contrast between Continental European and English-Speaking Countries*, 2 vols. (Oxford: Oxford University Press, 2007) (an incomparable mine of statistics). For the United Kingdom, see also the in-depth study by the Government Equalities Office, *An Anatomy of Economic Inequality in the UK* (London, 2010). For an overview of Organisation for Economic Co-operation and Development (OECD) countries, see *Growing Unequal? Income Distribution and Poverty in OECD Countries* (Paris: OECD, 2008). On the recent explosion of high incomes in France, see Camille Landais, *Les Hauts Revenus en France (1998–2006): Une explosion des inégalités?* (Paris: Paris School of Economics, 2007). The figures given below come from these works.

2. In France, the average disposable income (after transfers and taxes) of the wealthiest 0.01 percent rose to seventy-five times that of the bottom 90 percent.

3. Thomas Piketty, "On the Long-Run Evolution of Inheritance: France, 1820-2050" (working paper, Paris School of Economics, May 2010).

4. On this point see Marc Barbut, *La Mesure des inégalités: Ambiguïtés et paradoxes* (Geneva: Droz, 2007).

5. Data taken from the cited works of Thomas Piketty.

6. Jasper Roine and Daniel Waldenström, "The Evolution of Top Incomes in an Egalitarian Society: Sweden, 1903-2004," Working Paper Series in Economics and Finance, no. 625, Stockholm School of Economics, 2006.

7. In *Œuvres du comte P. L. Rœderer*, vol. 3 (Paris, 1854), pp. 8-9 (though written in 1815, the work was not published until 1830).

8. The words are Jacques Necker's, from his *Du Pouvoir exécutif dans les grands États* (1792), in *Œuvres complètes de M. Necker*, vol. 8 (Paris, 1821), p. 285.

9. See the international poll on perceptions of social justice in twelve countries, commissioned in 2010 by the Fondation Jean-Jaurès (France), the Brookings Institution (United States), and the Fondation européenne d'études progressistes (Brussels). Australia, the United States, and the Netherlands stood out as exceptions in the otherwise uniformly negative findings.

10. The results were presented in Michel Forsé and Olivier Galland, eds., *Les Français face aux inégalités et à la justice sociale* (Paris: Armand Colin, 2011). The data cited hereafter come from this work.

11. Bossuet famously said that "God laughs at men who complain of the consequences while cherishing the causes." This paradox can also be understood as a composition effect: heterogeneous sources of discontent can add up, whereas reasons to act and goals of action must be positively determined.

1. THE INVENTION OF EQUALITY

1. Abbé Sieyès, *Essai sur les privilèges* (1788), in *Qu'est-ce que le tiers état?* (Paris: PUF, 1982), p. 9.

2. Alexis de Tocqueville, *De la démocratie en Amérique,* vol. 2, ed. Eduardo Nolla (Paris: Vrin, 1990), p. 146; translated as *Democracy in America,* trans. Arthur Goldhammer (New York: Library of America, 2004) (henceforth cited as AG), p. 655.

3. Quoted in Sieyès, *Essai sur les privilèges,* p. 26.

4. See Daniel Teysseire, "De l'usage historico-politique de *race* entre 1680 et 1820, et de sa transformation," *Mots,* no. 33 (1982): 43.

5. See Arlette Jouanna, *L'Idée de race en France au xvie siècle et au début du xviie,* review ed., vol. 1 (Montpellier: Université Paul-Valéry, 1981), p. 16. See also André Devyver, *Le Sang épuré: Les préjugés de race chez les gentilshommes français de l'Ancien Régime (1560–1720)* (Brussels: Éditions de l'Université, 1973).

6. Sieyès, *Essai sur les privilèges,* p. 10.

7. See Jacques Guilhaumou, "Aristocrate(s), aristocratie (1789–1793)," in *Dictionnaire des usages socio-politiques (1770–1815),* fasc. 1 (Paris: Klincksieck, 1985).

8. On the importance of hierarchical order and the circumstances surrounding its critique, see Gordon S. Wood's chapters on "Hierarchy" and "The Assault on Aristocracy" in *The Radicalism of the American Revolution* (New York: Vintage Books, 1993).

9. Gordon S. Wood, *The Creation of the American Republic, 1776–1787* (New York: W. W. Norton & Company, 1976), p. 74.

10. Ibid., p. 122.

11. Quoted in Wood, *The Radicalism of the American Revolution,* p. 341.

12. Jean-Paul Rabaut Saint-Étienne, August 18, 1789, *Archives parlementaires,* ser. 1 (henceforth cited as *AP*), vol. 8, p. 452.

13. Tocqueville, *De la démocratie en Amérique,* vol. 1, p. 13; AG, p. 12.

14. Ibid., vol. 2, p. 28; AG, p. 496.

15. See Jeremy Waldron, *God, Locke, and Equality: Christian Foundations of John Locke's Political Thought* (Cambridge: Cambridge University Press, 2002).

16. On the importance of this text, see Jean Reviron, *Les Idées politico-religieuses d'un évêque du ixe siècle: Jonas d'Orléans* (Paris: Vrin, 1930).

17. Jack P. Greene, *All Men Are Created Equal: Some Reflections on the Character of the American Revolution* (New York: Oxford University Press, 1976).

18. Sylvain Maréchal, "Égalité naturelle." Maréchal was the future author of the celebrated *Manifeste des égaux* (1801); the article was signed by Louis de Jaucourt.

19. Here I am following the analysis of Buffon's thinking in Michèle Duchet, *Anthropologie et histoire au siècle des Lumières* (Paris: Maspero, 1971), pp. 230–234.

20. Buffon, *Œuvres* (Paris: Gallimard, "Bibliothèque de la Pléiade," 2007), p. 407.

21. Quoted in the article "Espèce" in the *Encyclopédie*.

22. See the article on "Similitude ou ressemblance" (similarity and resemblance) in the *Encyclopédie*.

23. On this point, see the incisive analyses of Célestin Bouglé, *Les Idées égalitaires* (Paris: Alcan, 1899). The best edition of this text is edited by Serge Audier, who provides a substantial preface (Bordeaux: Éditions Le Bord de l'eau, 2007).

24. Reproduced in *AP,* vol. 8, p. 404; emphasis added.

25. Letter dated 1731, in *Correspondance complète de Jean-Jacques Rousseau,* ed. Ralph Alexander Leigh, vol. 1 (Oxford: Voltaire Foundation, 1965), p. 13.

26. Rousseau, *Émile, ou De l'éducation* (1762), in *Œuvres complètes,* vol. 4 (Paris: Gallimard, "Bibliothèque de la Pléiade," 1990), p. 470.

27. Jean Starobinski, Introduction to the *Discours sur l'origine et les fondements de l'inégalité parmi les hommes* (Paris: Gallimard, "Folio," 1989), p. 15.

28. Published in 1689.

29. Lettre no. 62, January 20, 1721, John Trenchard and Thomas Gordon, *Cato's Letters,* in *The English Libertarian Heritage,* ed. D. L. Jacobson (New York: Bobbs-Merril, 1965), p. 131.

30. On this theme, see Bernard Bailyn, *The Ideological Origins of the American Revolution* (Cambridge, Mass.: Belknap Press of Harvard University Press, 1967), pp. 232–235.

31. The term "indentured" came from the form of this contract, which was initially executed in two copies on one sheet of paper and then cut in two, with one copy going to the immigrant and the other to the person financing his travel. The indented edge of the paper was sealed to prove the authenticity of the document, hence the name.

32. See Richard Brandon Morris, *Government and Labor in Early America* (New York: Harper Torchbooks, 1965), and Abbot Emerson Smith, *Colonists in Bondage: White Servitude and Convict Labor in America, 1607–1776* (Chapel Hill: University of North Carolina Press, 1947).

33. In speaking of exchanges in certain societies, Mauss wrote: "At bottom, these are mixtures. One mixes souls in things; one mixes things in souls. One mixes lives, and in that way persons and things combined emerge from their proper spheres and mingle: precisely this is the contract and exchange." See *Essai sur le don,* in Marcel Mauss, *Sociologie et anthropologie* (Paris: PUF, 1978), p. 173.

34. This was a favorite idea of Sieyès, who borrowed it from Adam Ferguson's *Essay on the History of Civil Society* (London, 1767).

35. On French representations of this liberalism, see Simone Meyssonnier, *La Balance et l'Horloge: La genèse de la pensée libérale en France au xviiie siècle* (Paris: Les Éditions de la Passion, 1989), esp. the passages devoted to Vincent de Gournay.

36. See Emma Rothschild, *Economic Sentiments: Adam Smith, Condorcet, and the Enlightenment* (Cambridge Mass.: Harvard University Press, 2001) esp. chapter on "Apprenticeship and Insecurity."

37. John Millar, *Observations sur les commencemens de la société,* trad. fr. (Amsterdam, 1773), p. 320.

38. See Michael Ignatieff, "John Millar and Individualism," in Istvan Hont and Michael Ignatieff, *Wealth and Virtue: The Shaping of Political Economy in the Scottish Enlightenment* (Cambridge: Cambridge University Press, 1983).

39. On this point, see the work of J. G. A. Pocock. For a discussion of Pocock's analysis, see the thesis of Marie P. McMahon, *The Radical Whigs, John Trenchard and Thomas Gordon* (Lanham, Md.:

University Press of America, 1990), esp. the chapter on "Cato and the Country Category."

40. James Steuart, *An Inquiry into the Principles of Political Economy* (1767), edited and with an introduction by Andrew S. Skinner, vol. 1 (Edinburgh: Oliver & Boyd, 1966), p. 203.

41. Ibid., p. 211.

42. Bertrand Barère, *Premier Rapport fait au nom du Comité de salut public sur les moyens d'extirper la mendicité dans les campagnes, et sur les secours que doit accorder la République aux citoyens indigents* (Paris, 22 Floréal an II), p. 3.

43. Nicolas de Condorcet, *Esquisse d'un tableau historique des progrès de l'esprit humain* (1794) (Paris: Vrin, 1970), pp. 203–204. With these words he began his description of the tenth and final epoch in the history of man, entitled "On the future progress of the human spirit."

44. Ibid., p. 204.

45. Ibid., p. 212. Furthermore, according to Condorcet, equality of education would help to reduce differences of talent to distinctions that would no longer create barriers between human beings. Although he was merely parroting common sense on this point, he was more original in envisioning ways in which circumstantial inequalities might be reduced: he imagined a system of old-age insurance based on an "application of the calculus of probabilities to live," which would make it possible to "fight chance with chance" in order to eliminate forms of dependency and misery due to life's accidents. Ibid., p. 213.

46. Ibid., p. 212.

47. Quotes are from the edition of *Olbie* included in Jean-Baptiste Say, *Œuvres diverses* (Paris, 1848), pp. 595–601.

48. Here I am following the richly documented work of Bernard Bailyn.

49. For a good description of this culture, see J. R. Pole, "Equality, Status, and Power," in *Thomas Jefferson's Virginia* (Williamsburg: Colonial Williamsburg Foundation, 1986).

50. For an introduction to this topic, see the chapter entitled "The Small Republic" in Herbert J. Storing, *What the Anti-Federalists Were For* (Chicago: University of Chicago Press, 1981).

51. On this point see James Livesey, "Agrarian Ideology and Commercial Republicanism in the French Revolution," *Past and Present* 157, no. 1 (1997).

52. "The people" is simultaneously the *sum* and *form* of the collection of individuals.

53. See his well-known comments in Karl Marx, *The Jewish Question* (1844) and the remarks of Cornelius Castoriadis, "Valeur, égalité, justice, politique: De Marx à Aristote et d'Aristote à nous," *Textures,* no. 12-13 (1975).

54. Sieyès, *Qu'est-ce que le tiers état?* (Paris: Au siège de la société, 1888).

55. See Claude Lefort, *L'Invention démocratique* (Paris: Fayard, 1981), p. 148.

56. For France, see Alain Garrigou, *Les secrets de l'isoloir* (Paris: Magnier, 2008). For Australia, see John Henry Wigmore, *The Australian Ballot as Embodied in the Legislation of Various Countries* (Boston: C. C. Soule, 1899). The use of a voting booth is called the "Australian ballot" in English-speaking countries because it was first used in the state of South Australia in 1857.

57. New light has been shed on the subject by Patrice Gueniffey, *Le nombre et la raison: La Révolution française et les élections* (Paris: Éditions de l'Ecole des hautes etudes en sciences sociales, 1993) and Philippe Tanchoux, *Les procédures électorales en France de la fin de l'Ancien Régime à la Première Guerre mondiale* (Paris: CTHS, 2004).

58. Condorcet was apparently the only person to propose a secret individual ballot as a reflection of his belief that the vote ought to be a deliberate exercise of individual reason. On this point, see Gueniffey, *Le nombre et la raison,* pp. 302-303.

59. See Henry Babeau, *Les Assemblées générales des communautés d'habitants en France, du xiiiᵉ siècle à la Révolution* (Paris, 1893).

60. See Serge Aberdam et al., *Voter, élire pendant la Révolution française, 1789-1799* (Paris: CTHS, 1999), p. 457.

61. Second-stage assemblies met more frequently and for longer periods, up to eighty days per year in 1790 and 1791.

62. Abbé Sieyès, "Notes sur l'éthocratie," in *Des manuscrits de Sieyès, 1770–1815*, vol. 2, ed. Christine Fauré (Paris: Champion, 2007), pp. 544–545. He also used these expressions in *Journal d'instruction sociale*, no. 5 (July 6, 1793): 146.

63. Speech by Jérôme Pétion de Villeneuve, August 11, 1791, *AP*, vol. 29, p. 358.

64. Petition from the voters of the Hérault, quoted in Jean Belin, *La Logique d'une idée-force: L'idée d'utilité sociale pendant la Révolution française* (Paris: Hermann, 1939), p. 459.

65. Ibid., p. 460; emphasis added.

66. Ibid., p. 137.

67. Speech of October 28, 1789 (*AP*, vol. 9, p. 596). The reflection on civic inscription as a ceremony of social insertion fits in with the individualist perspective of the inclusion of the individual in society. By contrast, as we will see, the great revolutionary festivals celebrated the people primarily as the collective subject of sovereignty.

68. Judith Shklar, *American Citizenship: The Quest for Inclusion* (Cambridge, Mass.: Harvard University Press, 1991), p. 27.

69. Mainly in primary assemblies (abstention in second-stage assemblies was much lower).

70. Shklar, *American Citizenship*, p. 16.

71. The words are those of Gay-Vernon, bishop of Limoges, quoted in Mona Ozouf, *La Fête révolutionnaire, 1789–1799* (Paris: Gallimard, 1976), p. 236.

72. *Rapport sur la confection du calendrier*, 24 octobre 1793, *AP*, vol. 77, p. 500.

73. The phrase is borrowed from Jean Starobinski, *1789, ou les Emblèmes de la raison* (Paris: Flammarion, 1979).

74. Ozouf, *La Fête révolutionnaire*, p. 152.

75. Ibid., p. 177.

76. Charles-Alexandre de Moy, *Des fêtes, ou quelques idées d'un citoyen français, relativement aux fêtes publiques et à un culte national* (Paris, an VII [1799]), p. 2.

77. On this point, see the very illuminating work of Michael Zuckerman, *Peaceable Kingdom: New England Towns in the Eighteenth Century* (New York: Alfred Knopf, 1970), and Zuckerman, "The Social Context of Democracy in Massachusetts," *William and Mary Quarterly* 24, no. 4 (October 1968).

78. Caraceux de La Chaolotais, *Essai d'éducation nationale* (Paris, 1763).

79. See the critical edition of the *Essai d'éducation nationale,* ed. Robert Granderoute (Paris: CNRS Éditions, 1996).

80. Honoré-Gabriel Riquetti De Mirabeau, *Travail sur l'éducation publique* (1791), in *Une éducation pour la démocratie: Textes et projets de l'époque révolutionnaire,* ed. Bronislaw Baczko (Paris: Garnier, 1982); emphasis added.

81. For an interpretation, see Michel de Certeau, Dominique Julia, and Jacques Revel, *Une politique de la langue: La Révolution française et les patois* (Paris: Gallimard, 1975).

82. See my discussion of "equalizing monopolies" in *L'État en France de 1789 à nos jours* (Paris: Seuil, 1990), pp. 106–108.

83. At the time, the word "assimilation" was used primarily in the fields of nutrition and physiology.

84. See his formulations in Abbé Seiyès "Sur le projet de décret pour l'établissement de l'instruction nationale," *Journal d'instruction sociale,* no. 5 (July 6, 1793): 146.

85. Paul Henri Thiry d'Holbach, *Éthocratie: Ou le gouvernement fondé sur la morale* (1776) (Paris: Éditions d'histoire sociale, 1967). The work defended the need for common mores in order to establish a patriotism based on justice, fraternity, and unity. Recall that Tocqueville would later come up with the celebrated phrase "habits of the heart." See Tocqueville, *De la démocratie en Amérique,* vol. 1, p. 223.

86. Fauré, *Des manuscrits de Sieyès,* vol. 2, p. 549.

87. Tocqueville was not the first to use this expression. The liberals of the Restoration used it before him. François Guizot, for example, spoke of "community of condition" to characterize modern society. The socialist Pierre Leroux also used it independently of the author of *Democracy in America*. It was also used more directly in one of the first works to treat American mores, Achille Murat's *Esquisse morale et politique des États-Unis* (1832) (see next chapter). For a precise history of the expression, it is important to note that Tocqueville, as he mentions in his manuscript, was struck "like the others" by the extreme equality of conditions in America. See Tocqueville, *De la démocratie en Amérique,* vol. 1, p. 3. The reference to the others was expunged from the published version, however.

88. Tocqueville, *De la démocratie en Amérique,* vol. 2, p. 98.

89. Sieyès, *Qu'est-ce que le tiers-état?* p. 88; emphasis added.

90. Adam Smith, *Theory of Moral Sentiments* (London: A. Millar, 1790), IV.1.10.

91. See John Shovlin, *The Political Economy of Virtue: Luxury, Patriotism, and the Origins of the French Revolution* (Ithaca, N.Y.: Cornell University Press, 2006).

92. Gabriel-François Coyer, *Dissertation sur le vieux mot de patrie* (1755), critical edition in Edmond Dziembowski, *Écrits sur le patriotisme: L'esprit public et la propagande au milieu du xviiie siècle* (La Rochelle: Rumeur des âges, 1997), pp. 45–49; emphasis added.

93. Montesquieu, *De l'esprit des lois* (1748), Book V, chap. 6, in *Œuvres complètes,* vol. 2 (Paris: Gallimard, "Bibliothèque de la Pléiade," 1979), p. 280.

94. Rousseau, *Discours sur l'économie politique* (1755), in *Œuvres complètes,* vol. 3, p. 258.

95. Rousseau, *Du contrat social,* Book II, chap. 11, in ibid., pp. 391–392.

96. See *Mémoire des pensées et des sentiments de Jean Meslier,* in *Œuvres complètes,* vol. 1 (Paris: Anthropos, 1971), p. 17.

97. See Shovlin, *The Political Economy of Virtue,* p. 195.

98. It was not until 1828 that it was published by Philippe Buonarroti in his *Conspiration pour l'égalité, dite de Babeuf I* (Paris, 1850).
99. Included in Benjamin Franklin, *Mélanges d'économie politique*, vol. 1 (Paris, 1847), pp. 650–656.
100. Franklin urged his fellow citizens to be "thrifty, industrious, and free."
101. On this vision of a society of virtue and frugality, see Wood, *The Creation of the American Republic, 1776–1787*, pp. 114–118.
102. Rousseau, *La Nouvelle Héloïse* (1761), in *Œuvres complètes*, vol. 2, p. 608. "Beggars," he continued, "are unhappy because they are always beggars."
103. Abbé Sieyès, *Fragments politiques* (approx. Spring 1793), in *Des manuscrits de Sieyès*, vol. 1, ed. Christine Fauré, p. 472.
104. Sieyès also spoke of "active equality" in this connection.
105. Rousseau, *La Nouvelle Héloïse*, part 5, VII, pp. 608–609.
106. Rabaut Saint-Étienne, "De l'égalité" (2nd article), *Chronique de Paris*, no. 21 (June 21, 1793): 43.
107. Ibid.
108. See Michel Borgetto, *La Notion de fraternité en droit public français* (Paris: LGDJ, 1993).
109. By the oath of July 14, 1790, all French citizens swore "to remain united by the indissoluble bonds of fraternity." Quoted in Marcel David, *Fraternité et Révolution française* (Paris: Aubier, 1987), p. 58.
110. Mona Ozouf, "Fraternité," in François Furet and Mona Ozouf, *Dictionnaire critique de la Révolution française* (Paris: Flammarion, 1988), p. 740.
111. Liveries were distinctively colored uniforms that the domestic servants of noble houses were obliged to wear.
112. *Protestation de cent trente-huit gentilshommes contre le décret du 19 juin 1790* (Paris, 1790). See also the individual protests, some of which were published in *AP*, vol. 16, pp. 379–386.
113. Protest of Roch-Hyacinthe, vicomte du Hautoy (*AP*, vol. 16, p. 380).

114. There was a large literature on this during the Revolution. See, for example, Nicolas Prevost, *Véritable civilité républicaine à l'usage des citoyens des deux sexes,* Rouen, Year II.

115. The quotes are from an article published in the *Mercure national* on December 14, 1790. Quoted in Alphonse Aulard, "Le tutoiement pendant la Révolution," *La Révolution française* 34 (June 1898). Note that Montesquieu himself regarded *"vous* as a defect of modern languages" and said that its use "shocked nature." Ferdinand Brunot, *Histoire de la langue française,* vol. 9, in *La Révolution et l'Empire* (Paris: Armand Colin, 1937), p. 689.

116. See Albert Soboul, *Les Sans-culottes parisiens en l'an II* (Paris: Librairie Clavreuil, 1958), p. 655.

117. Quoted in Alan Forrest, "Respect et reconnaissance dans la France révolutionnaire," in *La Considération,* ed. Claudine Haroche and Jean-Claude Vatin (Paris: Desclée de Brouwer, 1998), p. 70.

118. For an introduction to the abundant literature on the subject, see Claudine Haroche, "La civilité et la politesse: Des objets 'négligés' de la sociologie politique," *Cahiers internationaux de sociologie,* vol. 94, 1993.

119. Sieyès, *Fragments politiques,* pp. 470–471.

120. On this point, see Gordon S. Wood, *Empire of Liberty: A History of the Early Republic, 1789–1815* (New York: Oxford University Press, 2010).

121. See the definitions given by James Fenimore Cooper in "An Aristocrat and a Democrat," in *The American Democrat* (Cooperstown, N.Y., 1838). For him, the two terms encapsulated the opposition of "the smaller number" and "the greater number," of special interests and the general interest, of selfishness and generosity.

122. See the examples given in John Ashford, *"Agrarians" and "Aristocrats"* (Cambridge: Cambridge University Press, 1987).

123. For an overview of European visitors to the United States, see the anthology of words and images compiled by d'Aurelian Craiutu and Jeffrey C. Isaac, eds., *America through European Eyes: British and*

French Reflections on the New World from the Eighteenth Century to the Present (University Park: Pennsylvania State University Press, 2009).

124. On the little-known Jacquemont, see Aurelian Craiutu, "In Search of Happiness: Victor Jacquemont's Travels in America," *The European Legacy* 13, no. 1 (2008).

125. Achille Murat, *Esquisse morale et politique des États-Unis* (Paris, 1832), p. 371.

126. Michel Chevalier, *Lettres sur l'Amérique du Nord,* vol. 2 (Paris, 1836), p. 408.

127. It is worth noting that nearly all of these travelers were so struck by the distinctness of America that they saw it in contrast to what they took to be the common traits of Europeans. The comparison was always America versus Europe.

128. The Beaumont quotes are from Gustave de Beaumont, *Marie: Ou l'Esclavage aux Etats-Unis,* vol. 1 (Paris, 1835), pp. 224–228.

129. Herman Melville offered a striking illustration of what we might call "equality of elevation" in his novel *Mardi* (1849), in which he described the manners of a utopian republic called Vivanza, in which all citizens were equally entitled to be considered kings: "We are all Kings here; royalty breathes in the common air" (chap. 158).

130. Chevalier, *Lettres sur l'Amérique du Nord,* vol. 2, p. 410.

131. Even though "boss" came from the Dutch *boss,* which in fact meant "master." The semantic aspect was therefore decisive. On this hypocrisy, see the remarks of Cooper in *The American Democrat.*

132. Tocqueville, *De la démocratie en Amérique* II.3.5, vol. 2, p. 159; AG, p. 677.

133. On this point see Wood, *The Radicalism of the American Revolution,* pp. 342–343.

134. Joyce Appleby, *Inheriting the Revolution: The First Generation of Americans* (Cambridge, Mass.: Harvard University Press, 2000).

135. Frances Trollope, *Domestic Manners of the Americans,* vol. 2 (London, 1832), p. 298.

136. Achille Murat, *Exposition des principes du gouvernement républicain, tel qu'il a été perfectionné en Amérique* (Paris, June 1833), pp. 358–359. The book was dedicated to Andrew Jackson.

137. See Wood, *The Radicalism of the American Revolution,* p. 170.

138. This phrase, from a later period, was due to the German jurist Rudolf von Jhering, quoted in Bouglé, *Les Idées égalitaires,* p. 243.

139. Bear in mind that this was a *British* right, granted by the colonial authorities.

140. Estimates vary widely, from 40 to 80 percent. See Robert J. Dinkin, "The Suffrage," *Encyclopedia of the North American Colonies,* vol. 1, New York, 1993.

141. See d'Alexander Keyssar, *The Right to Vote: The Contested History of Democracy in the United States* (New York: Basic Books, 2000), pp. 22–23, which is the definitive reference on the subject.

142. See Chilton Williamson, *American Suffrage: From Property to Democracy, 1760–1860* (Princeton, N.J.: Princeton University Press, 1960).

143. Shklar, *American Citizenship,* p. 16.

144. See Keyssar, *The Right to Vote,* pp. 34–42.

145. François Guizot, speech to the Chamber, March 14, 1838, in *Histoire parlementaire de France,* vol. 3 (Paris, 1864), p. 153.

146. See my *Le Sacre du citoyen: Histoire du suffrage universel en France* (Paris: Gallimard, 1992).

147. *Bulletin de la République,* no. 4, March 19, 1848. Declaration drafted by Lamartine; emphasis added.

148. This faith in the socially regenerative effects of universal suffrage was also central to Chartist doctrine in Britain.

149. *Bulletin de la République,* no. 9, March 30, 1848.

150. Eugène Pottier, "Le vote universel," in *Œuvres complètes* (Paris, 1966), p. 48.

2. THE PATHOLOGIES OF EQUALITY

1. Jean de Sismondi, *De la richesse commerciale* (Geneva: Paschoud, 1803).

2. Jean-Baptiste Say, *Traité d'économie politique* (Paris: Deterville, 1819).

3. Jean de Sismondi, *Nouveaux principes d'économie politique,* vol. 1, 2nd ed. (Paris, 1827), p. xxii.

4. Ibid., vol. 2, p. 345.

5. J. de Sismondi, "Comment les manufactures contribuent-elles au bonheur national?" in *Études sur l'économie politique,* vol. 2 (Paris, 1837), p. 331. This passage contains an anticipation of the celebrated aphorism of Engels, according to which manufacturing produces both cotton and paupers.

6. M. Rubichon and L. Mounier translated some of these in *Extraits des enquêtes et des pièces officielles publiées en Angleterre par le Parlement depuis l'année 1833 jusqu'à ce jour, accompagnés de quelques remarques faites par les éditeurs,* 6 vols. (Paris, 1840–1843).

7. Baron d'Haussez, *La Grande-Bretagne en mil huit cent trente-trois,* 2 vols. (Paris, 1833).

8. Maurice Rubichon, *Du mécanisme de la société en France et en Angleterre* (Paris, 1833), p. 244.

9. Eugène Buret, *De la misère des classes laborieuses en Angleterre et en France,* vol. 2 (Paris, 1840), p. 50.

10. See Louis-Pierre Dufourny de Villiers, *Cahiers du quatrième ordre, celui des pauvres journaliers, des infirmes, des indigents, etc., l'ordre sacré des infortunés,* no. 1 (April 1789).

11. Buret, *De la misère des classes laborieuses,* vol. 2, p. 51.

12. Ibid., p. 46.

13. Saint-Marc Girardin, *Journal des débats,* December 8, 1831, reproduced in the author's *Souvenirs et réflexions d'un journaliste* (Paris, 1859). Subsequent quotes are from the same article. On the comparison of proletarians to ancient barbarians, see Pierre Michel, *Un mythe romantique, les barbares (1789–1848)* (Lyon: PUL, 1981).

14. Albert Laponneraye, *Lettre aux prolétaires,* February 1833, p. 1.

15. Quoted in Iouda Tchernoff, *Le Parti républicain sous la monarchie de Juillet* (Paris: Pedone, 1901), p. 203.

16. Société des amis du peuple, *Procès des Quinze* (Paris, 1832), p. 9.

17. On this point see "De la véritable démocratie," in Albert Laponneraye, *Mélanges d'économie sociale, de littérature et de morale,* vol. 2 (Paris, 1835), esp. pp. 180–183.

18. Quoted in Louis Chevalier, *Classes laborieuses, classes dangereuses* (Paris: Hachette, "Pluriel," 1978), p. 598.

19. Benjamin Disraeli, *Sybil, or the Two Nations* (London, 1845), esp. book 2, chap. 5.

20. Alban de Villeneuve-Bargemont, *Économique politique chrétienne* (1834; reprint, Bruxelles, 1837), p. 15.

21. Buret, *De la misère des classes laborieuses,* vol. 2, pp. 1–2.

22. Alphonse Grignon, *Réflexions d'un ouvrier tailleur sur la misère des ouvriers en général* (Paris, 1833), p. 2.

23. Prospectus, September 22, 1830.

24. See, for example, Charles Gilles, "Les mineurs d'Utzel," in the anthology *La Voix du peuple,* vol. 1 (Paris, 1848), p. 33.

25. Pierre-Joseph Proudhon, *Système des contradictions économiques, ou Philosophie de la misère* (1846), vol. 1, new ed. (Paris, 1923), p. 340.

26. Buret, *De la misère des classes laborieuses,* vol. 2, p. 49.

27. For example, Villeneuve-Bargemont referred to the aristocracy of money and industry as a new feudal elite, "far more despotic and aggressive and a thousand times harsher than the feudalism of the Middle Ages." See the chapter entitled "D'une féodalité nouvelle," in book 1 of his *Économie politique chrétienne.*

28. Buret, *De la misère des classes laborieuses,* vol. 2, pp. 23–25.

29. The formula originated in Proudhonian circles. On this point see my *Modèle politique français* (Paris: Seuil, 2004); trans. by Arthur Goldhammer as *The Demands of Liberty* (Cambridge, Mass.: Harvard University Press, 2005).

30. Abel Transon, *De la religion saint-simonienne: Aux élèves de l'École polytechnique* (Paris, 1830), p. 47.

31. See *La Voix du peuple,* vol. 1, p. 257, and vol. 2, p. 43.

32. Contemporary analyses often blurred the differences, however.

33. Charles Comte, *Traité de législation, ou Exposition des lois générales suivant lesquelles les peuples prospèrent, dépérissent ou restent stationnaires,* 4 vols. (Paris, 1826). See vol. 4.

34. Quoted in Villeneuve-Bargemont, *Économie politique chrétienne,* p. 154.

35. Ibid.

36. Félicité de Lamennais, *Le Livre du peuple* (Paris, 1838), p. 23.

37. See, for example, Louis Blanc, "De l'esclavage aux Colonies," *Revue du progrès* 3 (January 15, 1840).

38. See Charles Sellers, *The Market Revolution: Jacksonian America, 1815–1846* (New York: Oxford University Press, 1991), and John Lauritz Larson, *The Market Revolution in America: Liberty, Ambition, and the Eclipse of the Common Good* (New York: Cambridge University Press, 2010).

39. Jonathan A. Glickstein, *Concepts of Free Labor in Antebellum America* (New Haven, Conn.: Yale University Press, 1991), p. 43.

40. See Eric Foner, *Free Soil, Free Labor, Free Men: The Ideology of the Republican Party before the Civil War* (Oxford: Oxford University Press, 1970).

41. Historians today would probably agree that America in this period was defined by tension between a still-vigorous faith in the ability of each individual to master his own fate and the rise of capitalism, whose transformative power was not yet recognized.

42. Published in the *Boston Quarterly Review,* July 1840; reprinted in *The Early Works of Orestes A. Brownson: The Transcendentalist Years, 1840–1841,* ed. Patrick W. Carey, vol. 5 (Milwaukee, Minn.: Marquette University Press, 2004).

43. Ibid., p. 306.

44. An ideology is a system of representations that parries all critiques of a social order by making it seem that the principles on which it is based are self-evidently just. Socially determined outcomes are thus treated as irrefutable logical deductions.

45. Louis René Villermé, *Tableau de l'état physique et moral des ouvriers,* vol. 2 (Paris, 1840), p. 346.

46. Ibid., p. 343. Workers did not appreciate the improvement in their condition, he argued, because it created "new needs" that spurred desires and distorted judgment (ibid., p. 348).

47. Ibid., p. 344.

48. Buret, *De la misère des classes laborieuses,* vol. 1, p. 68.

49. He uttered these words in January 1832 during the inaugural lecture of his course on Germany. Quoted in Michel, *Un mythe romantique,* p. 215.

50. Honoré Antoine Frégier, *Des Classes dangereuses de la population dans les grandes villes,* 2 vols. (Paris, 1840).

51. Joseph-Marie de Gérando, *De la bienfaisance publique,* vol. 1 (Paris, 1839), p. 304. Note that in 1826 he spoke of indigence as a "factitious cause" of misery: "The unfortunate do indeed suffer, but by their own fault. This is the usual case, as well as the most important to study." See *Le Visiteur du pauvre,* 3rd ed. (Paris, 1826), p. 27.

52. Ibid., p. 302.

53. Ibid., p. 303.

54. Vol. 7, p. 362. Quoted in Gérando, *De la bienfaisance publique,* vol. 1, p. 305.

55. For an overview of contemporary attitudes toward the subproletariat, see Gareth Stedman Jones, *Outcast London: A Study in the Relationship between Classes in Victorian Society* (Oxford: Clarendon Press, 1971).

56. The use of the word "responsibility" in this sense came later, but what it referred to was incorporated at the time in the meaning of "virtue."

57. See Françoise Barret-Ducrocq, *Pauvreté, charité et morale à Londres au xixe siècle* (Paris: PUF, 1991).

58. Charles Dunoyer, *De la liberté du travail,* 3 vols. (Paris, 1845). Quotes are taken from *Œuvres de Charles Dunoyer* (Paris, 1870), which includes vols. 1 and 2.

59. Ibid., vol. 1, p. 345.

60. Ibid., p. 352. "It tends to ensure that the most industrious, energetic, and courageous, the best disciplined and most prudent, are also the happiest and freest of men."

61. A defining characteristic of ideology.

62. Dunoyer, *De la liberté du travail,* vol. 1, p. 352, for this and the following two citations.

63. Charles Dunoyer, *Des objections qu'on a soulevées ces derniers temps contre le régime de la concurrence* (Paris, 1841), p. 38.

64. Quotations here are from *Œuvres complètes de M. Necker,* vol. 10 (Paris, 1821).

65. Ibid., p. 466 (and p. 350 ff. for the following quote).

66. Alexis de Tocqueville, *De la démocratie en Amérique,* vol. 2, ed. Eduardo Nolla (Paris: Vrin, 1990), pp. 182, 265; translated as *Democracy in America,* trans. Arthur Goldhammer (New York: Library of America, 2004) (henceforth cited as AG), p. 818.

67. These two themes were not superimposed in the (Romantic) artistic critique of bourgeois platitude.

68. Nikolai Berdyaev, *The Philosophy of Inequality* (1923).

69. François Guizot, *Du Gouvernement de la France depuis la restauration et du gouvernement actuel,* 3rd ed. (Paris, 1821), p. xxxii.

70. Ibid., p. xxiv.

71. Ibid., pp. xxv–xxvi.

72. Ibid., p. 106; emphasis added. The phrase "factitious inequality" was also used by many other writers at the time. The contrast with natural inequality, which was deemed acceptable, was a central tenet of conservative-liberal ideology.

73. François Guizot, *Des moyens de gouvernement et d'opposition dans l'état actuel de la France* (Paris, 1821), pp. 157–158.

74. It is obviously important to point out the difference between scientific progress in general, the selective attention of the public, and the ideological use of science.

75. See Georges Lanteri-Laura, *Histoire de la phrenology: L'homme et son cerveau selon F. J. Gall* (Paris: PUF, 1970).

76. One should be careful to distinguish phrenology from craniometry. The latter involved measuring the size, weight, shape, and appearance of the skull. In many cases the same motives accounted for interest in both procedures.

77. Indeed, the word "talent" was directly applied to certain functions in Gall's classification.

78. On the reasons for Gall's intellectual and social success in France, see Alphonse Esquiros, *Paris, ou les sciences, les institutions et les mœurs au xixe siècle*, vol. 1 (Paris, 1847), pp. 288–425.

79. Some of his lectures were published as Pierre Leroux, *Cours de phrénologie* (Jersey, U.K., 1853).

80. Lanteri-Laura, *Histoire de la phrénologie*, pp. 149–150. Gall visited a prison and claimed to be able to detect "theft organs" by feeling the heads of prisoners.

81. See the lengthy article on phrenology by Napoléon Barthel in *Almanach de la communauté pour 1843* (Paris: Dézamy, 1843).

82. Stephen Jay Gould, *The Mismeasure of Man* (New York: Norton, 1981).

83. See Guy Avanzini, *Alfred Binet* (Paris: PUF, 1999), and François-Louis Bertrand, *Alfred Binet et son œuvre* (Paris: Alcan, 1930).

84. The ministry wanted an early means of detecting students who might experience great difficulty in school in order to orient them toward special courses of instruction.

85. Binet calculated the pupil's overall intellectual level by subtracting the mental age from the biological age. Later, it was proposed to divide the former by the latter (hence the idea of a "quotient"). This change was introduced by a German psychologist in 1912 and eventually adopted everywhere. For a technical overview of the subject, see Serge Nicolas and Bernard Andrieu, eds., *La Mesure de l'intelligence (1904–2004): Conférences à la Sorbonne à l'occasion du centenaire de l'échelle Binet-Simon* (Paris: L'Harmattan, 2005).

86. Simon's preface to Alfred Binet and Théodore Simon, *La Mesure du développement de l'intelligence chez les jeunes enfants* (Paris: Société Alfred-Binet, 1931), p. xxviii.

87. See the collection of articles edited by Ned Joel Block and Gerald Dworkin, *The IQ Controversy: Critical Readings* (New York: Pantheon Books, 1976). Walter Lippman expressed skepticism as early as 1922 in a series of articles published in *The New Republic*.

88. See Nicholas Lemann, *The Big Test: The Secret History of the American Meritocracy* (New York: Farrar, Straus & Giroux, 1999), and John Carson, *The Measure of Merit: Talents, Intelligence, and Inequality in the French and American Republics, 1750–1940* (Princeton, N.J.: Princeton University Press, 2007).

89. In *The Bell Curve: Intelligence and Class Structure in American Life* (New York: Free Press, 1994), Richard J. Herrnstein and Charles A. Murray claimed to show that IQ was the explanatory variable that determined social position and behavior. The book was particularly controversial for its assertion that ethnic groups can be differentiated by IQ.

90. To gauge the influence of social Darwinism, see Mike Hawkins, *Social Darwinism in European and American Thought, 1860–1945* (Cambridge: Cambridge University Press, 1997); Richard Hofstadter, *Social Darwinism in American Thought* (New York: Braziller, 1959); and Jean-Marc Bernardini, *Le Darwinisme social en France (1859–1918): Fascination et rejet d'une idéologie* (Paris: Éditions du CNRS, 1997).

91. See Louis-René de Caradeuc de La Chalotais, *Essai d'éducation nationale* (1763), esp. pp. 45–46. Quotations are from this work.

92. Denis Diderot, *Plan d'une université ou d'une éducation publique dans toutes les sciences* (1775), in *Œuvres complètes,* éd. chronologique, vol. 11 (Paris: Club français du livre, 1971). Quotes can be found on pp. 749–750 (emphasis added) and 849–850.

93. We find various versions of these sentiments in the work of Guizot and Victor Cousin. For example, Guizot explained the need for strict limits on access to secondary education: "For the happy, talented few who can usefully be rescued from their initial condition by scientific and classical education, how many mediocrities acquire tastes and habits incompatible with the condition to which they must revert and who, once removed from their natural sphere and made uncertain of their path in life, produce little and become ingrates and malcontents dependent on others and on themselves." Quoted in Pierre Rosanvallon, *Le Moment Guizot* (Paris: Gallimard, 1985), pp. 247–248.

94. See Pierre Rosanvallon, "Rationalisme politique et démocratie en France (XVIIIᵉ–XIXᵉ siècles)," *Zinbun: Annals of the Institute for Research in Humanities,* no. 29, 1994.

95. Reproduced in *Archives parlementaires,* ser. 1 (henceforth cited as *AP*), vol. 74, pp. 233–236. Subsequent quotations are taken from this text.

96. The phrase is from Victor Cousin, *De l'Instruction publique en Hollande* (Paris, 1837), p. 220.

97. See *Rapport de Fourcroy au Conseil des Cinq-Cents sur le projet de loi relatif à l'instruction publique,* 30 Germinal an X (April 19, 1802), in *Procès-verbaux du Comité d'Instruction publique, de la Convention,* reprint, vol. 1 (Paris: L'Harmattan, 1998), pp. 193–194.

98. Chambre des députés, *Tableau des élèves du gouvernement dans les Collèges royaux* (Paris, March 1834).

99. Hippolyte Carnot, *Le Ministère de l'Instruction publique et des Cultes, (February 24 to July 5, 1848)* (Paris, 1848), p. 19.

100. On the import and educational consequences of his principle that "all men are equal in intelligence," see Joseph Jacotot, *Journal de l'émancipation intellectuelle,* 2 vols. (1829–1830). See also the book about him by Jacques Rancière, *Le Maître ignorant: Cinq leçons sur l'émancipation intellectuelle* (Paris: 10/18, 2004).

101. Both his *Étude sur le mandarinat français* and his pamphlet *Des privilèges de diplôme et d'école,* were reprinted in Jean-Gustave Courcelle-Seneuil, *La Société moderne: Études morales et politiques* (Paris, 1892).

102. He used the expression in Henri Marion, "Réflexions sur les récompenses scolaires," *Revue internationale de l'enseignement* 11 (January–June 1886): 423.

103. Guizot, *Du gouvernement de la France depuis la restauration,* p. 106. He contrasted this with caste society, defined as a society "divided into distinct and immobile classes."

104. For a contemporary assessment of this difference, see Christian Baudelot and Roger Establet, *L'élitisme républicain en France* (Paris: La République des idées-Seuil, 2008).

105. Pierre Leroux, *Aux Philosophes: De la situation actuelle de l'esprit humain* (1831), quoted in David O. Evans, *Le Socialisme romantique: Pierre Leroux et ses contemporains* (Paris, 1948), p. 213.

106. Philarète Chasles, *Études sur les hommes et les mœurs au xix* siècle (Paris, 1849), p. 253.

107. Félix de La Farelle, *Plan d'une réorganisation disciplinaire des classes industrielles de la France* (1842), reprinted in *Du Progrès social au profit des classes populaires non indigentes*, 2nd ed. (Paris, 1847), p. 466.

108. Laurent de l'Ardèche, "De la foi et de l'examen," *Le Producteur* 2 (1826): 538.

109. See, for example, a two-part article by Prosper Enfantin, "Considérations sur les progrès de l'économie politique dans ses rapports avec l'organisation sociale," *Le Producteur* 4 and 5 (1826).

110. Robert Owen, *A New View of Society and Other Writings*, ed. Gregory Claeys (London: Penguin, 1991), pp. 358–359.

111. See the article "Concurrence" in the *Dictionnaire de sociologie phalanstérienne* by Édouard Silberling (Paris, 1911).

112. Louis Blanc, *L'Organisation du travail*, 5th ed. (1839; reprint, Paris, 1847), pp. 27–32.

113. Ibid., pp. 272–273.

114. On the "corporatist culture" of the early workers' movement, see, for France, William H. Sewell, *Work and Revolution in France: The Language of Labor from the Old Regime to 1848* (Cambridge: Cambridge University Press, 1980).

115. On Blanc's views, see Francis Démier, "Louis Blanc face à l'économie de marché," in *Louis Blanc, un socialiste en République* (Paris: Créaphis, 2005).

116. The quote is from Anthime Corbon in "De la concurrence," *L'Atelier*, January 30, 1850.

117. See Louis Blanc's account of the much-discussed tailors' cooperative in Clichy in *Histoire de la Révolution de 1848*, vol. 1 (Paris, 1880), pp. 194–199.

118. On these grounds Marx launched a violent attack on Proudhon in his *1844 Manuscripts*. For his critique of the rights of man, see

his classic analyses in *The Holy Family* (1844) and his 1843 response to Bruno Bauer's *The Jewish Question*.

119. See Claude Francis and Fernande Gontier, *Partons en Icarie: Des Français en utopie: une société idéale aux États-Unis en 1849* (Paris: Perrin, 1983), and *Recueil de prédications de la Religion saint-simonienne*, 2 vols. (Paris, 1832).

120. See Robert Owen, *Report to the County of Lanark* (London, 1820).

121. Friedrich Engels, *Description des colonies communistes surgies ces derniers temps* (1845), reprinted in Friedrich Engels and Karl Marx, *Utopisme et communauté de l'avenir* (Paris, 1976). Like Owen, Engels particularly admired the Shakers.

122. Friedrich Engels, *Discours d'Ebenfeld* (1845), in *Utopisme et communauté de l'avenir,* p. 35.

123. For a thorough study of the history of the term "communism," see Jacques Grandjonc, *Communisme/Kommunismus/Communism: Origine et développement international de la terminologie communautaire prémarxiste, des utopistes aux néobabouvistes, 1785–1842,* vol. 1: *Historique* (Trier, Germany: Karl-Marx-Haus, 1989).

124. Among the pamphlets I have in mind were those written by Jean-Jacques Pillot, Richard Lahautière, and Albert Laponneraye. The texts published by this group were collected in the second series of the collection *Les Révolutions du xixᵉ siècle (1834–1848),* vols. 6–8, *Révolutionnaires et néo-babouvistes de 1835 à 1847* (Paris: EDHIS, 1979). For an overview, see Alain Maillard, *La Communauté des égaux: Le communisme néo-babouviste dans la France des années 1840* (Paris: Kimé, 1999).

125. On Marx and the French neo-Babouvists, see Michael Löwy, *La Théorie de la révolution chez le jeune Marx* (Paris: Maspero, 1970).

126. *Le Populaire,* November 1844.

127. Théodore Dézamy, *Code de la communauté* (Paris, 1842), p. 11, for this and subsequent quotations.

128. Jules Gay, an associate of Dézamy, explained it this way in *Le Communiste:* "We want to unite all families in one big family, one

really big family: all children will be the children of all. All the elderly will be everyone's elderly. . . . In the general family, there must not be small individual families, for otherwise the general family would be torn apart." Quoted in Maillard, *La Communauté des égaux,* p. 109.

129. Étienne Cabet, *Voyage en Icarie* (1839), 5th ed. (Paris, 1848), p. 105.

130. Pierre Leroux, *Aux Politiques: De la politique sociale et religieuse qui convient à notre époque* (1832), in *Œuvres de Pierre Leroux,* vol. 1 (Paris, 1850; reprint, Geneva: Slatkine Reprints, 1978), p. 156.

131. Quoted by Bruno Viard in his introduction to the anthology of Pierre Leroux, *À la source perdue du socialisme français* (Paris: Desclée de Brouwer, 1997), p. 35.

132. Robert Owen, *Textes choisis,* trans. Paul Meier (Paris: Éditions sociales, 1963), p. 133.

133. Cabet, *Voyage en Icarie,* p. 197; see esp. chap. 25, "On Newspapers."

134. Ibid.

135. Here I do not discuss the differences among these authors concerning the way in which the communitarian order was to be established. Cabet counted on the pressure of public opinion, while others sought to cajole wealthy and powerful individuals into financing their experiments. Dézamy and the neo-Babouvists took a more revolutionary line, calling for a dictatorship of the proletariat.

136. See part four of *Code de la nature,* "Model of legislation in conformity with nature's intentions."

137. See Babeuf, *Fragment d'un projet de décret économique,* among the "supporting documents" for Buonarroti, *La Conspiration pour l'égalité, dite de Babeuf,* vol. 2.

138. Constantin Pecqueur, *La République de Dieu* (Paris, 1844), pp. 245, 314. Pecquer also observed that "unity of belief . . . is a condition of admission. Everyone is orthodox." Ibid., p. 245.

139. Étienne Cabet, *Douze lettres d'un communiste à un réformiste sur la communauté,* 3rd ed. (Paris, 1845), p. 6. Subsequent quotes are from p. 5.

140. "Do we not cultivate thousands of types of roses, daisies, and tulips, or plubs, apples, pears, and grapes? Why can't education do similar wonders for man, nature's cherished child and finest work?" Ibid. Cabet thus radicalized the hygienist-eugenicist ideals of the great reformist physicians of the revolutionary period.

141. Gracchus Babeuf, "Marchons franchement à l'Égalité," *Tribun du peuple,* no. 35, Year IV.

142. Robert Owen, "Report to the County of Lanark" (1820), in Owen, *A New View of Society and Other Writings,* p. 298.

143. Robert Owen, "Address to the Inhabitants of New Lanark," in Owen, *A New View of Society and Other Writings,* p. 124.

144. Here, I pass over the question of the parallel between frugality and abundance as both leading to an extinction of economics. For more, see my *Le Capitalisme utopique* (Paris, 1979), pp. 200-201.

145. Karl Marx and Friedrich Engels, *The German Ideology* (1845). Translated from the French.

146. Karl Marx and Friedrich Engels, *The Holy Family* (1844). Translated from the French.

147. Karl Marx, *Grundrisse* (Moscow: Moscow Books, 1939). Translated from the French; emphasis added.

148. See the chapter on him in Bronislaw Baczko, *Lumières de l'utopie* (Paris: Payot, 1978).

149. Reproduced in Léger-Marie Deschamps, *Le Vrai système,* an anthology of his writing edited by Jean Thomas and Franco Venturi (Paris: Droz, 1939). Quotes are from this edition.

150. Ibid., p. 118.

151. Ibid., p. 122 (p. 123 for the next quote).

152. Ibid., p. 169 (p. 170 for the next quote).

153. On his life and work, see Jean Boissel, *Victor Courtet (1813–1867), premier théoricien de la hiérarchie des races* (Paris: PUF, 1972), and Loïc Rignol and Philippe Régnier, "Races et politique dans l'histoire de France chez Victor Courtet de l'Isle," in *Études saint-simoniennes,* ed. Philippe Régnier (Lyon: PUL, 2002).

154. Victor Courtet, *La Science politique fondée sur la science de l'homme* (Paris, 1838), p. 204.

155. Ibid., p. 396. In a similar spirit, see Gustave d'Eichtal and Ismaÿl Urbain, *Lettres sur la race noire et la race blanche* (Paris, 1839).

156. In liberal and conservative circles, fear among property owners led only to ideological tracts. See, for example, Louis Reybaud, *Études sur les réformateurs contemporains* (1841), and Adolphe Thiers, *De la propriété* (1848). On the left, there was an exception to this rule in the form of a "debate on communism" in the columns of *L'Atelier,* the first important newspaper produced by workers. For a response, see Étienne Cabet, *Réfutation des doctrines de "L'Atelier"* (Paris, 1842).

157. Anthime Corbon, "De la concurrence," *L'Atelier,* January 30, 1850. Subsequent quotes are from this article.

158. Proudhon, *Système des contradictions économiques,* vol. 1, pp. 237, 247. Subsequent quotes are from the same chapter, "Des remèdes contre la concurrence."

159. On this point, see his arguments in the anthology *Solution du problème social* (Paris, 1848).

160. Friedrich List, *The National System of Political Economy,* English trans. by G. A. Matile (Philadelphia, 1856). List thus differed with Fichte, whose *Closed Commercial State* (1800) advocated autarchic protectionism of a political sort.

161. Ibid., p. 77.

162. François Guizot, speech of April 1, 1846 (during a debate about a commercial treaty with Belgium), *Histoire parlementaire de France,* vol. 5 (Paris, 1864), p. 120.

163. Guizot, speech of May 11, 1846, ibid., pp. 134–135.

164. For an informed overview of debates on this subject in this period, see David Todd, *L'Identité économique de la France: Libre-échange et protectionnisme, 1814–1851* (Paris: Grasset, 2008).

165. Charles Dupin, speech of April 14, 1836 (in tariff debate), *AP,* 2nd ser., vol. 102, p. 34.

166. Ibid., p. 35, for this and subsequent quotes.

167. Louis Reybaud, always on the lookout for expressions significant of a particular age, used it in his celebrated *Jérôme Paturot à la recherche d'une position sociale,* illustrated ed. (Paris, 1846), p. 238.

168. Christophe-Joseph-Alexandre Mathieu de Dombasle, *De l'avenir industriel de la France: Un rayon de bon sens sur quelques grandes questions d'économie politique,* 2nd ed. (Paris, 1834), p. 55.

169. Founded in 1846 by Auguste Mimerel, an industrialist from eastern France, who later became president of the Conseil Général des Manufactures. The organization's first objective was to defeat the proposed free-trade treaty with Belgium.

170. Mathieu de Dombasle, *De l'avenir industriel de la France,* p. 26.

171. The distinction is Dombasle's, ibid., pp. 55–57.

172. On this point, see the seminal work of Frank Trentmann, *Free Trade Nation: Commerce, Consumption, and Civil Society in Modern Britain* (Oxford: Oxford University Press, 2008).

173. See Adolphe Thiers, *Discours sur le régime commercial de la France* (Paris, 1851), pp. 22–24, and François Guizot, speech of April 1, 1846, in ibid., pp. 115–116.

174. Charles Dupin, *Bien-être et concorde des classes du peuple français* (1848), in *Mémoires de l'Académie des sciences morales et politiques,* vol. 7 (Paris, 1850), p. 219.

175. Auguste Mimerel, *Du paupérisme dans ses rapports avec l'industrie en France et en Angleterre* (Lille, n.d.), p. 14.

176. Unions began to develop as soon as the ban on them was lifted in 1825. The Labour Party was organized eighty years later, initially to represent the trade unions in the political sphere.

177. *L'Atelier,* November 1846 (vol. 2, p. 406).

178. Karl Marx, "On the Question of Free Trade," 1848. He ended his speech with the words "I vote in favor of free trade." In *Capital* he observed that protectionist duties had "bled the people white." (Book I, sec. 8, chap. 31).

179. *L'Atelier*'s position is significant in this respect. See especially the debate with Bastiat in the newspaper's columns in the fall of 1846. The paper had proposed a Society for the Defense of

Workers to approach the trade issue in terms of the social question rather than of economic theory. The government refused to authorize the society, however.

180. Martin Nadaud, *Léonard, maçon de la Creuse* (1889), reprinted with a preface by Jean-Pierre Rioux (Paris: Maspero, 1976).

181. Eugène Spuller, *Rapport présenté à la Commission d'enquête parlementaire sur la situation des ouvriers de l'agriculture et de l'industrie en France, et sur la crise parisienne,* in *Annales de la Chambre des députés: Documents parlementaires,* regular session of 1884, vol. 2 (annex no. 2695), p. 870. See the chapter entitled "Des concurrences."

182. Previously, the word "protection" referred to the local or guild level.

183. See the "Barodet" (an anthology of campaign platforms) for 1889. See also the comments of Antoine Prost, *Vocabulaire des proclamations électorales de 1881, 1885 et 1889* (Paris: PUF, 1974), pp. 72–74.

184. See his speech of November 23, 1891, on the general tariff in *Discours et opinions de Jules Ferry,* vol. 7 (Paris, 1898), p. 272. This was his key speech on the issue.

185. Quoted in Jean-Marie Mayeur, *Les Débuts de la IIIe République (1871–1898)* (Paris: Seuil, 1973), p. 205.

186. See Herman Lebovics, *The Alliance of Iron and Wheat in the Third French Republic, 1860–1914: Origins of the New Conservatism* (Baton Rouge: Louisiana State University Press, 1988), esp. chap. 2. See also Alan Milward, "Tariffs as Constitutions," in *The International Politics of Surplus Capacity: Competition for Market Shares in the World Recession,* ed. Susan Strange and Royer Tooze (London: Allen & Unwin, 1981).

187. Jules Ferry, preface to Léon Santupéry, *Le Tonkin et la mère-patrie* (1890), in *Discours et opinions de Jules Ferry,* vol. 5 (Paris, 1897), p. 558.

188. See J. A. Hobson, *Imperialism* (1902), and Lenin, *Imperialism, the Highest Stage of Capitalism* (1916), among others.

189. See Joseph Schumpeter, "Contribution à une sociologie des impérialismes" (1919), in *Impérialisme et classes sociales* (Paris: Flammarion, "Champs," 1984).

190. "One thing is worth emphasizing: nationalism is a form of protectionism," Barrès wrote in "L'erreur intellectuelle des socialistes," *Le*

Journal, January 22, 1897, in *L'Œuvre de Maurice Barrès,* vol. 5 (Paris, 1966), p. 400. Note that when the Action Française commented on Barrès's platform in 1898, it emphasized the link between nationalism and protectionism and was delighted that he "has combined the three ideas of nationalism, protectionism, and socialism in a highly attractive system." Quoted in ibid., p. 384.

191. Marc Crapez, *La Gauche révolutionnaire: Mythes de la plèbe et de la race* (Paris: Berg International, 1997), esp. pp. 221-224.

192. Their virulent anti-Semitism should be interpreted in the same light.

193. See Maurice Hollande, *La Défense ouvrière contre le travail étranger: Vers un protectionnisme ouvrier* (Paris, 1913), and Giuseppe Prato, *Le Protectionnisme ouvrier (l'exclusion des travailleurs étrangers),* French trans. (Paris, 1912).

194. On these bills, see two old theses: Yves Le Febvre, *L'Ouvrier étranger et la protection du travail national* (Paris, 1901), and Paul Larricq, *Des Mesures législatives proposées pour la protection du travail national* (Paris, 1904).

195. From an 1893 brochure comprising three articles published in *Le Figaro* between May and July of 1893, reproduced in *L'Œuvre de Maurice Barrès,* vol. 5.

196. See, for example, J. Berjont, *De l'envahissement des étrangers en France: La Provence italienne: naturalisations, criminalité, protection du travail national* (Imprimerie spéciale de la Ligue, 1903). Subsequent quotes are from this work.

197. Alexandre Bérard, *L'Invasion des étrangers et la taxe de séjour.* Report presented to the Société d'économie politique de Lyon, March 5, 1886. Subsequent quotes are from this report.

198. Rapport Pradon, in *Annales de la Chambre des députés: Documents parlementaires,* session ordinaire de 1888, vol. 1 (annex no. 2364 to session of February 2, 1888), pp. 184-187. Subsequent quotes are from this report.

199. The fundamental work on this is a thesis by Pierre-Jacques Derainne, *Le Travail, les migrations et les conflits en France: Représenta-*

tions et attitudes sociales sous la monarchie de Juillet et la Seconde République (Dijon: Université de Bourgogne, 1999).

200. See Laurent Dornel, *La France hostile: Socio-histoire de la xénophobie (1870–1914)* (Paris: Hachette, 2004).

201. See Gérard Noiriel, *Le Massacre des italiens: Aigues-Mortes, 17 août 1893* (Paris: Fayard, 2010).

202. Barrès, *Contre les étrangers*, p. 412.

203. Barrès, "L'erreur intellectuelle des socialistes," pp. 401–404.

204. Jules Michelet, *Tableau de la France*, in *Histoire de France: Le Moyen Âge* in *Œuvres complètes*, vol. 4 (Paris: Flammarion, 1974), p. 377.

205. Jean Dausset defines immunology as the "science of the self's defense against the non-self," in "La Définition biologique du soi," in *Soi et non-soi*, ed. Jean Bernard and Claude Debru (Paris: Seuil, 1990), p. 19.

206. Richard Hoggart, *The Uses of Literacy: Aspects of Working Class Life* (London: Chatto and Windus, 1957), p. 48. See also the illuminating analyses by Norbert Elias, "Les Relations entre établis et marginaux, essai théorique," in Norbert Elias and John L. Scotson, *Logiques de l'exclusion: Enquête sociologique au cœur des problèmes d'une communauté* (1965), trans. Pierre-Emmanuel Dauzat (Paris: Fayard, 1997).

207. See George C. Rable, *But There Was No Peace: The Role of Violence in the Politics of Reconstruction* (Athens: University of Georgia Press, 1984).

208. See Joël Michel, *Le Lynchage aux États-Unis* (Paris: La Table ronde, 2008). Lynching was especially common in areas where "poor whites" felt economically threatened.

209. Although federal antidiscrimination norms were enshrined in the Fifteenth Amendment, the right to vote was still in principle regulated by the states.

210. See Comer Vann Woodward, *The Strange Career of Jim Crow*, 3rd ed. (1955; reprint, New York: Oxford University Press, 1974).

211. For a recent overview of the subject, see John David Smith, ed., *When Did Southern Segregation Begin?* (Boston: Bedford, 2002).

212. "Jim Crow" originally referred to satirical shows in which whites played blacks.

213. See Douglas A. Blackmon, *Slavery by Another Name: The Re-enslavement of Black People in America from the Civil War to World War II* (New York: Anchor Books, 2009).

214. Woodward, *The Strange Career of Jim Crow*. In this work, first published in 1955, at the beginning of the struggle for civil rights, Woodward sought to show that the southern whites' claim that segregation was a very old system reflecting a "natural order" was without foundation.

215. Tocqueville, *Democracy in America*, vol. 1, pp. 264-265; AG, pp. 395-397.

216. Ibid., p. 265; AG, p. 396.

217. On this point, see Woodward, *The Strange Career of Jim Crow*, p. 92 ff. See also Michael McGerr, *A Fierce Discontent: The Rise and Fall of the Progressive Movement in America, 1870–1920* (New York: Free Press, 2003), esp. the chapter entitled "The Shield of Segregation."

218. On this point, see Joel Williamson, *New People: Miscegenation and Mulattoes in the United States* (New York: New York University Press, 1980), and *The Crucible of Race: Black-White Relations in the American South since Emancipation* (New York: Oxford University Press, 1984).

219. See William Cohen, *At Freedom's Edge: Black Mobility and the Southern White Quest for Racial Control, 1861–1915* (Baton Rouge: Louisiana State University Press, 1991).

220. As pointed out by Paul Schor, *Compter et classer: Histoire des recensements américains* (Paris: Éditions de l'EHESS, 2009).

221. See Howard N. Rabinowitz, *Race Relations in the Urban South, 1865–1890* (New York: Oxford University Press, 1978), and *The First New South, 1865–1920* (Arlington Heights, Ill.: Harlan Davidson, 1992). The author argues that although blacks opposed segregation, they often put more energy into gaining better schools or more effective welfare institutions than into achieving integration.

222. Gunnar Myrdal, *An American Dilemma: The Negro Problem and Modern Democracy*, 2 vols. (New York: Harper, 1944).

223. See Theodore W. Allen, *The Invention of the White Race*, 2 vols. (London: Verso, 1994–1997), and Grace Elizabeth Hale, *Making Whiteness: The Culture of Segregation in the South, 1890–1940* (New York: Vintage, 1999).

224. Colette Guillaumin, *L'Idéologie raciste, genèse et langage actuel* (Paris: Mouton, 1972), p. 40.

225. Gustave de Beaumont, *Marie, ou l'Esclavage aux États-Unis,* vol. 1 (Paris: C. Gosselin, 1835), pp. 303-304. Beaumont insisted on this point in his correspondence. See, for example, his letter to his mother of December 15, 1831 in Beaumont, *Lettres d'Amérique, 1831–1832* (Paris: PUF, 1973), pp. 196-197. In *Les États-Unis aujourd'hui* (Paris: Armand Colin, 1927), p. 93, André Siegfried observed a century later: "Less well-paid than in the North and with few legal protections in the workplace, the 'poor white' is nevertheless proud to feel that he belongs to an aristocracy."

226. Rousseau, *Constitution pour la Corse*, in *Œuvres complètes*, vol. 3 (Paris: Gallimard, Bibliothèque de la Pléiade, 1969), p. 909.

227. On this "fear of falling" among whites, see Margaret Kohn, "The Other America: Tocqueville and Beaumont on Race and Slavery," *Polity* 35, no. 2 (Winter 2002), and Laura Janara, "Brothers and Others: Tocqueville and Beaumont, US Genealogy, Democracy, and Racism," *Political Theory* 32, no. 6 (December 2004.

228. Werner Sombart, *Why Is There No Socialism in the United States?* (New York: M. E. Sharpe, 1979).

229. See, for example, Marx's letter to Siegfried Meyer and August Vogt, April 9, 1870, in Karl Marx and Friedrich Engels, *Letters to Americans, 1848–1895* (New York: International Publishers, 1953), p. 77.

230. For an overview, see the essays in Seymour Martin Lipset and Theodore Lowi in *Why Is There No Socialism in the United States?* ed. Jean Heffer and Jeanine Rovet (Paris: Éditions de l'EHESS, 1988).

231. For an overview, in addition to the work of Heffer and Rovet, see Seymour Martin Lipset and Gary Marks, *It Didn't Happen Here: Why Socialism Failed in the United States* (New York: Norton, 2000).
232. Note that American trade unionism developed by availing itself of nativist sentiment.
233. Chevalier, *Lettres sur l'Amérique du Nord*, vol. 2, p. 375.
234. See Martin Gilens, *Why Americans Hate Welfare: Race, Media, and the Politics of Antipoverty Policy* (Chicago: University of Chicago Press, 1999).
235. Alberto Alesina and Edward L. Glaeser, *Fighting Poverty in the US and Europe: A World of Difference* (New York: Oxford University Press, 2006).
236. On this point, see Robert Putnam, *"E Pluribus Unum:* Diversity and Community in the Twenty-First Century," *Scandinavian Political Studies* 30, no. 2 (2007). I will discuss this article later in the text.
237. Alesina and Glaeser, *Fighting Poverty*, p. 328. See also the similar conclusions in Gilens, *Why Americans Hate Welfare*.
238. Alesina and Glaeser, *Fighting Poverty*, p. 27.
239. See the data in "Chinese and Japonese in America," special issue of *The Annals of the American Academy of Political and Social* Science 34, no. 2 (September 1909).
240. See John P. Young, "The Support of the Anti-Oriental Movement" in "Chinese and Japanese in America," p. 12.
241. Quoted in Mary R. Coolidge, *Chinese Immigration* (New York: 1909), p. 109.
242. See Carol A. Horton, *Race and the Making of American Liberalism* (New York: Oxford University Press, 2005).

3. THE CENTURY OF REDISTRIBUTION

1. For details, see Jean Nicolas, *La Rébellion française: Mouvements populaires et conscience sociale, 1661–1789* (Paris: Seuil, 2002).
2. On this point, see the seminal article by Peter Mathias and Patrick O'Brien, "Taxation in Britain and France, 1715–1810: A

Comparison of the Social and Economic Incidence of Taxes Collected for the Central Governments," *Journal of European Economic History* 5, no. 3 (Winter 1976).

3. Émile de Girardin, *L'Impôt* (Paris, 1852), p. 249.

4. Adolphe Thiers, *De la Propriété* (Paris, 1848), p. 355.

5. Pierre-Joseph Proudhon, *Théorie de l'impôt* (Bruxelles, 1861), p. 49. On p. 50 he states explicitly that "taxation is an exchange."

6. In 1900, indirect taxes accounted for 80 percent of French fiscal receipts.

7. See Fakhri Shehab, *Progressive Taxation: A Study in the Development of the Progressive Principle in the British Income Tax* (Oxford: Clarendon Press, 1952); and Martin Daunton, *Trusting Leviathan: The Politics of Taxation in Britain, 1799–1914* (Cambridge: Cambridge University Press, 2001), and *Just Taxes: The Politics of Taxation in Britain, 1914–1979* (Cambridge: Cambridge University Press, 2002).

8. See David A. Wells (an early proponent of this line), "The Communism of a Discriminatory Income-Tax," *North American Review* 130 (1880).

9. See *Pollock v. Farmers' Loan and Trust Company* (1895), and, on this decision, the *Encyclopedia of the American Constitution*, vol. 3 (New York: Macmillan, 1986), pp. 1423–1424.

10. See the articles quoted in Randolph E. Paul, *Taxation for Prosperity* (Indianapolis, Ind.: Bobbs-Merrill, 1947), pp. 12–13.

11. Quoted in Ernest Sabine, *A History of Income Tax* (London: Allen & Unwin, 1966), p. 125.

12. Quoted in Robert Schnerb, "La politique fiscale de Thiers," in *Deux siècles de fiscalité française, xixe–xxe siècles*, ed. Jean Bouvier and Jacques Wolff (Paris, 1973).

13. Nicolas Delalande, *Les Batailles de l'impôt: Consentement et résistances de 1789 à nos jours* (Paris: Seuil, 2011).

14. Quoted in Henri Isaïa and Jacques Spindler, "La Création d'un système d'imposition des revenus," in *L'Impôt sur le revenu en question* (Paris: Litec, 1989), p. 35.

15. See Joseph A. Pechman, *Federal Tax Policy* (Washington, D.C.: Brookings Institution, 1971), and Sidney Ratner, *Taxation and Democracy in America* (New York: Octagon Books, 1980).

16. Charles Renouvier, *Manuel républicain de l'homme et du citoyen* (1848) (Paris: Garnier, 1981), p. 130. Renouvier concluded that the tax was a "way of transitioning from a regime of inequality to one of equality."

17. Quoted in Geoffrey Lee, *The People's Budget: An Edwardian Tragedy* (London: Shepheard-Walwyn, 2008), p. 36.

18. Philip Snowden, *The Socialist's Budget* (London: George Allen, 1907), p. 1. See the passages on the 1909 reform in Philip Snowden, *An Autobiography, 1864–1919,* vol. 1 (London: Nicholson & Watson, 1934), pp. 146-151.

19. See also Philip Snowden, *Labour and the New World* (London, 1921).

20. Snowden, *The Socialist's Budget,* p. 7.

21. For a comprehensive overview, see U.S. Department of Commerce and Labor, *Workmen's Insurance and Compensation Systems in Europe,* 24th Annual Report of the Commissioner of Labor, 1909, 2 vols. (Washington, D.C., 1911).

22. See Rosanvallon, *L'État en France de 1789 à nos jours.*

23. Speech by Charles Floquet, May 21, 1881, *Annales de la Chambre des députés,* regular session of 1881, vol. 2, p. 102.

24. The expression was used by Marc Sauzet, "Essai historique sur la législation industrielle de la France," 2nd art., *Revue d'économie politique* 6 (1892): 923–924.

25. Buret, *De la misère des classes laborieuses,* vol. 2, p. 475.

26. Ibid., p. 481.

27. Émile de Girardin, *La Presse,* November 19, 1849, p. 1.

28. Kaiser Wilhelm II, Message to the Reichstag, November 17, 1881, quoted in Édouard Gruner, *Les Lois d'assistance ouvrière en Allemagne* (Paris, 1887), p. 8.

29. In Germany, the SPD received 3.3 percent of the vote in 1871 and 9.7 percent in 1884, before jumping to 23 percent in 1893 and 32

percent in 1903. In France, the first electoral breakthrough of the socialists did not occur until 1893. In Great Britain, it was the growth of trade unions that counted: by 1895, 1.5 million workers were unionized, and in some sectors (textile mills in Lancashire, mines in Durham and Northumberland) unionization was virtually complete.

30. Translated into French by Henri Saint-Marc, "Étude sur l'enseignement de l'économie politique dans les universités des pays de langue allemande," part 1, *Revue d'économie politique* (1892): 248.

31. Gustav Schmoller, *Politique sociale et économie politique* (1898), trans. M. Polack (Paris: Giard & Brière, 1902), p. 131.

32. Paul Lafargue, *Idéalisme et matérialisme dans la conception de l'histoire* (Paris, 1895), pp. 43-44.

33. Bernstein Archives, quoted in Pierre Angel, *Eduard Bernstein et l'évolution du socialisme allemand* (Paris: Didier, 1961), p. 125.

34. Rosa Luxemburg, *Réforme sociale ou révolution?* (1898), in *Œuvres,* vol. 1 (Paris: Maspero, 1969), p. 80.

35. See Emmanuel Jousse, *Réviser le marxisme? D'Eduard Bernstein à Albert Thomas, 1896–1914* (Paris: L'Harmattan, 2007).

36. In 1886, Boulangists organized a Congress of French Workers in Marseille.

37. *Le Cri du peuple,* January 6, 1886, reprinted in Jules Guesde, *État, politique et morale de classe* (Paris: Giard & Brière, 1901), pp. 156–159.

38. *Le Cri du peuple,* February 10, 1886, in Guesde, *État, politique et morale de classe,* pp. 160-163.

39. *Le Cri du peuple,* August 26, 1886, in Guesde, *État, politique et morale de classe,* pp. 352-355.

40. Jules Guesde, "Protection et libre-échange," *L'Égalité,* February 11, 1880.

41. In 1891, an FWP resolution denounced "a so-called republican government, which, after shooting down French workers in Fourmies, is preparing to starve others with its tariffs on wheat,

bread, meat, coffee, and sugar." *Neuvième Congrès national du Parti ouvrier français tenu à Lyon du 26 au 28 novembre 1891* (Lille, 1891), p. 9.

42. Pascal Faberot on one of many bills concerning the employment of foreign labor: *Annales de la Chambre des députés: Débats parlementaires,* session ordinaire de 1897, vol. 1, session of February 2, 1897, p. 300.

43. The expression was used in the manifesto of the FWP's national council, published in *Le Socialiste,* July 1896.

44. See the resolutions of 1903, 1904, and 1906 in Bureau socialiste international, *Comptes rendus des réunions, manifestes et circulaires,* with an introduction by Georges Haupt 1900–1907, vol. 1 (Paris: Mouton, 1969), pp. 85–89, 96, 258–261.

45. Socialist International Congress in Amsterdam (August 14–20, 1904), *Rapports et projets de résolutions* (Brussels, 1904).

46. Jean Jaurès, speech of March 8, 1887, in *Discours parlementaires,* vol. 1 (Paris: Cornély, 1904), pp. 189–210.

47. See Joseph Chamberlain, *Imperial Union and Tariff Reform: Speeches Delivered from May 15 to November 4, 1903,* 2nd ed. (London, 1910).

48. John Atkinson Hobson, *Imperialism: A Study* (New York: James Pott & Co., 1902), p. 96.

49. Ibid., p. 89.

50. See Kautsky's article "Die moderne Nationalität" (1887), translated into French in Georges Haupt, Michael Löwy, and Claudie Weill, *Les Marxistes et la question nationale (1848–1914),* 2nd ed. (Paris: L'Harmattan, 1997), pp. 114–127.

51. Otto Bauer, *La Question des nationalités et la social-démocratie* (1907), 2 vols., trans. Nicole Brune-Perrin and Johannès Brune (Paris: EDI, 1987).

52. Ibid., vol. 1, p. 147.

53. See Bauer's theory of social forms in ibid., vol. 2, pp. 587–588.

54. See Janet Horne, *A Social Laboratory for Modern France: The Musée Social and the Rise of the Welfare State* (Durham, N.C.: Duke University Press, 2001).

55. See Christian Topalov, ed., *Laboratoires du nouveau siècle: La nébuleuse réformatrice en France, 1880–1914* (Paris: Éditions de l'EHESS, 1999).

56. The first group to receive benefits consisted of relatives of defenders of the fatherland. See Guy Thuillier, "Les secours aux défenseurs de la patrie (1792-1796)," in *Actes du CXIIIᵉ Congrès des sociétés savantes* (1988) (Paris: Association pour l'étude de l'histoire de la Sécurité sociale, 1989).

57. See William Beveridge, Norman Hill, et al., *War and Insurance* (London: Milford, 1927).

58. Quoted in Paul Starr, *Freedom's Power* (New York: Basic Books, 2007).

59. Ernst Jünger, *La Guerre comme expérience intérieure* (1922), in *Journaux de guerre*, vol. 1: *1914–1918* (Paris: Gallimard, "Bibliothèque de la Pléiade," 2008), p. 592.

60. See the chapter on "the fraternity of the trenches" in Antoine Prost, *Les Anciens Combattants et la société française, 1914–1939*, vol. 3 (Paris: Presses de la FNSP, 1977).

61. André Bridoux, *Souvenirs du temps des morts* (Paris: Albin Michel, 1930), p. 50.

62. Robert Musil, "La Nation comme idéal et comme réalité" (December 1921), in *Essais* (Paris: Seuil, 1978), p. 118.

63. Musil speaks of "millions of men who had previously lived only for their own interests and with ill-concealed anguish in the face of death, who now suddenly offered to die joyfully for the sake of the nation." Ibid., pp. 118-119.

64. On the demonization of the "German race" in France and vice versa, see Michael Jeismann, *La Patrie de l'ennemi: La notion d'ennemi national et la représentation de la nation en Allemagne et en France de 1792 à 1918*, trans. Dominique Lassaigne (Paris: CNRS Éditions, 1997).

65. Laurent Bonnevay, *Journal officiel* du 18 avril 1930, *Débats parlementaires: Chambre des députés*, session of April 17, 1930, p. 1945.

66. See Steven Bank, Kirk Stark, and Joseph Thorndike, *War and Taxes* (Washington, D.C.: Urban Institute Press, 2008), p. 61.

67. Ibid., p. 62.

68. See James T. Sparrow, "Buying Our Boys Back: The Mass Foundation of Fiscal Citizenship in World War II," *Journal of Policy History* 20, no. 2 (April 2008).

69. See Carolyn C. Jones, "Mass-Based Income Taxation: Creating a Taxpaying Culture, 1940–1952," in *Funding the Modern American State, 1941–1995: The Rise and Fall of the Era of Easy Finance,* ed. W. Elliot Brownlee (New York: Cambridge University Press, 1996).

70. Quoted by Antoine Prost, "Le bouleversement des sociétés," in Stéphane Audoin-Rouzeau and Jean-Jacques Becker, *Encyclopédie de la Grande Guerre (1914–1918): Histoire et culture* (Paris: Bayard, 2004), p. 1182. Retranslated from the French.

71. "The idea of society," he wrote, "is one of separate living beings that constantly support one another in common action." See Alfred Espinas, *Des Sociétés animales* (Paris: Baillère, 1877), p. 123. "The individual," he concluded, "is more the work of society than the author." Ibid., p. 433.

72. Émile Durkheim, inaugural lecture of his *Cours de science sociale* (1888), in *La Science sociale et l'Action* (Paris: PUF, 1970), p. 97.

73. Ibid., p. 109.

74. Léon Bourgeois, *La Politique de prévoyance sociale,* vol. 1 (Paris: Fasquelle, 1913), p. 68.

75. Leonard Trelawney Hobhouse, *Liberalism* (London: Williams & Norgate, 1911), p. 126.

76. Bourgeois, *La Politique de prévoyance sociale,* vol. 1, p. 58.

77. See chap. 2 of Léon Bourgeois, *Solidarité* (Paris: Armand Colin, 1896), entitled "Scientific Doctrine of Natural Solidarity."

78. Alfred Fouillée, *La Propriété sociale et la démocratie* (Paris: Hachette, 1884), p. 21. "Gutenberg still prints all the books read throughout the world," he added.

79. Alfred Fouillée, *La Science sociale contemporaine* (Paris: Hachette, 1880). See also another of his works, eloquently entitled *Le Socialisme et la sociologie réformiste* (Paris: Alcan, 1909), in which he

systematically explored the relation between the idea of a contractual organism and the idea of reparative justice. With these themes, Fouillée and Bourgeois rediscovered the intuitions of Pierre Leroux, a socialist of an earlier era who by their day had been forgotten, who may be considered as a forerunner of Solidarism. See in particular Leroux's discussions of the indivisibility of modern labor in *Le Carosse de M. Aguado* (Paris, 1848), pp. 13-70; solidarity in *De l'humanité*, vol. 1 (Paris, 1840), pp. 218-220; the link to earlier generations (ibid., pp. 270-283); equality and fraternity in *De l'égalité* (1848); and man's ties to nature.

80. Léon Bourgeois, "L'idée de solidarité et ses conséquences sociales" (lecture 3, December 4, 1901), in *Essai d'une philosophie de la solidarité* (Paris: Alcan, 1902), pp. 93-94.

81. "Man," Bourgeois argued, "is the repository of a legacy for which we must constantly account to society as a whole. He is guilty of bankruptcy or theft if he keeps for himself what he was able to acquire only through the labor and effort of previous generations." *La Politique de prévoyance sociale*, vol. 1, p. 68. This notion of debt allowed Bourgeois to reconcile a "liberal" worldview (limiting equality to the principle of equality before the law) with a "socialist" sensibility (leaning toward actual equality).

82. Hobhouse, *Liberalism*, p. 190.

83. Bourgeois, "L'idée de solidarité," p. 110.

84. Richard T. Ely, *Taxation in American States and Cities* (New York: Crowell, 1888), p. 15.

85. See Seligman's fundamental work *Progressive Taxation in Theory and Practice* (Baltimore: American Economic Association, 1894).

86. See Ajay K. Mehrotra, "Envisioning the Modern American Fiscal State: Progressive-Era Economists and the Intellectual Foundations of the US Income Tax," *UCLA Law Review* 52, no. 6 (August 2005) and "The Intellectual Foundations of the Modern American Fiscal State," *Daedalus* 138, no. 2 (Spring 2009).

87. The first was theorized by Adolph Wagner in Germany (see his *Traité de la science des finances,* vol. 3, trans. Paul Hallier [Paris: Giard & Brière, 1912], p. 39 ff.) and by Alfred Fouillée in France *(Le Socialisme et la sociologie réformiste).* The second was theorized by Fouillée and Bourgeois.

88. Programmatic speech to the Chamber of Deputies, November 4, 1895, *Journal officiel,* November 5, 1895, p. 2268.

89. See Wagner, *Traité de la science des finances,* vol. 3, pp. 362–363.

90. See James Meadowcroft, *Conceptualizing the State: Innovation and Dispute in British Political Thought, 1880–1914* (Oxford: Clarendon Press, 1995).

91. Edwin R. A. Seligman, *Essays in Taxation* (New York: Macmillan, 1895), p. 72.

92. Bourgeois, *La Politique de prévoyance sociale,* vol. 1, p. 69.

93. Léon Bourgeois, "Doctrine de la solidarité," *La Solidarité,* October 25, 1849.

94. See Vincent Viet, *Les Voltigeurs de la République: L'Inspection du travail en France jusqu'en 1914,* vol. 1 (Paris: Éditions du CNRS, 1994), p. 169.

95. Raymond Saleilles, *Les Accidents de travail et la responsabilité civile: Essai d'une théorie objective de la responsabilité délictuelle* (Paris, 1897), p. 4.

96. Peter W. J. Bartrip, *Workmen's Compensation in Twentieth Century Britain* (Aldershot, U.K.: Gower Publishing, 1987).

97. Peter W. J. Bartrip and Sandra B. Burman, *The Wounded Soldiers of Industry: Industrial Compensation Policy, 1833–1897* (Oxford: Clarendon Press, 1983).

98. R. H. Tawney, *Equality* (London: Allen & Unwin, 1931). Often reprinted since, Tawney's work played a crucial role in shaping the ideology of the Labour Party.

99. See their joint work, *New Fabian Essays* (London: Turnstile, 1952).

100. On his work and influence, see John Vaizey, *In Breach of Promise: Gaitskell, MacLeod, Titmuss, Crosland, Boyle; Five Men Who Shaped a*

Generation (London: Weidenfeld & Nicolson, 1983), and Nicholas Ellison, *Egalitarian Thought and Labor Politics: Retreating Visions* (London: Routledge, 1994).

101. Richard Titmuss, *The Meaning of Poverty,* quoted in David Reisman, *Richard Titmuss: Welfare and Society* (London: Palgrave, 2001), p. 189.

102. Carl Schmitt, *Théorie de la Constitution* (1928), trans. Lilyane Deroche (Paris: PUF, 1993), p. 371. Note that for "equality" Schmitt used the word *Gleichheit,* and for "homogeneity," *Gleichartigkeit.* Thus the two ideas were intimately connected in his very language.

103. See, for example, Carl Schmitt, *Parlementarisme et démocratie* (1923), trans. Jean-Louis Schlegel (Paris: Seuil, 1988), p. 108.

104. Ibid.

105. Carl Schmitt, *État, mouvement, peuple* (1933), trans. Agnès Pilleul (Paris: Kimé, 1997), p. 48. "Without the principle of racial identity," he wrote, "the National Socialist state could not exist, and its legal system would be unthinkable." Ibid., p. 59.

106. Schmitt, *Théorie de la Constitution,* p. 391.

107. See Juliette Courmont, *L'Odeur de l'ennemi, 1914–1918* (Paris: Armand Colin, 2010).

108. Voir John Ikenberry, "Workers and the World Economy," *Foreign Affairs* (May–June 1996).

109. See the chapter "Abolition of Want as a Practicable Post-War Aim," in William Beveridge, *Social Insurance and Allied Services* (London: Twentieth Century Press, 1943), pp. 164–170.

110. Ibid., p. 171.

111. See William Beveridge, "A New Spirit for Total War" and "New Britain," in *The Pillars of Security and Other War-Time Essays and Addresses* (London: Allen & Unwin, 1943).

112. In the summer of 1940, the British spoke of the "spirit of Dunkirk" in describing the novel solidarity created by the war. (The reference was of course to the thousands of volunteers who heroically crossed the Channel to assist in the evacuation of

300,000 British soldiers trapped by the German army on French beaches near the city of Dunkirk.)

113. *Journal officiel: Débats de l'Assemblée consultative provisoire,* session of July 31, 1945, p. 1674.

114. See, for example, the programmatic statement by Pierre Laroque, the French Beveridge, "Le Plan français de Sécurité sociale," *Revue française du travail,* no. 1, 1946.

115. *Journal officiel: Documents de l'Assemblée consultative provisoire,* session of July 5, 1945, Annex no. 507, p. 665.

116. The simultaneous victory of the Soviet Union and the Western Allies raised this issue, as did the constitution of a communist bloc in Eastern Europe. The electoral success of the French and Italian Communist Parties also weighed heavily.

117. See Richard Whiting, *The Labour Party and Taxation: Party Identity and Social Purpose in Twentieth-Century Britain* (Cambridge: Cambridge University Press, 2000).

118. Richard Henry Tawney, *Equality,* 4th ed. (London: Allen & Unwin, 1952), pp. 143–144.

119. Ibid., p. 213.

120. Ibid., p. 214.

121. See Sven Steinmo, "The Evolution of Policy Ideas: Tax Policy in the 20th Century," *British Journal of Politics and International Relations* 5, no. 2 (May 2003).

122. See Richard M. Titmuss, *Income Distribution and Social Change* (London: Allen & Unwin, 1962).

123. Tawney, *Equality,* p. 144.

124. Karl Polanyi, *The Great Transformation: The Political and Economic Origins of Our Time* (Boston: Beacon Press, 1957), p. 250.

125. Andrew Shonfield, *Modern Capitalism: The Changing Balance of Private and Public Power* (New York: Oxford University Press, 1969), p. 377. Meanwhile, Peter Drucker wrote that "the concept of profit maximization makes no sense." See *Management: Tasks, Responsibilities, Practices* (New York: Harper & Row, 1974), p. 59.

126. John Kenneth Galbraith, "Le nouvel État industriel, présentation, critiques et conséquences," *Revue économique et sociale de Lausanne,* August 1969 (reprinted in *Problèmes économiques,* January 15, 1970, p. 14).
127. Shonfield, *Modern Capitalism,* p. 378.
128. See another classic of the period, Edward S. Mason, ed., *The Corporation in Modern Society* (Cambridge, Mass.: Harvard University Press, 1960).
129. John Kenneth Galbraith, *The New Industrial State* (1967; reprint, Princeton, N.J.: Princeton University Press, 2007), p. 101.
130. Ibid., p. 115.
131. Peter Drucker anticipated this development in the 1940s. In *The Future of Industrial Man* (New York: John Day, 1942), he wrote: "At the heart of the modern firm, the decision-making power, the power of the managers, is not in the hands of any individual. It is literally baseless, unjustified, unchecked, and irresponsible."
132. Galbraith, *The New Industrial State,* p. 87.
133. Ibid., pp. 75–76.
134. He wrote that "the goal of an organization is to make ordinary people capable of extraordinary things." Drucker, *Management,* p. 455.
135. Galbraith, *The New Industrial State,* p. 120.
136. Ibid., p. 192. "Within the technostructure . . . the factors making for identification . . . have a clear run." Ibid., p. 164.
137. This theme was developed in Galbraith's earlier work, *The Affluent Society* (New York: Houghton Mifflin, 1958).
138. Galbraith, *The New Industrial State,* p. 125.
139. Ibid., p. 127.

4. THE GREAT REVERSAL

1. Denis Kessler, "Adieu 1945, raccrochons notre pays au monde!" *Challenges,* October 4, 2007. "The list of reforms?" he wrote. "It's simple. Take everything that was done from 1944 to 1952, without

exception. It's all there. The goal today is to turn our back on 1945 and methodically dismantle the program of the National Council of the Resistance!"

2. I borrow the expression "veil of ignorance" from John Rawls, who used it in describing the procedure for formulating the rules of justice.

3. My argument here was first set forth in *La Nouvelle Question sociale: Repenser l'état-providence* (Paris: Seuil, 1995).

4. John Rawls, *A Theory of Justice* (Cambridge, Mass.: Harvard University Press, 1973).

5. The adoption of the "generalized social contribution" in 1990 marked a return to the principle of making social contributions proportional to income, with different categories of income treated in the same way.

6. See Pierre Ranval, *Hiérarchie des salaires et lutte des classes* (Paris: Cerf, 1972), which clearly laid out what was at stake in contemporary thinking about these issues.

7. See, for example, the special issue on "La hiérarchie" in *CFDT-Aujourd'hui,* no. 8, July–August 1974, which included ideas from worker activists as well as intellectuals such as Cornelius Castoriadis, Renaud Sainsaulieu, and Eugène Enriquez.

8. In France, one thinks of the antitax movements led by Pierre Poujade and Gérard Nicoud in the period 1950–1970.

9. Robert Kuttner, *Revolt of the Haves: Tax Rebellions and Hard Times* (New York: Simon & Schuster, 1980), and Isaac William Martin, *The Permanent Tax Revolt: How the Property Tax Transformed American Politics* (Stanford, Calif.: Stanford University Press, 2008).

10. On the growth of inequality in the United States as a deliberate consequence of policy and not just of globalization, see Larry M. Bartels, *Unequal Democracy: The Political Economy of the New Gilded Age* (Princeton, N.J.: Princeton University Press, 2008), and Jacob S. Hacker and Paul Pierson, *The Winner-Take-All Politics: How*

Washington Made the Rich Richer and Turned Its Back on the Middle Class (New York: Simon & Schuster, 2010).

11. See Serge Paugam and Marion Selz, "La perception de la pauvreté en Europe depuis le milieu des années 1970," *Économie et statistique,* nos. 383-384-385, 2005.

12. See his "Manifesto" in the June 10, 2009, issue of the *Frankfurter Allgemeine Zeitung,* from which the following quotes are taken.

13. See Yann Moulier-Boutang, ed., *Le Capitalisme cognitif: La nouvelle grande transformation* (Paris: Éditions Amsterdam, 2008), along with arguments that Toni Negri has developed in his recent work.

14. We see similar diversification of manufactured goods and a proliferation of "singular" products defined primarily by quality. See Lucien Karpik, *L'Économie des singularités* (Paris: Gallimard, 2007).

15. Denis Segrestin, *Les Chantiers du manager* (Paris: Armand Colin, 2004), p. 102.

16. Pierre-Michel Menger called attention to this change in *Portrait de l'artiste en travailleur: Métamorphoses du capitalisme* (Paris: La République des idées/Seuil, 2003).

17. Although, it was in reference to the state of isolation and decomposition that the term "individualism" would be forged in the 1820s.

18. Simmel used the German word *Gleichheit,* which connotes both equality and similarity. On this point, see his comments in *Sociologie: Études sur les formes de socialisation* (1908) (reprint, Paris: PUF, 1999), pp. 702-706. Conversely, Simmel used the phrase "individualism of dissimilarity" to denote Romantic individualism, which sought a radical distinction of the self and separation from others.

19. Ibid., p. 702.

20. In the eighteenth-century concept of individuality, Simmel wrote, "personal liberty did not exclude but rather included

equality, *because the 'real' person is identical in each individual.*"See Georg Simmel, "L'individu et la société dans certaines conceptions de l'existence des xviiie et xixe siècles," in *Sociologie et épistémologie* (Paris: PUF, 1981), p. 150; emphasis added. "Liberty and equality," he also wrote, "were seen to be two obviously harmonious faces of a single human ideal." Ibid., p. 145.

21. Georg Simmel, "L'individu et la liberté" (1917), reprinted in *Philosophie de la modernité* (Paris: Payot, 2004), p. 210; emphasis added.

22. On the psychology of distinction at the court of Louis XIV, see the *Memoirs* of the Duke de Saint-Simon.

23. See Nathalie Heinich, *L'Élite artiste: Excellence et singularité en régime démocratique* (Paris: Gallimard, 2005).

24. Stendhal, *Vie de Henry Brulard* (1835) (Paris: Gallimard, "Folio," 1981), p. 161.

25. On the artist and the constitution of the modern self, see Charles Taylor, *Sources of the Self: The Making of the Modern Identity* (Cambridge, Mass.: Harvard University Press, 1992), and Jerrold Seigel, *Bohemian Paris: Culture, Politics, and the Boundaries of Bourgeois Life, 1830–1930* (Baltimore, Md.: Johns Hopkins University Press, 1999).

26. See Gabriel Tarde, *Les Lois de l'imitation* (Paris: Alcan, 1890). Tarde's work on fashion made him a pioneer in applying psychological analysis to the economy. See his remarkable *Psychologie économique,* 2 vols. (Paris: Alcan, 1902).

27. See esp. the important work of Daniel Kahneman.

28. See Jean-Paul Fitoussi and Pierre Rosanvallon, *Le Nouvel âge des inégalités* (Paris: Seuil, 1995), esp. chap. 2.

29. This is why blogs have proliferated on the Internet. On this issue, see Patrice Flichy, *Le Sacre de l'amateur: Sociologie des passions ordinaires à l'ère numérique* (Paris: La République des idées/Seuil, 2010).

30. David Hume, *An Enquiry Concerning the Principles of Morals* (Oxford: Oxford University Press, 1975), sec. 3, part 2.

31. Michael Young, *The Rise of the Meritocracy, 1870–2033* (London: Thames and Hudson, 1971).

32. See the article *"mérite"* in the *Dictionnaire de théologie catholique* (Paris: Letouzey et Ané, 1908).

33. See Marie Duru-Bellat, *Le Mérite contre la justice* (Paris: Presses de Sciences Po, 2009), and "L'Emprise de la méritocratie scolaire: quelle légitimité?" *Revue française de sociologie* 50, no. 2 (2009).

34. The expression is borrowed from François Dubet, *L'École des chances: Qu'est-ce qu'une école juste?* (Paris: La République des idées/ Seuil, 2004), p. 36.

35. Roger Caillois, *Les Jeux et les Hommes: Le masque et le vertige,* rev. and exp. ed. (Paris: Gallimard, 1967).

36. Ibid., p. 58. Subsequent quotes are from p. 224.

37. Between 2005 and 2010, six winners of the transnational Euro-Millions lottery pocketed prizes greater than €100 million (the record being €130 million). In Italy, the national lottery had a record payoff of €177 million in 2010. In France, the twenty-eight million players in the various national lotteries spent more than €10 billion.

38. The point has been emphasized by Roger Caillois as well as in Olivier Ihl, *Le Mérite et la République* (Paris: Gallimard, 2007), pp. 323–325.

39. In France, a person who supplies illegal drugs to an athlete is subject to up to five years in prison and a fine of €75,000. Use of illegal drugs is punishable by up to one year in prison and a fine of €3,750.

40. One can readily imagine Hegel using sports as a central example if the *Phenomenology of Spirit* were written today.

41. On this point, see my *Capitalisme utopique: Histoire de l'idée de marché* (1979), new ed. (Paris: Seuil, "Points," 1999).

42. Friedrich A. Hayek, *Law, Legislation, and Liberty: The Mirage of Social Justice,* vol. 2 (Chicago: University of Chicago Press, 1976), p. 8.

43. Ibid.

44. Ibid., p. 9. "It is thus due to the freedom of choosing the ends of one's activities that the utilization of the knowledge dispersed through society is achieved." Ibid.

45. Society does not exist for Hayek: "Society is not a person who acts; it is the organized structure of activities that arises when its members observe certain abstract rules." Ibid., p. 95.

46. See esp. François Ewald and Denis Kessler, "Les noces du risque et de la politique," *Le Débat,* no. 109, March–April 2000. Kessler served as a high official in an association of French employers, while Ewald is an historian and social theorist of insurance who began his career as Michel Foucault's assistant at the Collège de France. Subsequent citations refer to this article.

47. Simone de Beauvoir, *Pour une morale de l'ambiguïté* (Paris: Gallimard, 1947).

48. Charles Coquelin and Gilbert-Urbain Guillaumin, eds., *Dictionnaire de l'économie politique* (Paris: Guillaumin, 1853), vol. 1, article "Concurrence."

49. In this sense there has been a return to the utopian liberalism of the eighteenth century in the form of a critique of established authority. This return is therefore the opposite of conservatism.

50. Although there are also socially instituted differences owing to the existence of a minimum wage, the influence of networks of graduates of elite universities, etc.

51. See Xavier Gabaix and Augustin Landier, "Why Has CEO Pay Increased So Much?" *Quarterly Journal of Economics* 123, no. 1 (February 2008).

52. For an overview of work on this question, see Frédéric Palomino, *Comment faut-il payer les patrons?* (Paris: Cepremap-Éditions Rue d'Ulm, 2011), and Maxence Brischoux, "Rémunération des dirigeants: Quels déterminants économiques et sociaux," *Revue Banque,* no. 723, April 2010.

53. See the seminal article by Sherwin Rosen, "The Economics of Superstars," *American Economic Review* 71, no. 5 (December 1981).

54. See Robert H. Frank and Philip J. Cook, *The Winner-Take-All Society: Why the Few at the Top Get So Much More Than the Rest of Us* (New York: Free Press, 1995). For an informed introduction to this literature, see Pierre-Michel Menger, *Le Travail créateur: S'accomplir dans l'incertain* (Paris: Seuil/Gallimard, 2009), chap. 4, "Talent et réputation: Les inégalités de réussite et leurs explications dans les sciences sociales."

55. See Voir Peter L. Bernstein, "Le Système fantastique des produits dérivés," in *Plus forts que les dieux: La remarquable histoire du risque* (Paris: Flammarion, 1998).

56. See James Mackintosh, "Hedge Fund Stars Shine High Above the Crowd," *The Financial Times,* September 11-12, 2010.

57. See Olivier Godechot, *Working Rich: Salaires, bonus et appropriation du profit dans l'industrie financière* (Paris: La Découverte, 2007). Godechot has recently argued that the large rewards going to top people in the financial sector are responsible for the dramatic increase in the share of income going to the very top of the income distribution.

58. The arts are a partial exception to this rule. In the world of art, large disparities of income are more readily tolerated and even legitimated because the link between the person and the work is more obvious than that between a CEO and the success of his or her company.

59. What John Rawls called "equality of fair opportunity." See John Rawls, *Justice as Fairness: A Restatement* (Cambridge, Mass.: Harvard University Press, 2001), section 13.

60. Amartya Sen, *The Idea of Justice* (Cambridge, Mass.: Harvard University Press, 2011).

61. Ronald Dworkin, "What is Equality?" (Part 1: "Equality of Welfare"; Part 2: "Equality of Resources"), *Philosophy and Public Affairs* 10, nos. 3 and 4 (Summer and Autumn 1981). Reprinted in *Sovereign Virtue: The Theory and Practice of Equality* (Cambridge, Mass.: Harvard University Press, 2000).

62. In Dworkin's terms, a fair income distribution should be "ambition-sensitive and endowment-insensitive."

63. This is the significance of his famous "difference principle." If inequalities of talent do in fact exist, those who possess superior talents should be able to profit from them only on condition that this benefits the least favored members of the society.

64. Dworkin, Cohen wrote, "has, in effect, performed for egalitarianism the considerable service of incorporating within it the most powerful idea in the arsenal of the anti-egalitarian right: the idea of choice and responsibility." See "On the Currency of Egalitarian Justice," *Ethics* 99, no. 4 (July 1989): 933.

65. The choice/chance distinction is more stringent than Dworkin's contrast between preferences and resources because Cohen argues that preferences may not be the result of deliberate choice.

66. In addition to Cohen, see the work of John E. Roemer and Richard J. Arneson, who have continued down this path. Note that Dworkin has always refused to be characterized as a luck egalitarian and that Cohen himself preferred to speak of the need for a "level playing field." For an overview of this school of thought, see Jean-Fabien Spitz, *Abolir le hasard? Responsabilité individuelle et justice sociale* (Paris: Vrin, 2008).

67. John E. Roemer, "Equality and Responsibility," *Boston Review*, April–May 1995.

68. John E. Roemer, "A Pragmatic Theory of Responsibility for the Egalitarian Planner," *Philosophy and Public Affairs* 22, no. 2 (Spring 1993). On the notion of responsibility in this context, see also Samuel Scheffler, *Boundaries and Allegiances: Problems of Justice and Responsibility in Liberal Thought* (New York: Oxford University Press, 2001).

69. On this point, see Jonathan Wolff, "Fairness, Respect, and the Egalitarian Ethos," *Philosophy and Public Affairs* 27, no. 2 (Spring 1998).

70. *Archives parlementaires,* ser. 1 (henceforth cited as *AP*), vol. 68, p. 663.

71. "The principle of fair opportunity can be only imperfectly carried out, at least as long as the institution of the family exists." John Rawls, *A Theory of Justice* (Oxford: Oxford University Press, 1973), p. 75.

72. Mirabeau, *Discours sur l'égalité des partages dans les successions en ligne directe*, April 2, 1791, in *AP*, vol. 26, pp. 510-515. Subsequent citations refer to this article.

73. This system would have been financed by a tax on large inheritances. Billaud-Varenne also envisioned a ceiling on inheritances. See the chapter "On Property" in his *Éléments du républicanisme* of June 1793 (reproduced in *AP*, vol. 67).

74. See Stanley N. Katz, "Republicanism and the Law of Inheritance in the American Revolutionary Era," *Michigan Law Review* 76, no. 1 (November 1977).

75. See his letter to James Madison of 1789, in which he noted that "the fruits of the land belong to the living."

76. Thomas Paine, "Agrarian Justice," in *The Complete Writings of Thomas Paine*, ed. Philip S. Foner, vol. 1 (New York: Citadel Press, 1945), pp. 605-623.

77. John Stuart Mill, *Principles of Political Economy*, 1848 (reprint, Oxford: Oxford University Press, 2008), II.2, sec. 4.

78. One of the most frequently cited plans in Europe was that of the Socialist Eugenio Rignano, who proposed taxing wealth amassed through work and savings at 50 percent compared to a 100 percent rate on wealth stemming from inheritance. Thus inherited wealth would end after one generation. See his *Pour une réforme socialiste du droit successoral*, French trans. (Paris: Rieder, 1918).

79. This was the cornerstone of Hayek's critique of equality of opportunity. See *Law, Legislation, and Liberty*, vol. 2, p. 157.

80. Laurent de l'Ardèche, "L'hérédité," in *Religion saint-simonienne: Recueil de prédications*, vol. 2 (Paris, 1832), p. 189. On this theme, see the thesis of André Robert, *Le Saint-simonisme et l'Hérédité* (Paris, 1908).

81. *Doctrine de Saint-Simon: Exposition (première année, 1829),* new ed., with introduction and notes by Célestin Bouglé and Élie Halévy (Paris: Rivière, 1924), p. 287.

82. See Abel Transon, "L'éducation," in *Religion saint-simonienne,* vol. 1, p. 563.

83. Saint-Amand Bazard and Prosper Enfantin, *Lettre à Monsieur le Président de la Chambre des députés,* Paris, October 1, 1830, in response to attacks alleging that Saint-Simonians favored the communal ownership of property. John Stuart Mill vigorously criticized the fundamental duality of Saint-Simonian doctrine in his *Principles of Political Economy.*

84. Tawney, *Equality,* p. 105.

85. Young, *Meritocracy.*

5. THE SOCIETY OF EQUALS

1. For an overview, see Nicholas Ellison, *Egalitarian Thought and Labour Politics: Retreating Visions* (London: Routledge, 1994), and Anthony Giddens and Patrick Diamond, eds., *The New Egalitarianism* (London: Polity Press, 2005). In French, see the thesis of Jérôme Tournadre-Plancq, *Au-delà de la gauche et de la droite, une troisième voie britannique* (Paris: Dalloz, 2006).

2. On January 11, 1998, to a group of California computer executives.

3. Richard Wilkinson and Kate Pickett, *The Spirit Level: Why More Equal Societies Almost Always Do Better* (London: Allen Lane, 2009). See also Richard Wilkinson, *The Impact of Inequality: How to Make Sick Societies Healthier* (London: Routledge, 2005). For an in-depth discussion of the methodological problems raised by these works, see David Runciman, "How Messy It All Is," *London Review of Books,* October 22, 2009.

4. On this point see Jean Starobinski, "Tout le mal vient de l'inégalité," *Europe,* nos. 391–392, November–December 1961.

5. See Michael Sandel, *Liberalism and the Limits of Justice,* 2nd ed. (Cambridge: Cambridge University Press, 1998).

6. In the 1980s it was more common to contrast this "communitarian" approach with the "liberal" approach.

7. See Iris Marion Young, *Justice and the Politics of Difference* (Princeton, N.J.: Princeton University Press, 1990).

8. For a caricatural version, see Walter Benn Michaels, *The Trouble with Diversity: How We Learned to Love Identity and Ignore Inequality* (New York: Metropolitan, 2006), and for a more developed discussion, Sheri Berman, *The Primacy of Politics: Social Democracy and the Making of Europe's 20th Century* (New York: Cambridge University Press, 2006), and Tony Judt, *Ill Fares the Land* (New York: Penguin Press, 2010).

9. Engels put it this way: "The real content of the proletarian demand for equality is the abolition of classes." Friedrich Engels, *Anti-Dühring* (Paris: Éditions sociales, 1963), p. 139.

10. Tawney, *Equality,* p. 113.

11. George Orwell, *Homage to Catalonia* (London: Secker and Warburg, 1938).

12. In the 1990s, New Labour revived the theme of classless society but with a weaker and above all more ideological meaning.

13. For an enlightening legal commentary, see Danièle Lochak, "Réflexions sur la notion de discrimination," *Droit social,* November 1987.

14. French electoral law took this course concerning the right to vote for women. The Constitution of 1946 stated explicitly that women have the right to vote, not that all individuals above a certain age may vote. The object of the measure was not the individual woman but women as a group.

15. On this duality, consider the French choice to submit the issue of homosexual marriage to the legislature.

16. Rétif de La Bretonne, *Les Gynographes, ou Idées de deux honnêtes femmes sur un projet de règlement proposé à toute l'Europe pour mettre les femmes à leur place, et opérer le bonheur des deux sexes* (The Hague, 1777), p. 41; emphasis added.

17. See my discussion of this point in *Le Sacre du citoyen.*

18. This was the basis of the idea that male suffrage represented the family in an organic sense.

19. Germaine de Staël, *De la littérature considérée dans ses rapports avec les institutions sociales* (1800), part 2, chap. 4, "Des femmes qui cultivent les lettres," in *Œuvres complètes de madame la baronne de Staël-Holstein,* vol. 1 (Paris, 1838), p. 301.

20. Laure Bereni and Éléonore Lépinard, " 'Les femmes ne sont pas une catégorie:' Les stratégies de légitimation de la parité en France," *Revue française de science politique* 54, no. 1 (February 2004), and Joan W. Scott, *Parité! Sexual Equality and the Crisis of French Universalism* (Chicago: University of Chicago Press, 2005).

21. John Stuart Mill, *The Subjection of Women* (1869; reprint, Mineola, N.Y.: Dover, 1997), chap. 2.

22. See Irène Théry, *La Distinction de sexe: Une nouvelle approche de l'égalité* (Paris: Odile Jacob, 2007). Théry rightly treats gender as a "modality of actions and relations." Ibid., p. 447.

23. Étienne Balibar, *La Proposition de l'égaliberté: Essais politiques, 1989–2009* (Paris: PUF, 2010), p. 83.

24. Simone de Beauvoir raised this possibility in *The Second Sex,* trans. Constance Borde and Sheila Malovany (New York: Vintage, 2011), where she argued that gender differences would cease to be significant in the future and that men and women would then become "truly alike."

25. On this point, see my discussion in *La Nouvelle Question sociale.*

26. See Jacques Lenoble and André Bertin, *Dire la norme: Droit, politique et énonciation* (Paris: LGDJ, 1990).

27. For an attempt to do this, see Frédéric Worms, *Le Moment du soin: À quoi tenons-nous?* (Paris: PUF, 2010).

28. On this ambiguity, see Robert Castel, "L'autonomie, aspiration ou condition," review of Alain Ehrenberg, in *La Société du malaise* (Paris: Odile Jacob, 2010), http://www.laviedesidees.fr, March 26, 2010, and Ehrenberg's response, "Société du malaise ou malaise dans la société" (ibid., March 30, 2010).

29. See, for example, Jon Elster, *Traité critique de l'homme économique,* vol. 1: *Le Désintéressement* (Paris: Seuil, 2009), trans. Arthur Goldhammer as *Critique of Homo Economicus:* vol. 1, *Disinterestedness* (Cambridge: Cambridge University Press, 2011), and *L'Irrationalité,* vol. 2 (Paris: Seuil, 2010).

30. For an introduction, see Serge-Christophe Kolm and Jean Mercier-Ythier, eds., *Handbook of the Economics of Giving, Altruism and Reciprocity,* vol. 1: *Foundations,* and vol. 2: *Applications* (Amsterdam: Elsevier, 2006). In France the *Revue du MAUSS* has been spurred interest in these subjects.

31. See Peter Kropotkin, *Mutual Aid: A Factor of Evolution* (reprint, New York: Forgotten Books, 2008).

32. For a recent overview, see Oren Harman, *The Price of Altruism: George Price and the Search for the Origins of Kindness* (New York: Norton, 2010).

33. See, for example, Frans de Waal, *L'Âge de l'empathie: Leçons de la nature pour une société solidaire* (Paris: Les Liens qui libèrent, 2010).

34. The first expression can be found in Howard P. Becker, *Man in Reciprocity* (New York: Praeger, 1956), and the second in Samuel Bowles and Herbert Gintis, "Is Equality Passé? Homo Reciprocans and the Future of Egalitarian Politics," *Boston Review,* December 1998–January 1999.

35. Alexis de Tocqueville, *De la démocratie en Amérique,* vol. 2, ed. Eduardo Nolla (Paris: Vrin, 1990), p. 93; translated as *Democracy in America,* trans. Arthur Goldhammer (New York: Library of America, 2004) (henceforth cited as AG).

36. Alvin W. Gouldner, "The Norm of Reciprocity: A Preliminary Statement," *American Sociological Review* 25 (April 1960): 171.

37. Georg Simmel, "Excursus sur la sociologie des sens," in *Sociologie,* p. 630. Ibid. for the following quote.

38. Martha Nussbaum, *The Fragility of Goodness: Luck and Ethics in Greek Tragedy and Philosophy* (New York: Cambridge University Press, 1986); Carole Uhlaner, "Relational Goods and Participation:

Incorporating Sociability into a Theory of Rational Action," *Public Choice* 62, no. 3 (1989). See also Pierpaolo Donati, *Relational Sociology: A New Paradigm for the Social Sciences* (London: Routledge, 2010).

39. Tocqueville, *De la démocratie en Amérique,* I.2.8, vol. 1, p. 214; AG, p. 316.

40. See Dan M. Kahan, "The Logic of Reciprocity: Trust, Collective Action, and Law," in Herbert Gintis, Samuel Bowles, Robert Boyd, and Ernst Fehr, *Moral Sentiments and Material Interests: The Foundations of Cooperation in Economic Life* (Cambridge, Mass.: MIT Press, 2006).

41. Richard Sennett, *Respect in a World of Inequality* (New York: W. W. Norton, 2003), p. 64. "If society fears waste, it even more fears—whether rationally or irrationally—being sucked dry by unjustified demands." Ibid.

42. See "Les assureurs s'alarment de la banalisation des fraudes," *Le Monde,* January 30, 2011.

43. See Pierre Lascoumes, *Une Démocratie corruptible: Arrangements, favoritisme et conflits d'intérêts* (Paris: La République des idées/Seuil, 2011).

44. See Christina Fong, Samuel Bowles, and Herbert Gintis, "Strong Reciprocity and the Welfare State," in *Handbook of the Economics of Giving, Altruism and Reciprocity,* vol. 2: *Applications,* ed. Serge-Christophe Kolm and Jean Mercier-Ythier (Amsterdam: Elsevier, 2006).

45. Émile Benveniste, *Le Vocabulaire des institutions indo-européennes,* vol. 1 (Paris: Minuit, 1969), pp. 335–337. Benveniste distinguishes the Latin model of communal citizenship from the Greek model in which the city comes first. See also Benveniste, "Deux modèles linguistiques de la cité," in *Problèmes de linguistique générale,* vol. 2 (Paris: Gallimard, 1980), pp. 272–280.

46. *Le Monde,* November 11, 2010.

47. Éric Maurin, *Le Ghetto français* (Paris: La République des idées/ Seuil, 2004). Maurin argues that "the French ghetto is not so

much a theater of confrontation between included and excluded as a theater in which each group seeks to flee or avoid the group immediately below it in the scale of difficulties. Thus it is not simply workers fleeing unemployed immigrants but also top earners fleeing the upper middle class, the upper middle class fleeing middle managers, middle managers refusing to mingle with employees, etc. In other words, everyone has a fairly active accomplice in the segregation process." See ibid., p. 6.

48. See Gary Becker, "A Theory of Marriage: Part I," *Journal of Political Economy* 81, no. 4 (July–August 1973).

49. For an overview, see Thierry Paquot, ed., *Ghettos de riches: Tour du monde des enclaves résidentielles sécurisées* (Paris: Perrin, 2009).

50. Bill Bishop, *The Big Sort: Why the Clustering of Like-Minded America Is Tearing Us Apart* (New York: Houghton Mifflin, 2008).

51. *Munire* means "to fortify or protect" in Latin. The expression is due to Greg Eghigian, "Homo munitus," in *Socialist Modern,* ed. Paul Betts and Katherine Pence (Ann Arbor: University of Michigan Press, 2007).

52. In the United States, some towns saw internal secession movements, as wealthy neighborhoods sought to become independent municipalities, so as not to have to deal with their poorer neighbors. In France, some well-to-do towns have refused to allow the construction of affordable housing, despite laws requiring that a certain percentage of the total dwelling space be set aside for this purpose.

53. See Pierre Lévêque and Pierre Vidal-Naquet, *Clisthène l'Athénien* (Paris: Les Belles Lettres, 1973), and the collective work *Clisthène et la démocratie athénienne* (with a preface by Jean-Pierre Vernant) (Paris: Macula 1995).

54. For example, Solon canceled peasant debts while requiring all citizens to join in the defense of the city.

55. Ephraim David, "The Spartan *syssitia* and Plato's *Laws*," *American Journal of Philology* 99, no. 4 (Winter 1978), and Klaus Schöpsdau,

"Des repas communs pour les femmes en utopie platonicienne," *Revue française d'histoire des idées politiques,* no. 16, 2002.

56. Aristotle, *Politics,* VII, 10, 1330a1.

57. Article "*Représentants.*"

58. The Jacobin spirit was able to tolerate the idea of "administrative decentralization" while rejecting "political decentralization."

59. This measure represented a serious limitation on universal suffrage, because the number of big taxpayers allowed to deliberate with the municipal council was equal to the number of elected members of the council. Adopted in 1818, the measure was strengthened in 1837. It was not rescinded until 1882, two years before the adoption of an important law on municipal government in 1884.

60. For more on this point, see my "La commune entre société civile et société politique," in *Le Modèle politique français: La société civile contre le jacobinisme de 1789 à nos jours* (Paris: Seuil, 2004), pp. 360–368; in English, *The Demands of Liberty: Civil Society in France Since the Revolution,* trans. Arthur Goldhammer (Cambridge, Mass.: Harvard University Press, 2007).

61. See Maurice Hauriou's important comment on the Gignac Canal case in *Notes d'arrêts sur décisions du Conseil d'État et du tribunal des conflits, publiées au recueil Sirey de 1892 à 1928,* vol. 1 (reprint, Paris: La Mémoire du droit, 2000), pp. 413–422.

62. See the beginning of book III of Aristotle's *Politics.*

63. Robert Putnam, "*E Pluribus Unum:* Diversity and Community in the Twenty-First Century."

64. Célestin Bouglé devotes a chapter to this in his *Idées égalitaires.*

65. Even the validity of the correlation has been disputed. See Marc Hooghe et al., "Ethnic Diversity and Generalized Trust in Europe: A Cross-National Multi-Level Study," *Comparative Political Studies* 42, no. 2 (February 2009).

66. See the remarks by Émile Benveniste, *Le Vocabulaire des institutions indo-européennes,* vol. 1, pp. 96–98.

67. Rousseau, *Émile*, in *Œuvres complètes*, vol. 4 (Paris: Gallimard, "Bibliothèque de la Pléiade," 1969), p. 503, and *Lettres morales*, in ibid., p. 1114.

68. Max Stirner, *Der Einzige und sein Eigentum;* quoted from the 1845 French translation, *L'Unique et sa propriété* (reprint, Paris, 1899), p. 247.

69. "Idiorrhythmia," which etymologically means "one's own rhythm," is a term that Barthes borrowed from Jacques Lacarrière's description in *L'Été grec* (1976) of monasteries in which monks lived separately from one another. See Voir Roland Barthes, *Comment vivre ensemble: Cours et séminaires au Collège de France (1976–1977)* (Paris: Seuil/IMEC, 2002), p. 36.

70. On the idea of friendship in Antiquity, see Jacques Follon, "L'amitié dans la pensée antique," in Jean-Christophe Merle and Bernard Schumacher, *L'Amitié* (Paris: PUF, 2005). See also Pierre Aubenque, "Sur l'amitié chez Aristote," appendix to *La Prudence chez Aristote* (Paris: PUF, 1963).

71. Aristotle, *Nicomachean Ethics*, 1159b25–35.

72. In Plato, *Lysis*, 214a, we read that friendship results from the "movement of like to like."

73. Aristotle, *Nicomachean Ethics*, 1163b15.

74. Similarly, one might say that no man can be a friend of his father's, because the elective bond would be overwhelmed by the priority of the kinship bond.

75. Quoted in Follon, "L'amitié dans la pensée antique," p. 23.

76. Jacques Derrida, *Politiques de l'amitié* (Paris: Galilée, 1994), p. 259.

77. Which I will develop in a forthcoming work.

78. It may be worth noting that such an idea of equality lies behind certain eugenicist proposals for achieving human homogeneity.

79. See Michael Walzer, *Spheres of Justice: A Defense of Pluralism and Equality* (New York: Basic Books, 1983).

80. On this point, however, see Nancy Fraser's interesting efforts to overcome the difficulty.

81. We would also do well to review past experiments in dealing with this issue, some of which were mentioned in an earlier chapter of this work.

82. The term "decommodification" comes from Gösta Esping-Andersen, *The Three Worlds of Welfare Capitalism* (Princeton, N.J.: Princeton University Press, 1990).

83. Philanthropy is the extension of *philia,* or friendship, to the entire human race.

84. See François Bourguignon, *La Mondialisation de l'inégalité* (Paris: La République des idées/Seuil, 2011).

85. This figure and the following one are taken from PNUD, *Rapport sur le développement humain* (Brussels: De Boeck, 1999).

Index